Topics in Mathematics for Elementary Teachers

A Technology-Enhanced Experiential Approach

Topics in Mathematics for Elementary Teachers

A Technology-Enhanced Experiential Approach

Sergei Abramovich
State University of New York at Potsdam

INFORMATION AGE PUBLISHING, INC.
Charlotte, NC • www.infoagepub.com

Library of Congress Cataloging-in-Publication Data

Abramovich, Sergei.
  Topics in mathematics for elementary teachers : a technology-enhanced experiential approach / Sergei Abramovich.
      p. cm.
  Includes bibliographical references.
  ISBN 978-1-60752-460-1 (pbk.) – ISBN 978-1-60752-461-8 (hardcover) – ISBN 978-1-60752-462-5 (e-book)
  1. Mathematics–Study and teaching (Elementary) I. Title.
  QA135.6.A23 2010
  372.7–dc22

                                                        2010006701

CONTENTS

PREFACE

This book reflects the author's experience in teaching a mathematics content course for pre-service elementary teachers (hereafter referred to as teachers). The book addresses a number of recommendations of the Conference Board of the Mathematical Sciences (2001) for the preparation of teachers, demonstrating how mathematics can be approached "at least initially . . . from an experientially based direction, rather than an abstract/deductive one" (p. 96). Such an approach, when enhanced by the use of technology, makes it easier for teachers to grasp the meaning of generalization and to appreciate the creation of an increasing number of concepts on higher levels of abstraction. Moreover, by situating mathematical ideas in computationally supported environments, teachers can develop an appreciation of the role of formal proof in mathematics.

The proposed technology-enhanced approach has the potential to reduce mathematics anxiety among teachers and help them develop confidence in teaching mathematics through modeling and problem solving. A strong experiential component of the book, made possible by the use of concrete objects (often referred to as manipulatives) and digital technology, including spreadsheets, The Geometer's Sketchpad, Graphing Calculator 3.5 (produced by Pacific Tech), and Kid Pix Studio Deluxe, allows a balance of informal and formal approaches to mathematics that will enable teachers to learn how the two approaches complement each other. Classroom observations of teachers' learning of mathematics as a combination of experiment and theory confirm that this approach elevates one's mathematical understanding to a higher level. The book demonstrates not only the importance of mathematics content knowledge for teachers, but better yet, how this knowledge can be gradually developed in the context of exploring grade-appropriate activities and tasks and using computational and manipulative environments to support these explorations.

Most of the chapters are motivated by a problem/activity typically found in elementary mathematics curricula and/or standards (either National or New York State, the context in which the author prepares teachers). By exploring such problems in depth, teachers can learn fundamental mathematical concepts and ideas hidden within a seemingly mundane problem/activity. The need to have experience in going beyond traditional expectations for learning is due to the constructivist orientation of contemporary mathematics pedagogy, which encourages students to ask questions about the mathematics they study. Theoretically, this approach is based on the notion of a hidden mathematics curriculum—a positive learning framework which includes tacit concepts and structures underlying the traditional mathematical content communicated to students through formal schooling. In particular, through this approach, prospective teachers can learn to appreciate a common mathematical structure of seemingly disconnected problems scattered across K–8 mathematics curricula. Furthermore, each chapter (except the last one) includes an activity set that can be used for the development of the variety of assignments for teachers.

The book emphasizes the importance of teaching mathematics to teachers through modeling with new technologies in a variety of problem-solving contexts. The very notion of modeling is understood as the development of isomorphic relationships between mathematical concepts. This abstract concept has rather concrete meanings and can serve as a conceptual underpinning of mathematical modeling. Through this process, one creates a model (either physical or symbolic), explores its properties, develops methods of investigation, comes up with meaningful results, and then interprets these results in the language of the original system. An additional aspect of modeling that underlies the pedagogical approach of the book concerns two ways in which isomorphic relationships can be extended. One way is to change the structure of the object (situation), develop a new model, and refine the corresponding methods of exploring the model. Another way is to change the structure of model first, and then change the object (situation), develop new results, and then see how to modify the object (situation) in order to make new results applicable to it. This idea is integrated in many activities throughout the book.

Finally, the last chapter includes programming details for most of the spreadsheets used in the book, demonstrating how this generic software can be utilized as an agent of a mathematical activity appropriate for teachers to engage in. The material of this chapter can be included in a special course for teachers on the use of technology in the teaching of mathematics. By learning to design computational environments using the capability of spreadsheets, teachers can use mathematical concepts as tools in computing applications. The combination of context, mathematics, and computing enables teachers to connect mathematical concepts with their situational referents. This process of teachers' conceptual development in mathematics, for which technology serves as an agency, includes several stages: competence in the use of technology, appreciation of the interplay between experiential and theoretical knowledge, ability to connect seemingly unrelated ideas, and the acquisition of experience in technology-motivated conjecturing and follow-up formal demonstration. Teachers' success at each stage is documented in the book through their (solicited) reflections on the learning of mathematics by using a technology enhanced experiential approach emphasized by the author in various teacher education courses.

The material included in the book is original, in terms of the approach used to teach mathematics to teachers, and it is based on a number of journal articles published by the author in the United States and elsewhere. Mathematics educators interested in integrating hands-on activities and digital technology into the teaching of mathematics will find this book useful. Mathematicians who teach mathematics to teachers as part of their teaching load will be interested in the material included in this book, as it connects childhood mathematics content and mathematics for teachers.

CHAPTER 1

PARTITION OF WHOLE NUMBERS

Reasoning with Manipulatives and Computational Experiments

Teaching elementary mathematics requires both considerable mathematical knowledge and a wide range of pedagogical skills.

—Conference Board of the Mathematical Sciences (2000, p. 55)

1. MOTIVATION: A STUDENT GROUP PROBLEM

Partition of a whole number is a representation of this number as the sum of other whole numbers. This definition points to the operation of addition—the first operation studied in arithmetic. Despite the elementary nature of addition, partitioning problems may differ significantly in complexity: from partitioning a whole number in the sums of two whole numbers, to partitioning into the sums of three whole numbers, to partitioning into all possible sums of whole numbers. Problems of that type belong to the theory of partitions—the area of mathematics that borders number theory and combinatorics.

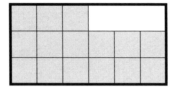

Figure 1.1   A manipulative-based solution to the student group problem.

Partitioning problems often emerge from simple real-life situations like the one that students might face on the first day of a class when they are asked to arrange themselves into study groups to do presentations of articles assigned by the instructor. For example, consider a class of 15 students to be arranged in six study groups. How can this be done? Is the solution unique? An obvious (yet not explicitly stated, and, thereby, hidden) constraint is that the groups should be as close to the same size as possible. Although many teachers view this task as a division-with-adjustment problem (divide the number of groups into the number of students to see to which interval between two consecutive integers the quotient belongs—these integers determine the sizes of the groups), we suggest solving the problem by using concrete objects (e.g., square tiles) and manipulating them until they are arranged in six groups. Such a solution, appropriate for the kindergarten level, is pictured in Figure 1.1.

In turn, the diagram of Figure 1.1 can be described symbolically as

$$15 = 3 + 3 + 3 + 2 + 2 + 2.$$

This means that 15 students have to be arranged in three groups of three students in each, and three groups of two students in each. In that way, the student group problem was solved using just common sense.

2. DIFFERENT VARIATIONS OF THE STUDENT GROUP PROBLEM

If the order in which the groups will be doing presentations makes a difference, then the diagram of Figure 1.2, representing a different partition of 15 into the summands two and three,

$$15 = 3 + 2 + 2 + 2 + 3 + 3,$$

can be interpreted as follows: The first and the last two presentations will be delivered by the groups of three students, and the remaining presentations by the groups of two students.

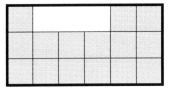

Figure 1.2   Another way of doing six presentations.

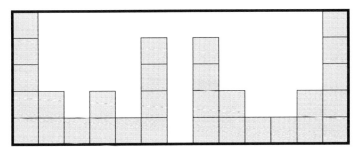

Figure 1.3   Two contextually incoherent solutions to the student group problem.

Furthermore, if we give up an implicit assumption of groups being as close to the same size as possible, other partitions of 15 into six summands are possible (two of them are pictured in Figure 1.3), and, thereby, new situations can be explored. The following two variations of the student group problem stem from abolishing this implicit assumption.

Variation 1

Is it possible for 15 students to do five presentations if study groups should all be different in size? What is the largest number of presentations 15 students can carry out if study groups should all be different in size?

To answer the first question, one can add the first five counting numbers to see that their sum is equal to 15. Figure 1.4 shows such a partitioning of 15, this number representing the smallest number of students that can be arranged in five groups of different size. Numerically,

$$15 = 1 + 2 + 3 + 4 + 5.$$

This brings about an answer to the second question: 15 students cannot do more than five presentations in groups of different size. Note that 21 is the smallest number greater than 15 that can be partitioned in the sum of six different numbers: $21 = 1 + 2 + 3 + 4 + 5 + 6$.

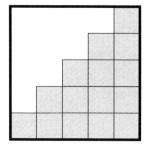

Figure 1.4   Doing presentations in groups of different size.

The next few variations of the student group problem deal with the question "*How many?*"—a typical inquiry for the theory of partitions.

Variation 2

How many ways can 15 students be arranged in four study groups of different size? What is the smallest number of students that could be in the largest group out of four groups?

The first question affords multiple answers. For example,

$$15 = 1 + 2 + 3 + 9, \ 15 = 1 + 2 + 4 + 8, \text{ and } 15 = 2 + 3 + 4 + 6.$$

The answer to the second question is six, as, for example, the last partitioning equation indicates (note the partition $15 = 1 + 3 + 5 + 6$ gives the same result). It remains to be shown how all such partitions can be found in a systematic way. To this end, all partitions of 15 into four summands can be put in groups, depending on the smallest summand used in a partition. There are five partitions of 15 that start with one; besides the two partitions listed above, we have

$$15 = 1 + 2 + 5 + 7, \ 15 = 1 + 3 + 4 + 7, \text{ and } 15 = 1 + 3 + 5 + 6.$$

Note that the sum that starts with one may not have four as the second smallest number, as already $1 + 4 + 5 + 6 > 15$.

Interestingly, there is a single partition of 15 that starts with two (it is listed above). Finally, there are no partitions of 15 that start with three. Indeed, the sum of four consecutive integers starting with three is greater than 15.

One can see that the way all the above six partitions were found, although it was based on a systematic reasoning, may not be recommended for partitioning larger numbers. In particular, this demonstrates the complexity of problems involving partitions. Consequently, the teachers have to be very careful when designing variations of partitioning problems to be used in the classroom.

Variation 3

How many ways can 15 students be arranged in three study groups?

This situation can be explored computationally by using a spreadsheet (see the last section of this chapter). The use of technology and the numerical evidence it generates allows one to make conjectures and develop connections to the concept of triangular numbers appearing later in the book. It will be found that when the order of three summands, in which the number n is partitioned, matters, there exist

$$\frac{(n-2)(n-1)}{2}$$

such partitions.

Variation 4

How many ways can 15 students be arranged in the study groups of different size (in the range one through fifteen), assuming that the order in which the groups will be presenting matters?

While there are many types of easy-to-understand partitioning problems, when it comes to large numbers, not all problems have easy solutions, let alone enable transparent, hands-on solutions. In this chapter, using concrete objects (manipulatives) and concepts from the elementary school curriculum, a rigorous method will be gradually developed that would allow one to resolve Variation 4 for any number of students. As the Conference Board of the Mathematical Sciences (2001) put it, "[T]he challenge is to work from what teachers *do* know—the mathematical ideas they hold, the skills they possess, and the contexts in which these are understood—so they can move from where they are to where they need to go" (p. 57). With this in mind, we will begin with a simple problem, which can be solved by making an organized list—one of the basic problem-solving strategies.

3. A POSTAGE PROBLEM: MAKING AN ORGANIZED LIST

Problem 1: *A post office has stamps of denominations 1 cent, 2 cents, 3 cents, and 4 cents. How many ways can Andy make postage of 4 cents out of these*

*four types of stamps if the order in which the stamps are arranged on an enve-
lope matters? Solve this problem by making an organized list (that is, answer
the question by actually listing all combinations of the stamps).*

As a clarification, Figure 1.5 shows two different ways of making 4 cents
in postage using the stamps.

One can find other combinations of the stamps that can be placed on
an envelope and, in doing so, develop an organized list like the one shown
in Figure 1.6. In all, there are eight different combinations of stamps (put
on an envelope in different orders) that can be used to mail a letter with
the 4-cent postage. As the postage and the number of stamps available grow
larger, this experiential, organized list approach becomes ineffective. In order to develop an effective way of solving problems of that type, in the next
section, we will consider a task adapted from Classroom Idea 1B for grades

Figure 1.5 Two possible solutions to Problem 1.

Combinations of stamps	Postage
2¢ & 2¢	4 cents
3¢ & 1¢	4 cents
1¢ & 3¢	4 cents
2¢, 1¢, & 1¢	4 cents
1¢, 2¢, & 1¢	4 cents
1¢, 1¢, & 2¢	4 cents
1¢, 1¢, 1¢, & 1¢	4 cents
4¢	4 cents

Figure 1.6 Solving Problem 1 through an organized list.

1–2 of New York State mathematics core curriculum (New York State Education Department, 1998).

4. MANIPULATIVE TASK AS A SPRINGBOARD TOWARD CONCEPTUALIZATION

Task: *Provide students with four two-color counters. Have students create different combinations of red and yellow counters, record each combination they find, and stop when they believe they have found all of them.*

This task was given to a second grade pupil of average mathematical abilities. The pupil's response is shown in Figure 1.7. It represents a physical model constructed through trial and error that is short of one combination only. A complete solution to the task is presented in Figure 1.8, which

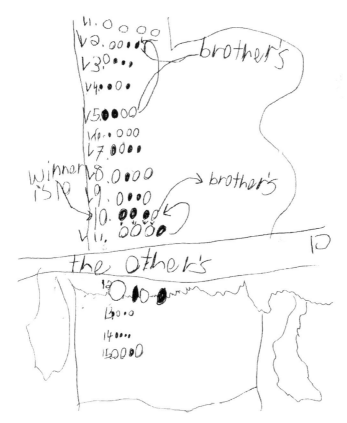

Figure 1.7 A second-grader's solution to the alternative task.

represents a manipulative-based organized list totaling to 16 combinations of counters. This approach, bounded by four counters, does not allow one to understand how the number of combinations depends on the number of counters. In the specific case of four counters, the question to be answered is: How are the numbers 4 and 16 related? In general, given the number of counters, how many different combinations of red and yellow counters can be created?

Very often prospective teachers suggest a simple relationship: $4^2 = 16$. The case of two counters explored through the same approach (Figure 1.9) supports this guess as $2^2 = 4$. This might suggest the following generalization (based on inductive reasoning): By using n two-sided counters, one can create n^2 combinations of red and yellow counters. Unfortunately, this

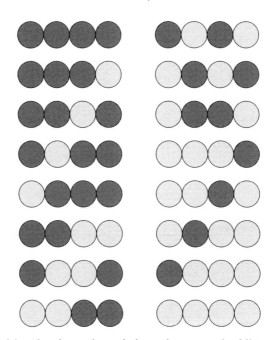

Figure 1.8 Solving the alternative task through an organized list.

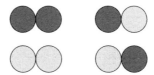

Figure 1.9 The case of two counters.

general conclusion is incorrect. (See Chapters 6 and 10 for the discussion of the deficiency of reasoning by induction—generalizing from a number of observed instances). Indeed, already the case of a single counter (typically overlooked by prospective teachers) provides a counterexample to the "*n*-squared" conjecture. How can one be helped to refine the conjecture?

5. TREE DIAGRAM AND THE RULE OF PRODUCT

In order to develop a method of counting combinations of red and yellow counters that is invariant across different numbers of counters, a special tool—called *tree diagram*—can be employed. A tree diagram represents a multiplicative structure used to organize counting according to the rule: *If an object A can be selected in* m *ways, and if, following the selection of A, an object B can be selected in* n *ways, then the ordered pair (A, B) can be selected in* mn *ways.*

Applying this rule (sometimes referred to as the rule of product) to Figure 1.10, one can conclude that because color for the first counter can be chosen in two ways ($m = 2$), and following the choice of color for the first counter, color for the second counter can be chosen in two ways also ($n = 2$), the total number of combinations of red and yellow counters is equal to the product 2×2. Similarly, applying the rule of product to three counters, as shown in the diagram of Figure 1.11, results in the product $2 \times 2 \times 2$.

Indeed, the first two counters (object A) can be selected in four ways ($m = 4$) and, following this selection, the third counter (object B) can be selected in two ways ($n = 2$), thereby yielding the product of three twos. This suggests that, for the purpose of generalization, the number 16 should be presented not as 4^2, but rather as $2 \times 2 \times 2 \times 2$. In other words, the number 2, representing the number of sides of a counter, should be multiplied by itself as many times as the number of counters involved. This conclusion matches the case of a single counter for which the number of combinations of red and yellow counters is equal to two. The same is true in the case of three counters.

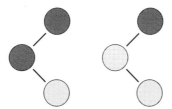

Figure 1.10   A tree diagram for two counters.

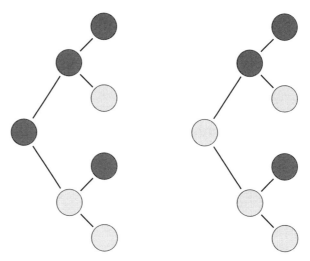

Figure 1.11 A tree diagram for three counters.

6. MOVING TOWARDS GENERALIZATION

So far, we have observed the four matching relationships between the number of counters and the number of combinations of red and yellow. They are presented in the chart of Figure 1.12. Would this doubling pattern continue? Why or why not?

A challenge for a teacher is "to build on children's capacities to articulate their observations [, which] requires teachers who understand the importance of generalization and who command a variety of methods of justification and forms of representations" (Conference Board of the Mathematical Sciences, 2001, p. 75). One of such powerful forms of representation is based on *recursive reasoning*—a rigorous method that allows for the reduction of a problem to a similar one, yet involving the smaller number of objects. When this kind of reduction does not depend on a number of objects involved, it does provide a tool for generalization.

With this in mind, one can prove (using recursive reasoning) that the number of combinations of red and yellow counters doubles as one moves from n to $n + 1$ counters. This can be done for a particular value of n in order for such a transition to be visually demonstrated and physically carried out with manipulatives. Let us show that the transition from three counters to four counters results in the doubling of the number of combinations of red and yellow for the former case. As shown in Figure 1.13, all combinations of four counters can be put in two groups depending on the color of the first (far-left) counter. Then, the number of combinations of red and

Number of counters	Number of combinations
1	2
2	2×2
3	$2 \times 2 \times 2$
4	$2 \times 2 \times 2 \times 2$

Figure 1.12 Recording a doubling pattern.

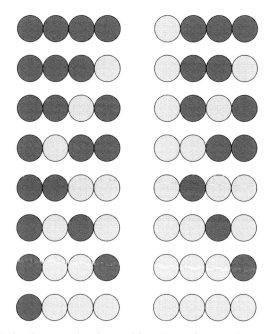

Figure 1.13 Reduction to a simpler problem through recursive reasoning.

yellow counters in each group is equal to that number in the case of three counters as only three counters are allowed to be manipulated. This shows how the doubling phenomenon occurs through the transition from three to four counters.

Likewise, in the general case, one can reason that all combinations of $n + 1$ counters can be put in two groups depending on the color of the first (far-left) counter. Then, the number of combinations of red and yellow counters in each group is equal to the number of combinations among n red and yellow counters. A similar reasoning technique will be employed for other situations throughout the book (e.g., for the introduction of Fibonacci numbers in Chapter 7).

7. NUMERICAL MEANING OF THE MANIPULATIVE TASK

One may wonder as to how the above activities with two-sided counters are related to the main topic of this chapter—the partition of whole numbers into summands. How can all the knowledge developed through the use of manipulatives be put to work for partitioning the number 15 into all possible sums of other whole numbers with regard to their order? How can one make a transition from visualization to symbolizing?

In order to answer these questions, note that the true intellectual accomplishment of the second grader, whose solution is presented in Figure 1.7, is manifested by his reflective analysis of the model, particularly by the use of the term "brothers." Using this term, the second grader really attempted to give a mathematical meaning to the model—the main purpose of using concrete objects as modeling tools. In fact, a hidden meaning of the task is to create conditions for generalization by moving from a physical model to its symbolic interpretation. By interpreting each combination of counters numerically, one can develop the understanding of what changes and what remains invariant when the number of counters involved becomes a variable quantity.

For example, the second combination in Figure 1.7 can be described in terms of the action on counters as follows: Two yellow counters when added to two red counters give the total of four counters. In a decontextualized form, this verbal description can be represented numerically as $2 + 2 = 4$. But the fifth combination in Figure 1.7, being associated by the child with the second combination, has the same numerical meaning! By pairing "brothers," one puts all red-yellow combinations of four counters in eight groups, each of which has a unique numerical interpretation. One can see that the physical model (almost completely) constructed by the second grader can be associated with the following eight representations of four as a sum of counting numbers with regard to the order of summands:

$$4 = 1 + 1 + 1 + 1$$
$$4 = 1 + 1 + 2$$
$$4 = 1 + 2 + 1$$
$$4 = 2 + 1 + 1$$
$$4 = 1 + 3$$
$$4 = 3 + 1$$
$$4 = 2 + 2$$
$$4 = 4$$

This result looks familiar—it was already found (Figure 1.6) by solving Problem 1 (section 3). It has also been found that n counters allow for 2^n combinations of red and yellow counters. Each such combination can be paired with another one so that each pair of "brothers" has a unique numerical meaning—representation of n as the sum of other numbers. Therefore, the number n can be partitioned into the sums of other numbers in 2^{n-1} ways. In particular, the number 15 can be partitioned into the sums of other numbers (counting $15 = 7 + 8$ and $15 = 8 + 7$ as different partitions) in $2^{15-1} = 16{,}384$ ways. This gives the answer to the problem posed in Variation 4; namely, 15 students can be arranged in 16,384 different study groups of all possible sizes to do presentations in all different orders. Obviously, this problem could not have been solved through making an organized list.

8. USING TECHNOLOGY IN DEVELOPING SYSTEMATIC REASONING

Although an organized list as a problem-solving tool has obvious limitations, one's ability to construct such a list indicates the ability to reason systematically, to construct valid arguments, and to appreciate the need for proof in the context of arithmetical problem solving. These are important problem-solving skills that prospective elementary teachers should be prepared to demonstrate in the classroom in order to foster these skills in their students. This section will show how technology can be used as a tool that supports the development of systematic reasoning. To begin, consider the following problem.

> **Problem 2:** *It takes 41 cents in postage to mail a letter. A post office has stamps in denominations of 5 cents, 7 cents, and 10 cents. How many combinations of the stamps could Anna buy to send a letter if the order in which the stamps are arranged on an envelope does not matter?*

In solving this problem by using situated addition in the context of making an organized list, one can find three partitions of 41 into the summands 5, 7, and 10:

$$41 = 7 + 7 + 7 + 5 + 5 + 5 + 5,$$
$$41 = 7 + 7 + 7 + 5 + 5 + 10,$$
$$41 = 7 + 7 + 7 + 10 + 10.$$

The goal of finding these partitions, however, is to move beyond mundane arithmetic toward the reflective analysis of the relationship among the numbers involved. It is through such an extension that one makes a transition from calculations to their analysis as a way of developing a method. With this in mind, the following simple question can be raised: What do the three partitions have in common? A possible answer is that in each partition, the number 7 enters three times. How can one explain this phenomenon? To this end, one can inquire:

- *Is it possible to make 41-cent postage without using a 7-cent stamp?*
- *Is it possible to make 41-cent postage using a single 7-cent stamp only?*
- *Is it possible to make 41-cent postage using two 7-cent stamps?*
- *Is it possible to make 41-cent postage using more than three 7-cent stamps?*

Answers to these questions require more than just using addition. Three other arithmetical operations—subtraction, multiplication, and division—are required here, as well. Subtracting 7 from 41 yields 34—a number that cannot be partitioned into the remaining summands 5 and 10, as it is not a multiple of five, or, alternatively, is not divisible by five. Indeed, counting by fives (or by tens) would not result in 34; alternatively, 34 is not a multiple of five (or ten); in other words, 34 is not divisible by five (or by ten). Subtracting 7 from 41 twice yields 27—another number that, for the same reason as 34, cannot be partitioned into the summands 5 and 10.

Continuing in the same vein, one can conclude that only by using three 7-cent stamps can 41-cent postage be made. This kind of reasoning provides a *proof* that the above three partitions of 41 into the three summands bring about a complete solution to the postage problem. Mathematically speaking, the equation $7x + 5y = 41$ has only one solution: $x = 3$ and $y = 4$. Likewise, the only integer solution of the equation $7x + 10y = 41$ is $x = 3$ and $y = 2$.

One can use a spreadsheet to numerically model Problem 2, enabling the generation of other context-bounded partitioning problems at a click of a slider. Such a spreadsheet is pictured in Figure 1.14. It displays three

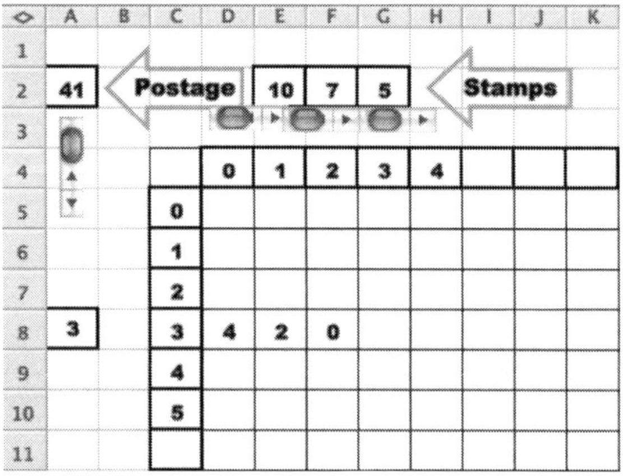

Figure 1.14 Generating three partitions of 41 into the summands 5, 7, and 10.

numbers in the range D5:K11, each of which, when taken with a corresponding number from the ranges C5:C10 and D4:H4, yields a partition of 41 into the summands 10, 7, and 5. For example, the triple (3, 4, 0), the elements of which are located, respectively, in cells C8, D8, and D4, represents a partition of 41 (cell A2) into three sevens (cell F2), four fives (cell G2), and zero tens (cell E2).

The geometry of numbers generated by the spreadsheet demonstrates that all solutions include the number from cell C8 that represents the number of 7-cent stamps used in each of the three combinations. One can also see that each combination may include either no 10-cent stamps, or one 10-cent stamp, or two 10-cent stamps. Using either three or four 10-cent stamps would not allow one to complete the postage with stamps of the other two denominations. Therefore, instead of asking questions about the number of 7-cent stamps, one can ask questions about the number of 10-cent stamps. This kind of reasoning represents a familiar strategy of reduction. Just as the above problem with four counters was reduced to the problem with three counters, a problem with three stamps can be reduced to several problems with two stamps.

This reduction approach proves especially effective when more than three partitions result. For example, *How many ways can one change a quarter into pennies, nickels, and dimes?* The spreadsheet pictured in Figure 1.15 re-

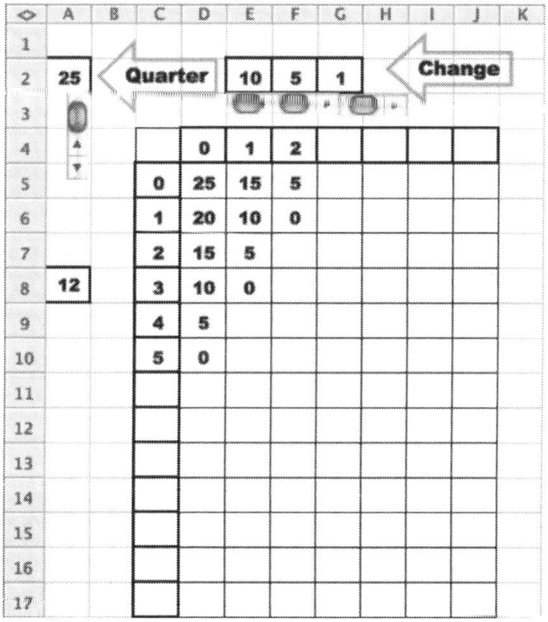

Figure 1.15 A spreadsheet reveals a reduction strategy.

veals the reduction strategy consisting of reducing the problem with three coins to three problems with two coins: (1) when no dimes (cell D4) are included in the change—in this case, one can change a quarter into pennies and nickels in six ways (ranges D5:D10 and C5:C10 display, respectively, the number of pennies and nickels); (2) when one dime (cell E4) is included in the change—in this case, one can change the remaining 15 cents into pennies and nickels in four ways (ranges E5:E8 and C5:C8 display, respectively, the number of pennies and nickels); (3) when two dimes (cell F4) are included in the change—in this case, one can change the remaining 5 cents into pennies and nickels in two ways (ranges F5:F6 and C5:C6, respectively, display the number of pennies and nickels). In that way, technology provides a medium that supports the development of systematic reasoning that can be used as a justification of the completeness of a solution to a problem in the absence of technology. Indeed, through such a reduction, all 12 combinations of coins that add up to a quarter can be found without technology by using four arithmetical operations in an applied problem-solving context.

The ease of transition in the spreadsheet environment from one problem to another, followed by an immediate change of modeling data, suggests using a spreadsheet as a problem-posing tool. The National Council of Teachers of Mathematics (1991) suggested that technology has the potential "to enhance and extend mathematical learning and teaching . . . in the areas of problem posing and problem solving in activities that permit students to design their own explorations and create their own mathematics" (p. 134). This vision of the potential of technology can be extended to mathematics teacher education. By clicking at the sliders that control four parameters involved—a partitioning number and three summands in which the number is to be partitioned—one can generate a multitude of numerical problems and their solutions. Once a problem and its solution are displayed in the spreadsheet template, a teacher can make a decision whether the problem is didactically coherent (Abramovich & Cho, 2008) to be offered to young learners.

In that way, technology provides teachers with research-like skills in the development of instructional materials for the elementary mathematics classroom. Such skills are important for making intelligent decisions under the demands of standards-based curricula. By being engaged in problem-posing activities, teachers learn to use technology for constructing worthwhile extensions of the existing curriculum. The programming of the problem-posing spreadsheets is discussed in Chapter 13.

9. EXPERIENTIAL APPROACH TO THE PARTITION OF INTEGERS

In this section, the following outstanding question posed at the beginning of this chapter (Variation 3) will be answered. Here, we formulate it in terms of partitions: *How many ways can 15 be partitioned in three summands with regard to their order?* (That is, the equations $15 = 4 + 4 + 7$ and $15 = 4 + 7 + 4$ are considered two different partitions of 15.) This question can be explored numerically within a spreadsheet enabling one to have an answer not only for 15, but also for many other numbers. (Note: Three is the smallest number that can be partitioned into three summands.) In other words, given n, a spreadsheet will generate all whole number solutions to the equation $x + y + z = n$, calculate the number of solutions for each n, and then construct a table representation (which can be converted into a graph) of the function that relates n to the number of solutions of this equation.

Such a spreadsheet is pictured in Figure 1.16. It displays in a numeric form not only all 91 (cell A1) partitions of 15 (cell B4) in three summands (for

◇	A	B	C	D	E	F	G	H	I	J	K	L	M	N	O
1	91		3	4	5	6	7	8	9	10	11	12	13	14	15
2			1	3	6	10	15	21	28	36	45	55	66	78	91
3															
4		15	1	2	3	4	5	6	7	8	9	10	11	12	13
5		1	13	12	11	10	9	8	7	6	5	4	3	2	1
6		2	12	11	10	9	8	7	6	5	4	3	2	1	
7		3	11	10	9	8	7	6	5	4	3	2	1		
8		4	10	9	8	7	6	5	4	3	2	1			
9		5	9	8	7	6	5	4	3	2	1				
10		6	8	7	6	5	4	3	2	1					
11		7	7	6	5	4	3	2	1						
12		8	6	5	4	3	2	1							
13		9	5	4	3	2	1								
14		10	4	3	2	1									
15		11	3	2	1										
16		12	2	1											
17		13	1												

Figure 1.16 Partitioning integers in three summands with regard to order.

example, the triple of cells B10, F10, F4 shows the partition $15 = 6 + 5 + 4$; one can then locate within the spreadsheet other five combinations of 4, 5, and 6 that sum up to 15), but also the relationship between the partitioning numbers $n = 3, 4, \ldots, 15$ (range C1:O1) and the corresponding number of solutions of the equation $x + y + z = n$ (range C2:O2) counted, recorded, and saved on the previous iterations. As it turns out, the latter range is filled with triangular numbers (see Chapter 8).

This brings about an interesting conjecture obtained computationally through spreadsheet modeling: *The number of partitions of n into three different summands with regard to their order is equal to t_{n-2}—the triangular number of rank* n – 2. As will be shown in Chapter 8,

$$t_{n-2} = \frac{(n-2)(n-1)}{2}.$$

A mathematical proof of this conjecture requires a number of means that are beyond the elementary level. Yet, as many mathematics educators have continuously emphasized, the importance of proof for mathematics does not necessarily mean that the teaching of mathematical ideas without rigorous proof has to be avoided, even when these very ideas are accessible to learners. As the German mathematician Carl Friedrich Gauss (1777–1855), one of the greatest mathematicians in the history of mankind, put it, "In arithmetic the most elegant theorems frequently arise experimentally as the result of a more or less unexpected stroke of good fortune, while their proofs lie so deeply embedded in darkness that they defeat the sharpest inquiries" (cited in Wells, 1986, p. 7). Technology can open a window to complex, yet simply formulated ideas without teaching proofs that often require the use of complicated mathematical machinery. Several simple proof techniques are discussed in Chapter 10.

10. ACTIVITY SET

1. Using ten linking cubes, construct five towers and arrange them from the lowest to the highest. There may be more than one way to do that. Construct all such combinations of five towers using the ten cubes. Record your combinations (the sets of towers). For each set of towers, find the mean number of stories, the median number of stories, and the mode number of stories.
2. Andy claimed that he constructed a set of five towers out of the ten cubes. Assuming that it is equally likely for one to construct any set of five towers out of the ten cubes, what is the probability that Andy's towers are all the same size?

3. Using eight linking cubes, construct four towers and arrange them from the lowest to the highest. There may be more than one way to do that. Construct all such combinations of four towers using the eight cubes. Record your combinations (the sets of towers). For each set of towers, find the mean number of stories, the median number of stories, and the mode number of stories. Describe what you have found.

4. Anna claimed that she constructed a set of four towers out of the eight cubes. Assuming that it is equally likely for one to construct any set of four towers out of the eight cubes, what is the probability that Anna's towers are all the same size?

5. A dollar was changed into 16 coins, consisting of nickels and dimes only. How many coins of each kind were in the change?

6. It takes 60 cents in postage to mail a letter. The post office has stamps in denominations of 4 cents, 8 cents, and 28 cents. How many combinations of the stamps could Roger buy to send a letter?

7. Fourteen linking cubes are used to make four different size towers. How many ways can that be done? What is the smallest possible number of stories that could be in the highest tower?

8. George claimed that he constructed four different size towers out of fourteen linking cubes. Assuming that it is equally likely for one to construct any set four different size towers out of fourteen cubes, what is the probability that the lowest tower in his set is a two-cube tower?

9. Twenty linking cubes are used to make five different size towers. How many ways can that be done? What is the smallest possible number of stories that could be in the highest tower?

10. Rita claimed that she constructed five different size towers out of twenty linking cubes. Assuming that it is equally likely for one to construct any set of five different size towers out of twenty cubes, what is the probability that the lowest tower in her set is a three-cube tower? What is the probability that the median size tower in her set is a four-cube tower?

11. How many ways can one change a $50 bill using $20, $10, and $5 bills? Assuming that it is equally likely for one to receive change in any combination of the bills, what is the probability of receiving exactly six banknotes?

12. You want to buy a 40-cent piece of candy at Kinney's. You have a piggy bank full of quarters, dimes, and nickels. What are the different combinations of these coins you could take with you to the store to pay for the piece of candy?

13. Last Saturday, Steve's Video Store rented two types of new movies: "Alice in Wonderland" and "Legion." A manager knows that the total sales for renting these movies last Saturday were $100, and that the store rented them in the price range from $3 to $6. Furthermore,

it is known that "Alice in Wonderland" was a more expensive movie than "Legion." Other than that, the manager does not have any records related to last Saturday's rentals, and wants to regain at least part of the renting history by using a spreadsheet. Help the manager find answers to the following questions: What is the maximum number of movies that could have been rented? What are the prices in this case? What is the minimum number of movies (greater than zero) that could have been rented? What are the prices, in this case? How many different combinations of $5 "Alice in Wonderland" and $3 "Legion" movies might there have been rented? What rent prices were not possible within the above range?

CHAPTER 2

COMBINATORIAL MODELS

From Trial and Error to Theory

For efficient learning, an exploratory phase should precede the
phase of verbalization and concept formation.

—George Pólya (1963, p. 609)

1. INTRODUCTION

Combinatorics is one of the oldest branches of what is now called discrete
mathematics, and it goes back to the 16th century, when games of chance
played an important role in the life of a society. The need for a theory of
such games stimulated the creation of specific counting techniques and
mathematical concepts related to new real-life situations. This, in turn, laid
a foundation for the theory of probability, the basic elements of which,
beginning from the use of fractions as tools in measuring chances (likeli-
hood) of a particular event, are included in elementary school curriculum
(National Council of Teachers of Mathematics, 2000). Just like with many
other mathematical topics, teachers need to experience how combinatorics
can be approached "from a concrete and experientially based, rather than
an abstract/deductive, direction" (Conference Board of the Mathematical
Sciences, 2001, p. 24). This chapter provides some teaching ideas for how
basic models of combinatorics can be developed.

2. MOTIVATION

Consider the following problem recommended by the National Council of Teacher of Mathematics (2000) for grades 1–2.

> **Brain Teaser:** *I have pennies, nickels, and dimes in my pocket. If I take three coins out of my pocket, how much money could I have taken?*

Although the original focus of the brain teaser is to promote practice in situated addition, its mundane context allows for much more mathematical thinking to be involved and multiple problem-solving strategies to be discussed. In addition, the appropriate use of technology may help the teachers recognize unexpected links between different contexts and appreciate the meaning of mathematical concepts that create such links. More specifically, the use of a spreadsheet-based tree diagram makes it possible to reveal hidden connections between the brain teaser and the manipulation of multicolored Unifix® Cubes.

The chart of Figure 2.1, completed through the combination of trial and error and systematic reasoning, suggests that there exist ten different sums made out of three coins of the given denomination. However, as the number of coins taken from the pocket, as well as the types of coins, increase, the chart-based approach becomes ineffective. For example, if one takes ten coins out of a pocket filled with pennies, nickels, and dimes, how much money (or, better, how many different sums of money) could have been taken? This question is difficult to answer by using a chart (i.e., by distributing ten asterisks among three boxes in all possible ways). In this chapter,

Penny	Nickel	Dime	Total
***			3 cents
	***		15 cents
		***	30 cents
*	*	*	16 cents
**	*		7 cents
**		*	12 cents
*	**		11 cents
*		**	21 cents
	*	**	25 cents
	**	*	20 cents

Figure 2.1 A chart-based solution to the brain teaser.

using grade-appropriate strategies and concepts, a method of answering questions of that type without using a chart will be developed. Most importantly, proceeding from concepts taught at the early elementary level, this method will be gradually developed by considering more and more advanced mathematical concepts.

To begin, consider the following alternative activity recommended by the New York State Education Department (1998) for grades pre-K–K:

> *Have students work in pairs. Give each pair of students three linking cubes in three different colors. Explain that one child will tell the other how to make a three-cube rod by naming the color that should be used at the top, middle, and the bottom of the rod. Children should hold up their rods to identify positional terms.* (p. 21)

This activity is designed to help young children develop spatial sense through identifying positional terms of colors in a rod. One can recognize, however, a broader mathematical and pedagogical content in the manipulation of the cubes. Indeed, through this activity, one creates different rods, in terms of the distribution of colors within a rod. Drawing on the power of colors in teaching mathematical concepts (Cuisenaire & Gattegno, 1963), one can extend the activity to the following grade-appropriate inquiries into the learning environment, enabling young learners of mathematics to go "beyond the information given" (Bruner, 1973). Below, in reference to diagrams, three types of patterns—brick, mix, and stripe—will be used instead of colors.

- Is there more than one 3 cube rod with brick pattern at the bottom of a rod?
- How many 3-cube rods can be constructed with brick pattern at the bottom of a rod?
- How many 3-cube rods can be constructed with mix pattern at the bottom of a rod?
- How many 3-cube rods can be constructed with stripe pattern at the bottom of a rod?
- How many *different* 3-cube rods can be constructed out of the three patterns?
- Assuming that there are at least three cubes in each pattern, what is the total number of 3-cube rods that can be constructed?

Figure 2.2 shows that there are two towers with brick pattern at the bottom, two towers with mix pattern at the bottom, and two towers with stripe pattern at the bottom. In all, there exist six different arrangements of three patterns in a three-cube rod. This strategy of finding an answer was based on the idea of reducing the problem to three simpler problems, each of

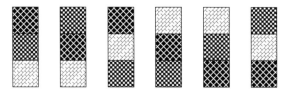

Figure 2.2 Constructing three-cube rods out of three colors.

which has an easy answer. Such a reduction to a simpler problem is commonly known as one of the most important problem-solving techniques (Pólya, 1945).

3. TREE DIAGRAM AND THE RULE OF PRODUCT

Alternatively, the number of different arrangements of patterns can be found by constructing a tree diagram—a multiplicative structure introduced in Chapter 1 and used there to organize counting. Figure 2.3 shows the use of a tree diagram in counting the total number of cubes through applying the rule of product (Chapter 1, section 5) three times. Indeed, the bottom cube can be selected in three ways; following this selection, the middle cube can be selected in two ways (thus, the first two cubes can be selected in six ways), and the top cube, following the selection of the first two, can be selected in one way only. So, three cubes can be selected in $3 \times 2 \times 1 = 6$ ways.

The product $3 \times 2 \times 1$ has a special notation, 3!, which reads "three factorial." Due to the commutative property of multiplication,

$$3 \times 2 \times 1 = 1 \times 2 \times 3 = 3!.$$

In general, the notation $n!$ (reads "n factorial") is used to represent the product of the first n consecutive counting numbers:

$$1 \times 2 \times 3 \times \ldots \times n = n!.$$

One can try to solve the brain teaser using a tree diagram. To this end, the spreadsheet pictured in Figure 2.4 can be used. One can recognize the difference between the problem with cubes and the problem with coins: Whereas all cubes in a rod have different patterns, the coins can be repeated (a sum may include coins of the same denomination). Yet, the tree diagram generates sums that repeat each other. One can program a spreadsheet to display sums in the increasing order, thereby clearly displaying 10 *different* sums out of 27 total. Note that just as there exist six three-cube rods

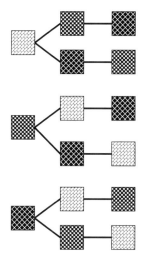

Figure 2.3 A tree-diagram representation of the number of three-cube rods.

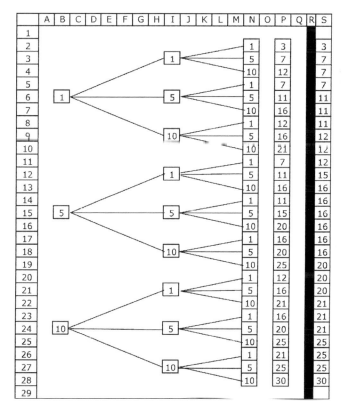

Figure 2.4 A numerical tree diagram for the brain teaser.

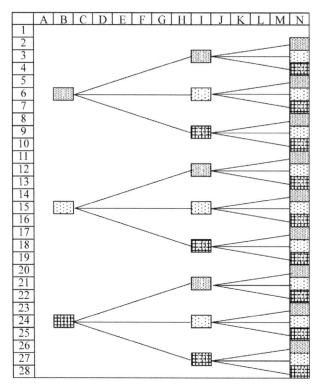

Figure 2.5 Conditional formatting of a tree diagram within a spreadsheet.

constructed out of three different patterns, 16 cents can be made out of pennies, nickels, and dimes in six ways. In that way, a tree diagram provides another medium for solving the brain teaser. However, this medium, just like the chart pictured in Figure 2.1, is not an effective problem-solving tool. Indeed, the number of repeated sums increases along with the number of coins of different denominations, as well as with the number of coins taken from the pocket.

One can also use the conditional formatting feature of a spreadsheet to replace a numeric spreadsheet with an iconic one, in which numbers are replaced by patterns. Such a spreadsheet is shown in Figure 2.5. Its programming is discussed in Chapter 13.

4. PERMUTATION OF LETTERS IN A WORD

Many real-life situations deal with the concept of permutations—all the possible arrangements of a collection of elements, each of which contains every element once, with two such arrangements differing only in the order of their elements. Commonly, the symbol $P(n)$ denotes the number of permutations of n elements. In this section, the following type of question will be explored: *How many ways can one permute letters in the word CAT?* This problem is similar to the problem of finding the number of different three-cube rods made out of three cubes of different colors/patterns. Indeed, each of the three letters can be associated with one of the three colors/patterns, and thereby, the tree diagram of Figure 2.3 (or the diagram of Figure 2.2) can be used to represent the permutation of letters in the word CAT.

So, in the case when all letters in an n-letter word are different, according to the rule of product, there exist $n!$ ways to arrange letters in the word. Alternatively, $n!$ distinct rods can be constructed out of n cubes of different colors/patterns, that is, $P(n) = n!$. For example, as $P(6) = 6! = 1 \times 2 \times 3 \times 4 \times 5 \times 6 = 720$, there exist 720 ways to arrange letters in the word METHOD. Such a large number of permutations of six letters indicates that as the number of letters in a word increases, making an organized list as a method of finding the number of permutations is a hopeless approach. One of the characteristic features of combinatorics is that it enables one to find the number of solutions to a problem without actually listing all the solutions. That is why combinatorics is often referred to as the art of counting without counting.

But what if a word has repeating letters? For example, how many ways can one permute letters in the word INN? If all three letters were different, the answer would have been six permutations. However, the presence of two N's should reduce this answer to the following three permutations: INN, NIN, and NNI. In order to develop a counting strategy that is different from making an organized list, one can first draw two tree diagrams—symbolic and iconic—for the problem of permuting letters in the word INN.

Figure 2.6 shows that in the word INN, there are 3 permutations of the letters; yet, according to Figure 2.3, in the word CAT, there are 6 permutations of the letters. Comparing iconic tree diagrams of Figure 2.3 and Figure 2.7, one can see that when the stripe pattern is replaced by the mix pattern, each path on the tree is repeated twice because the two mix-patterned cubes are indistinguishable. In that way, in order to count the number of permutations of letters in the word INN, one has to divide 2! into 3!, as, due

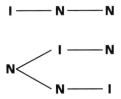

Figure 2.6 A letter-based tree diagram.

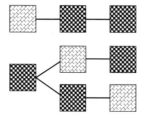

Figure 2.7 A color-based tree diagram.

to the rule of product, 2! represents the number of permutations of two objects. In doing so, one gets

$$\frac{3!}{2!} = \frac{1 \times 2 \times 3}{1 \times 2} = 3.$$

This way of counting permutations in a word with repeating letters can also be explained as follows. Let the number of permutations of letters in the word INN be equal to P. For each such permutation, two N's can be permuted in 2! ways. By the rule of product, the number of permutations of letters in a 3-letter word is equal to $P \times 2!$. On the other hand, the number of permutations in a 3-letter word is equal to 3!. This yields the equation $P \times 2! = 3!$, whence

$$P = \frac{3!}{2!} = 3.$$

The following words can be used to illustrate the strategy of counting permutations of letters in words with repeating letters. For example, in the word CALL, the letters can be arranged in

$$\frac{\overset{\text{letters total}}{\overbrace{4!}}}{\underset{\text{two L's}}{\underbrace{2!}}} = \frac{1 \times 2 \times 3 \times 4}{1 \times 2} = 12 \text{ ways;}$$

in the word PAPA, the letters can be arranged in

$$\frac{\overset{\text{letters total}}{\overbrace{4!}}}{\underset{\text{two P's}}{\underbrace{(2!)}} \times \underset{\text{two A's}}{\underbrace{(2!)}}} = \frac{1 \times 2 \times 3 \times 4}{(1 \times 2) \times (1 \times 2)} = 6 \text{ ways;}$$

in the word LETTER, the letters can be arranged in

$$\underset{\substack{\underbrace{(2!)}_{\text{two E's}} \times \underbrace{(2!)}_{\text{two T's}}}}{\overset{\overbrace{6!}^{\text{letters total}}}{}} = \frac{1 \times 2 \times 3 \times 4 \times 5 \times 6}{(1 \times 2) \times (1 \times 2)} = 180 \text{ ways};$$

in the word COMMITTEE, the letters can be arranged in

$$\underset{\substack{\underbrace{(2!)}_{\text{two M's}} \times \underbrace{(2!)}_{\text{two T's}} \times \underbrace{(2!)}_{\text{two E's}}}}{\overset{\overbrace{9!}^{\text{letters total}}}{}} = \frac{1 \times 2 \times 3 \dots \times 9}{8} = 45,360 \text{ ways.}$$

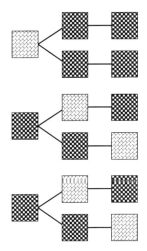

Figure 2.8 A tree diagram for the word INN shows three repeated arrangements of colors.

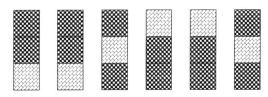

Figure 2.9 Using towers to show three repeated arrangements of colors in the word INN.

5. COMBINATIONS WITHOUT REPETITIONS

Modeling of many real-world situations deals with the concept of combination—the selection of a certain number of elements from a given collection, regardless of their order. Whereas the concept of permutation focuses on the ordering of a certain number of objects (e.g., sorting books *on* a bookshelf), the concept of combination focuses on the selection of a subset of a certain number of objects (e.g., selecting books *from* a bookshelf). Commonly, C_n^m denotes the number of ways to select m objects out of n objects ($n \geq m$).

Consider the following problem, which illustrates the concept of combination.

A Library Problem: *How many ways can one check out three library books out of five books by different authors?*

The chart of Figure 2.10 shows that if the letters Y and N mean, respectively, "yes" (checking out a book) and "nay" (not checking out a book), then the number of ways three books can be checked out from a five-book collection on display is equal to the number of permutations of letters in the word YYYNN. The latter is a five-letter word with three Y's and two N's. Therefore, the number of permutations sought can be calculated as follows:

$$\underbrace{\frac{\overbrace{5!}^{\text{letters total}}}{\underbrace{(3!)}_{\text{three Y's}} \times \underbrace{(2!)}_{\text{two N's}}}} = \frac{1 \times 2 \times 3 \times 4 \times 5}{(1 \times 2 \times 3) \times (1 \times 2)} = 10.$$

Note that a five-letter word, YYNNN, can be used to model the situation of checking out two books out of five books by different authors. Indeed,

$$\frac{\overbrace{5!}^{\text{letters total}}}{\underbrace{(3!)}_{\text{three N's}} \times \underbrace{(2!)}_{\text{two Y's}}} = 10$$

for the word YYNNN. Put another way,

$$C_5^3 = \frac{5!}{3!(5-3)!} = \frac{5!}{2!(5-2)!} = C_5^2 = 10.$$

In general,

$$C_n^m = C_n^{n-m} = \frac{n!}{m!(n-m)!}.$$

Begle	Katz	Ma	Polya	Vygotsky
Y	Y	N	Y	N
N	N	Y	Y	Y
Y	N	N	Y	Y
.	.	.	.	.
.	.	.	.	.
.	.	.	.	.

Figure 2.10 Selection of books as a permutation of letters.

Frequently, teachers suggest solving the library problem by using a tree diagram. The shortcoming of such an approach is two-fold. First, the increase of the number of books by just one book would double the size of a tree diagram. Second, a tree diagram would display the arrangements of books rather than their combinations (when the order is immaterial).

6. COMBINATIONS WITH REPETITIONS

The best way to introduce a new concept is to begin with a situation that can be resolved by either using a prerequisite knowledge or constructing a physical model that represents the situation. Then, drawing on the limitations of the physical model (experiment), one can motivate the concept, which, once developed in a theoretical mode, can be verified over the experiential results. With this in mind, consider the following problem

A Grocery Store Problem: *How many ways can one buy two drinks out of three types: Cola, Pepsi, and Sprite?*

This new situation is close to combinations, since the order in which the drinks are selected is irrelevant. However, the difference between the library and the grocery store is that, whereas one can buy two cans of Cola, Pepsi, or Sprite, two copies of the same book may not be checked out. Let us investigate how the change of context affects the model used to describe this context in mathematical terms. To begin, we create an experiential model of the situation, as shown in Figure 2.11. The importance of an experiential model, developed for a small number of objects, is that it can be used later as the confirmation of a theoretical model in that particular case.

The chart pictured in Figure 2.12 shows, using a modification of the "Y/N" model, that two drinks out of three types can be selected in six ways. As before, the letter Y indicates the choice of a drink; otherwise, the letter N is used. Now, we have to develop a model and offer a theory confirming the

Cola	Cola
Pepsi	Pepsi
Sprite	Sprite
Cola	Pepsi
Cola	Sprite
Pepsi	Sprite

Figure 2.11   An experimental solution to the grocery store problem.

Cola	Pepsi	Sprite
Y	**Y**	N
Y	N	**Y**
N	**Y**	**Y**
YY	N	N
N	**YY**	N
N	N	**YY**

Figure 2.12   The "Y/N" model applied to the grocery store problem.

experimental finding displayed in Figure 2.11. Unfortunately, what can also be seen from the chart of Figure 2.12 is that using the "Y/N" model results in the variation of the number of letters in a word as one moves from one selection of two drinks to another. For example, whereas the selection of any two different drinks is represented by a three-letter word, YYN, the selection of, say, two cans of Cola is represented by a four-letter word, YYNN. This suggests that the old model used to describe combinations without repetitions in the context of the library cannot be used for the description of combinations with repetitions in the context of the grocery store. So, the change of context requires the change of model.

An interesting classroom episode is worth noting, in this regard. One pre-teacher was observed claiming that the "Y/N" model would still work in the context of the grocery store. To support this claim, she presented a chart pictured in Figure 2.13, explaining that her model not only includes

Cola	Cola	Pepsi	Pepsi	Sprite	Sprite
Y	N	**Y**	N	N	N
Y	N	N	N	**Y**	N
N	N	**Y**	N	**Y**	N
Y	**Y**	N	N	N	N
N	N	**Y**	**Y**	N	N
N	N	N	N	**Y**	**Y**

Figure 2.13   One student's "refinement" of the "Y/N" model.

three types of drinks, but, better still, it allows for a six letter word with two Y's and four N's to describe any selection of two drinks.

As always, it is easier to explain why something is correct than incorrect. In other words, to find a counterexample may not always be an easy pedagogical (as well as mathematical) task. The presence of a physical (experiential) model of Figure 2.11 is helpful in this regard, as the new symbolic model (Figure 2.13) can be verified over the experiment. Indeed, the number of permutations of letters in a word with two Y's and four N's is equal to

$$\frac{6!}{(2!)\times(4!)} = 15$$

(these, in particular, include the words YNYNNN and NYYNNN; the latter being absent from the chart of Figure 2.13). Yet, the chart of Figure 2.11 (an experiential model) indicates that there exist only six ways to select two drinks out of three types.

Just like a tree diagram generates extra combinations (without repetitions), the "Y/N" model, suggested by the pre-teacher for the grocery store problem, yields an incorrect answer. In other words, the pre-teacher's model (Figure 2.13) and the physical model (Figure 2.11) are not isomorphic. This episode points to the importance of a physical experiment as a means of verifying the correctness of a theoretical model.

The deficiency of the "Y/N" model that was described above motivates the development of a new model for the grocery store problem. Yet, this new model should be capable of preserving the main idea of using the technique of permuting letters in a word. A possible solution is not to use the letter N (replacing a variable characteristic by an invariant one) in a word because the number of N's, as we have observed, depends on a selection. A characteristic that is invariant across all selections of two drinks is the number of drink types. With this in mind, the letter S can be introduced to serve as a separator between any two types of drinks. Such a modified chart is pictured in Figure 2.14, where, for instance, the word YSYS describes the selection of Cola and Pepsi. In that way, a four-letter word with two Y's and two S's describes a possible selection of two drinks out of three types. The total number of such selections (often referred to as combinations with repetitions) is equal to

$$\frac{4!}{(2!)\times(2!)} = 6$$

(the number of permutations of the letters in the word YYSS). This answer, obtained through the "Y/S" model, coincides with the experimental result shown in Figure 2.11.

Figure 2.15 describes the above approach of moving from an old model to a new one in terms of mathematical modeling. The first step in this approach is to provide a counterexample that shows the deficiency of an old model (theory). Through searching for a new model, one can come across different theoretical models. Having a physical experiment to guide the search for a new model is of critical importance. It is this experiment that allowed for the informed rejection of the model suggested by the pre-teacher, as well as for the whole class verification of another model that the course instructor had to offer.

Cola		Pepsi		Sprite
Y	S	**Y**	S	
Y	S		S	**Y**
	S	**Y**	S	**Y**
YY	S		S	
	S	**YY**	S	
	S		S	**YY**

Figure 2.14 Replacing N (nay) with S (separator).

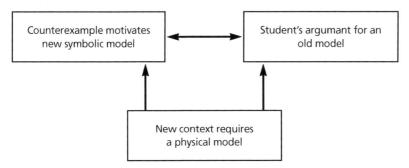

Figure 2.15 The complexity of searching for a new model.

7. SOLVING THE BRAIN TEASER THROUGH THE "Y/S" MODEL

The "Y/S" model can be applied to the brain teaser, our original problem. Indeed, in taking three coins out of a pocket filled with coins of three denominations, one makes the selections of three objects out of three types, when repetitions of objects are allowed. Apparently, three types of coins require two separators. So, the "Y/S" model for the brain teaser is a five-letter word with three Y's and two S's. The number of permutations of letters in such a word is equal to

$$\frac{5!}{(3!) \times (2!)} = 10.$$

This theoretically obtained result coincides with the one developed experimentally, the correctness of which was confirmed by observation. The advantage of having a theory is that it can be effectively applied to similar problems with data not conducive to experimentation. For example, by taking five coins out of a pocket filled with pennies, nickels, dimes, and quarters, one could have 56 different sums. Indeed, the "Y/S" model is represented by the word YYYYYSSS, the letters of which can be permuted in

$$\frac{8!}{(5!) \times (3!)} = 56 \text{ ways.}$$

Using the symbol $\bar{C}_n^r$ to denote the number of r-combination of n elements with repetitions (where r may be greater than n), the solution to the brain teaser can be expressed as

$$\bar{C}_3^3 = \frac{(3+(3-1))!}{3!(3-1)!} = 10.$$

In general,

$$\bar{C}_n^r = \frac{(r+n-1)!}{r!(n-1)!}.$$

Regarding the last example, we have

$$\bar{C}_4^5 = \frac{(5+4-1)!}{5!(4-1)!} = 56.$$

Note that the number of coins selected is greater than the number of coin types.

8. TEACHERS' VOICES FROM THE CLASSROOM

Many teachers believe that modeling activities involving manipulatives are associated with mathematics taught to only young children. It appears that the age level does not limit such modeling of mathematical content. Indeed, throughout the whole K–12 curriculum, the use of manipulatives as modeling tools facilitates one's conceptual understanding and the development of problem-solving skills. This approach allows one to develop a physical model and then internalize it through appropriate mathematical interpretation. As one teacher put it,

> I think using manipulatives helps the understanding of formal mathematics because it brings you back to the base of the problem and allows you to visually see what is going on in the problem. You can take the simple problem with the manipulatives and apply it to more difficult problems.

This remark suggests that the teacher has developed an appreciation of using concrete materials in modeling. Moreover, the remark indicates that the teacher considers a physical model as a springboard into an extended context that may include generalization.

By using tools of technology in mathematical modeling, teachers can discover isomorphic relationships among different concepts. Through such an experiential approach to mathematics, one can construct an "empirical situation in which [familiar] objects are differently related to one another" (Dewey, 1929, p. 86). An example of this type of empirical situation is the connection between a letter-based and manipulative-based tree diagrams.

Reflecting on the activities, a teacher noted, "In mathematics, it is important to experiment and formulate ideas about a solution for the problem. Once you have experimented, it is important to extend this knowledge into theoretical knowledge. When you create a theory, this theory can be applied to many different types of problems." This note shows the teacher's understanding of the value of modeling in developing theoretical knowledge from an experiment.

Furthermore, through experimentation made possible by the use of concrete materials, one can see new directions in which mathematical explorations can proceed, discover connections among concepts, and experience mathematics as a body of knowledge that makes sense. In the words of another teacher, "Throughout this class, I have also seen that there are a lot of connections in math. Learning about one topic or idea can carry over to another area. These connections help students to gain a more concrete understanding of mathematics." The use of the word *concrete* by the teacher indicates the emergence of meaning through constructing isomorphic relationships that make mathematical concepts less abstract. Promoting sense-making modeling pedagogy in mathematics teacher education courses does foster teachers' modeling abilities and, ultimately, can positively affect how mathematics is taught in schools.

9. ACTIVITY SET

1. How many ways can one permute letters in the words EERIE, ERROR, ERRATA, OCCURRENCE, and RECURRENCE?
2. Three different size towers are constructed out of six linking cubes. In how many different orders can these towers be arranged?
3. Three different size towers are constructed out of six linking cubes. What is the probability that the median size tower is two cubes high?
4. Four different size towers are constructed out of ten linking cubes. In how many different orders can these towers be arranged?
5. Five different size towers are constructed out of fifteen linking cubes. In how many different orders can these towers be arranged?
6. Five different size towers are constructed out of fifteen linking cubes. What is the probability that the median size tower is three cubes high?
7. How many ways can Rachel put three rings on the fingers of her right hand, excluding the thumb?
8. How many ways can Rachel put five rings on the fingers of her right hand, excluding the thumb?
9. How many ways can 2 books be bought by 3 people? Use manipulatives to solve the problem. Then use a tree diagram to solve the problem.
10. How many ways can 3 books be bought by 2 people? Use manipulatives to solve the problem. Then use a tree diagram to solve the problem.

11. How many ways can 6 books be bought by 3 people?

12. Three segments are given whose lengths are 1, 2, and 3 centimeters. Using any of the given lengths as many times as you wish, determine how many equilateral triangles with side 5 centimeters can be constructed.

13. Three segments are given whose lengths are 2, 3, and 5 centimeters. Using any of the given lengths as many times as you wish, determine how many equilateral triangles with side 16 centimeters can be constructed.

CHAPTER 3

EARLY ALGEBRA
WITH *KID PIX*

*The teacher must orient his work not on yesterday's development
in the child but on tomorrow's.*

—L. S. Vygotsky (1987, p. 211)

1. INTRODUCTION

This chapter describes how *Kid Pix Studio Deluxe* (referred to below as *Kid Pix*)—graphics software for creative activities of young children—can be used in a rather sophisticated problem-solving context that may be construed as an early application-oriented algebra. The context unites various seemingly unrelated problem-solving tasks across the K–12 mathematics core curriculum of New York State. As it turns out, these real-life tasks are structurally identical and, thereby, can be embedded into a single, grade-two-appropriate context. The material of this chapter is a reflection on the author's (and his students') work with young children in a computer laboratory of a rural elementary school in upstate New York (Abramovich, 2005).

Topics in Mathematics for Elementary Teachers, pages 39–50
Copyright © 2010 by Information Age Publishing

2. CURRENT TRENDS IN DEVELOPING TECHNOLOGY-ENHANCED ALGEBRA CURRICULA

Current K–12 mathematics curricula frequently include problems and tasks from which algebraic activities relevant to the world outside mathematics emerge. When such tasks can integrate the use of technology, the on-task behavior of the learners of mathematics can be greatly enhanced. Usually, technology uses in algebra are associated with either graphing or symbolic manipulation—activities appropriate for the middle and secondary levels. However, by fostering informal mathematical reasoning skills in the description of patterns generated by students when using technology in context, computer-enabled and contextualized algebra can be introduced into curriculum in early grades. Seeing young children's growth and performance in an applied problem-solving context is a key factor for teachers to implement a problem-based curriculum with intuitive uses of algebraic thinking. This, in turn, has a potential to provide groundwork for stressing the importance of transition from visual to symbolic, as a way of preparing young learners of mathematics for the use of variables.

One of the goals of teaching mathematics at the elementary level is to foster intuitive problem-solving strategies that can be adapted for learning formal mathematics at a higher level. However, the challenge of developing an algebra curriculum for young children is the design of learning environments structured by the duality of moving from particular to general and using context as the mediator of mathematical symbolism. As far as *Kid Pix* is concerned, the following two questions will be addressed below:

- *How can visual images developed by young children mediate the transition to mathematical symbolism associated with algebra?*
- *How can mathematical symbolism be guided by the meanings of real-life situations?*

3. INTERPLAY BETWEEN INFORMAL AND FORMAL MATHEMATICS

The problem-solving focus of current standards for school mathematics in North America (National Council of Teachers of Mathematics, 2000) has influenced regional mathematics curricula, starting from the early elementary level. Analysis of the curriculum of New York State (New York State Education Department, 1998) indicates that almost any mathematical activity/task at the primary level has a companion at a higher level. The general awareness of such a connection and specific knowledge of how to use it is very important for successful mathematics teaching. Concrete activity is what stimulated the development of mathematics over the centuries; thus, teaching should take this into consideration. The approach to teaching formal mathematics through decontextualization of concrete activities is grounded in a pedagogical tradition that views children as building formal knowledge on the foundations of the abilities that they use in an informal, intuitive manner. Most notably, this view was articulated by Vygotsky (1987), who, using language acquisition as a paradigm case, argued that the role of formal schooling is to make a student learn "conscious awareness of what he does . . . [that is, the student] learns to operate on the foundation of his capacities in a volitional manner" (p. 206).

In the case of arithmetic, there is ample evidence that young children come to possess many informal skills long before they learn to apply them in a formal way. For example, according to New York State mathematics core curriculum, children acquire the skill of counting, say, by twos before they learn the concept of multiplication; they are engaged in building same size towers using cubic blocks prior to formalizing this activity as division; similarly, they discover different ways in which a set of the blocks could be arranged as rectangles or rectangular prisms before the idea of factoring is introduced. Besides informal arithmetic, young children can be engaged in informal algebra activities through content-bounded problem solving that elicits their curiosity and intellect. Familiarity with the pedagogy of engaging children in activities that manifest the integrity of mathematical content is important for success in implementing an early algebra curriculum. A pedagogy based on the use of graphics software can significantly enhance these activities, thus illustrating an appropriate application of technology.

4. RECURRING MATHEMATICAL STRUCTURE ACROSS GRADES

Consider the following three problems from the K–12 mathematics curriculum of New York State.

Problem 1 (recommended for primary school): *A pet store sold only birds and cats. One day the store's owner asked his clerk to count how many animals there were in the store. The clerk counted 16 legs. How many cats and birds might there have been?*

Problem 2 (recommended for middle school): *Julie sold 125 frozen juice bars and 150 ice cream cones on Saturday. She made a total of $500. Julie sold each ice cream cone for $2.25. Write an equation you can use to find the cost of each frozen juice bar. Solve the equation you wrote to find the cost of one frozen juice bar.*

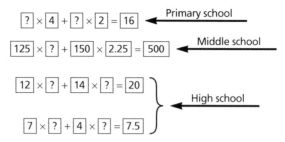

Figure 3.1 Recurring mathematical structure across grades.

> **Problem 3 (recommended for high school):** *Mary purchased 12 pens and 14 notebooks for $20. Carlos bought 7 pens and 4 notebooks for $7.50. Find the price of one pen and the price of one notebook algebraically.*

Analyzing the three problems, one can recognize that, regardless of context, a similar structure is recurring across grades. This structure, presented in the diagram of Figure 3.1, is based on linear combinations of contextually related objects put in two groups according to their specific properties. In primary school, such objects are cats and birds; in middle school, frozen juice bars and ice cream cones; and in high school, pens and notebooks. There are three main didactic differences among the problems: the context, the magnitude of the numbers involved, and a number system used at each grade level. This implies that all three problems can be introduced at the primary level, provided that the context, magnitude, and number system are didactically coherent (Abramovich & Cho, 2008) for that grade level.

Indeed, a question mark in the middle school part of Figure 3.1 refers to the price of a juice bar, something that may be considered as the bar's type. In terms of pets, this question mark indicates that one type of animal is unknown. In much the same way, the question marks in the high school part of Figure 3.1 refer to the prices of pens and notebooks. In terms of pets, missing prices indicate that both animal types are unknown. The following two problems represent the conversion of the middle and secondary school problems, respectively, into primary school problems. The artificial names given to the creatures, trimp and grimp, are vicarious variables or informal unknowns representing the number of legs that each creature has.

> **Problem 2.1:** *Julie, a pet store owner, sold two types of animals on Saturday; two of them were cats and three of them were some other type of animal. She counted 23 legs. How many legs did the other animal have?*
>
> **Problem 3.1:** *Mary, a pet store clerk, sold five trimps and two grimps, which had the total of 18 legs. Carlos, another clerk, sold four trimps and three*

$$\boxed{?} \times \boxed{4} + \boxed{?} \times \boxed{2} = \boxed{16}$$

$$\boxed{3} \times \boxed{?} + \boxed{2} \times \boxed{4} = \boxed{23}$$

$$\boxed{5} \times \boxed{?} + \boxed{2} \times \boxed{?} = \boxed{18}$$

$$\boxed{4} \times \boxed{?} + \boxed{3} \times \boxed{?} = \boxed{20}$$

Figure 3.2 Primary-school-appropriate common structure.

grimps, which had the total of 20 legs. How many legs does a trimp have and how many legs does a grimp have?

Now we can present Problems 1, 2.1, and 3.1 through a diagram (Figure 3.2) similar to that of Figure 3.1. Being coherent in structure, the diagram of Figure 3.2 is also coherent in terms of the number system used. Conceptually, the difference among the parts of the diagram resides in the fact that, depending on what factor is missing in a linear combination, the finding of the missing factor requires the application of either the measurement or the partition model for division (see Chapter 6). It appears that the latter model is more difficult to implement on the plane of action, and this explains the hidden complexity of using the vicarious variables introduced through Problem 3.1.

5. KID PIX AS A PROBLEM-SOLVING TOOL

One of the powerful educational features of *Kid Pix* resides in its capacity to accommodate three modes of knowledge representation: enactive, iconic, and symbolic. To clarify, note that according to Bruner (1964), mathematics learning begins with a set of physical actions in which mathematical structures emerge from a purposeful manipulation of concrete objects. Such actions then become represented and summarized in the form of particular images. Finally, with the help of symbolic notation that remains invariant across transformations in imagery, one comes to grasp the formal properties of the objects involved. It is through the process of developing three modes of knowledge representation that one grows intellectually and, thus, elevates learning of mathematics to a higher ground.

Using *Kid Pix* in the context of Problem 1 by young children supports Bruner's theory of mathematics learning and has the potential to bring about a qualitative change in the use of technology with the children. To this end, the use of *Kid Pix* can be extended to include mathematical activities presented in Problems 2.1 and 3.1 also. By editing custom tools of *Kid Pix*, one can create new rubber stamps to support the drawing of artificial creatures. For example, in order to accommodate the exploration of Problems 2.1 and 3.1, artificial creatures with a number of legs varying in the range one through nine can be created.

6. THE EMERGENCE OF A SYSTEM IN RESOLVING INDETERMINATE PROBLEMATIC SITUATIONS

How do young children solve problems with more than one correct answer using graphics software? How can problem-solving performance at the elementary level and that at higher levels be connected?

The analysis of Figure 3.3 indicates the presence of rudiments of advanced mathematical thinking in the children's intuitive approach to finding solutions to what, in formal terms, is a linear indeterminate equation in two variables, $2x + 4y = 16$. Indeed, this approach parallels a formal (geometric) method of solving the equation in whole numbers, which begins with finding two specific points that belong to its graph (Figure 3.4), namely, the points of concurrency of the graph with the coordinate axes (points with no birds belong to the cats' axis, points with no cats belong to the birds' axis). In order to complete the solution, one has to find all lattice points that reside on the segment connecting the two points. Such search for the lattice points can be recognized in the children's suggestions to each other (observed by the author): "Use more cats!" or "Use more birds!" As a result, the children constructed all five combinations of animals jointly having sixteen legs (Figure 3.5).

This example shows how the emergence of systematic thinking can be found in young children's intuitive strategies and how those strategies can be identified with more advanced lines of reasoning in a formalized context of solving indeterminate equations. It confirms observations by many researchers that young children are capable of powerful mathematical reasoning manifested through their seemingly naive actions upon developmentally appropriate objects of thought. Recognition and appreciation of young children's informal mathematics in a problem-solving situation

16 legs

Figure 3.3 Rudiments of advanced mathematical thinking.

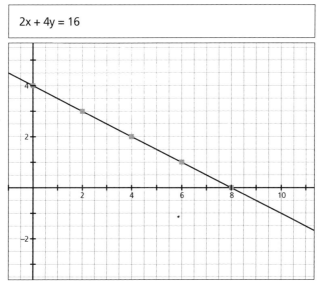

Figure 3.4   A graphic representation of the combinations of 16 animals.

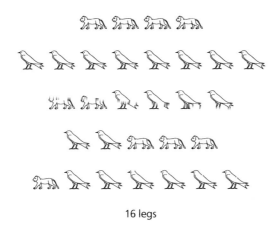

16 legs

Figure 3.5   Complete solution to Problem 1.

can help their intuitive thoughts to develop into a formal realization at the secondary level. Yet, revealing these mathematically rich manifestations of intuitive thinking by children is not an easy task for teachers. Thus, in the context of mathematics education, the above observations (and those to follow) can be used to help teachers understand the mathematical thinking of young children.

7. DEVELOPING SKILLS IN USING ALGEBRAIC
SYMBOLISM

One can observe young children moving with relative ease from representing a problematic situation through graphics (iconic representation) to its representation through written symbols. Traditional approach to applied algebra problem-solving is to start with writing equations (mathematical models) and continue with solving these equations using strictly defined syntactic actions on a notation system. Such an approach is not possible until higher grades, though. Furthermore, the grasp of the deductive structure of moving from general to specific (from algebraic equation to its numeric solution) is often extremely difficult for young children to follow, because of the technical complexity of correct application of mathematical machinery. In the context of Problems 2.1 and 3.1, learners can move in the opposite direction by being inducted into the use of symbolism through drawing with *Kid Pix*. How can that be achieved?

One can distinguish, using Vygotsky's (1978) terminology, the introduction of "first-order symbols...directly denoting objects of actions, and...second-order symbolism, which involves the creation of written signs for the spoken symbols of words...[and] develops [by] shifting from drawing of things to drawing of words" (p. 115). Whereas variables can be introduced to children as first-order symbols (a notation that reflects quantity associated with the objects of their actions), equations that relate these variables to each other were introduced as second-order symbols (a notation that reflects relationships between the quantified objects). *Kid Pix* provides young children with tools that enable them to make a shift from using first-order symbols to acquiring second-order symbolism. It is through meaningful play that children can move from creating graphics-based solutions of problematic situations to writing true algebraic equations (mathematical sentences) that rigorously model the situations. A practical implication of the approach of teaching second-order symbolism through play is that it can be done earlier than usual—a recommendation by Vygotsky for the teaching of writing. Such a recommendation can be extended to other school subjects, including algebra. Indeed, the construction of equations as symbolic representations of concrete situations can be introduced early in mathematics education, provided that appropriate computer tools, like *Kid Pix*, can accommodate children's move from drawing objects of actions to drawing symbolic relations that quantitatively describe these objects.

The use of *Kid Pix* enables young children to develop functions of both first and second-order symbolism by using "talking" letters and numerals as cognitive mediators. The success in developing these functions by the children using *Kid Pix* can be explained in terms of the "method of double stimulation" (Vygotsky, 1962). Indeed, one can note that in the course of moving from icons to symbols, two sets of stimuli were involved: The first set included rubber stamps of letters/numerals as objects of the children's activity, and the second set included verbal representations of the stamps that were employed to mediate the activity. "Talking" letters/numerals represent a sign system that served as an enhancement of young children's internal speech. Thus, in the mediated process of writing mathematical sentences, "the child is able to include stimuli that do not lie within the immediate visual field" (Vygotsky, 1978, p. 26). In this, Vygotsky insisted on the importance of semiotic mediation in the development of human consciousness. A representation of the solution to Problem 2.1 through the combination of drawings and grade-appropriate symbols of arithmetic is shown in Figure 3.6. In solving the problem, a second-grader used a two-step approach, in which rudiments of both measurement and partition models for division can be recognized. The second step clearly involves informal division—a partition of fifteen objects into three equal groups.

Finally, Figure 3.7 shows an even more impressive result—the second-grader was capable of implicitly solving a system of two simultaneous equations and then explicitly representing the equations through the use of meaningful (to her) symbols, T and G, associated with the artificial creatures, *trimps* and *grimps*. A trial and error approach, which was not directly taught to the children, but rather emerged as an intuitive problem-solving strategy, enabled the second-grader, in fact, to solve the system of equations as a riddle: partition eighteen objects into five groups with one cardinality and two groups with another cardinality and then, using the same group-

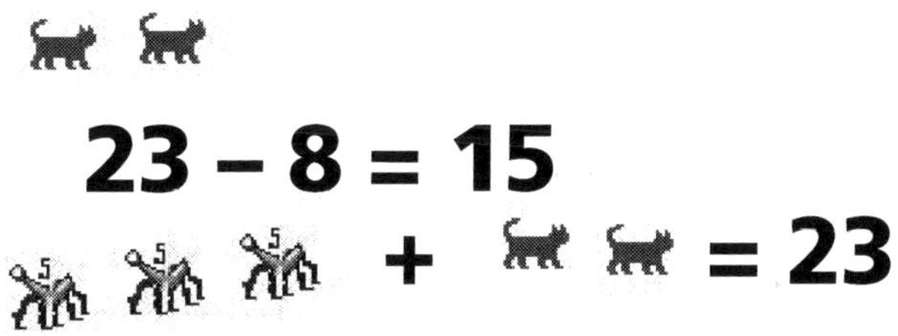

Figure 3.6 Solution to Problem 2.1..

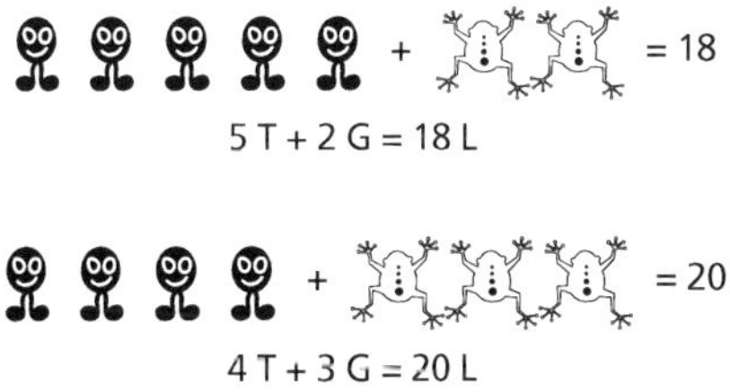

Figure 3.7 Emerging symbolism of simultaneous equations in the 2nd grade.

ing principle, partition twenty objects into four and three such groups. This partitioning perspective (discussed in Chapter 1) may be considered a method of solving systems of two simultaneous equations in whole numbers, something that is not commonly taught even at the secondary level. In such a way, a partitioning problem-solving strategy developed with the help of *Kid Pix* can be adapted as a formal method for solving high school algebra problems.

To conclude, note that despite overall success in resolving the riddle, a challenge for the second-grader was to recognize that if the first partition is a correct one, then the second partition should not involve trial and error, but rather a pure check-in strategy. More specifically, because from the pictorial representation of the partitioning of eighteen legs it follows that a *trimp* has two legs and a *grimp* has four legs, one may develop the second combination of creatures by testing whether four and three such *trimps* and *grimps*, respectively, give the total of twenty legs. This kind of reasoning, however, has not been observed, for it was beyond the reasoning ability of the second-grader.

8. ORIENTATION ON TOMORROW'S DEVELOPMENT OF YOUNG CHILDREN

The use of *Kid Pix* in the context of activities described in this chapter enables multiple pedagogical ideas to be used in the classroom. One such idea is to demonstrate that graphics software, like *Kid Pix*, is a grade-appropriate tool for enhancing early algebra curricula. In the last two decades, especially since the inception of Curriculum and Evaluation Standards for School Mathematics (National Council of Teachers of Mathematics, 1989), many authors have focused on the role that graphing software could play in the teaching and learning of algebra. While computers could not and should not replace students' abilities to solve algebraic equations in a traditional way (through syntactic actions), exploring new approaches to teaching algebra at the elementary level has potential to rouse cognitive abilities of young children to a higher level. Furthermore, through the use of graphics software, several informal problem-solving skills that can be adapted at the secondary level naturally develop.

Another pedagogical idea behind the activities was to demonstrate to the teachers (participating as tutors) how to orient a computer-mediated instruction to the development of residual mental power in young children that can be used in the absence of a tutor. In general, the goal of such pedagogy is to ensure that today's collaboration with a more knowledgeable other creates a zone of proximal development, and, thus, facilitates an independent performance tomorrow (Vygotsky, 1987). As Berg (1970) argued, although Vygotsky did not make clear how instruction could utilize the zone of proximal development, "he would perhaps recommend that teachers and pupils work together to solve problems and to do activities that pupils couldn't do themselves. The teachers' job would be to provide cues and clues to help the pupil get over hurdles he couldn't get over himself" (p. 385). It is precisely this kind of pedagogy that was learned first hand by the teachers through their practicum.

The described use of graphics software as a tool for doing mathematics makes it possible to substitute computer-mediated tasks for algebraic tasks so that for those commonly struggling with the subject matter, the unity of content and pedagogy would be particularly advantageous. By using various tools and features included in an expanded tool kit of the software, young children can represent mathematical situations at different levels of sophistication and grow intellectually as activities proceed. The fact that the children are able to self-structure and—most importantly—goal-organize their problem solving activities while mediating them by tools and signs of the software is a testament to their intellectual growth. Such a growth has been due to a pedagogy that, by early introduction of context-bounded algebra into a mathematics classroom, is strongly oriented on tomorrow's development of young children.

9. ACTIVITY SET

Using Kid Pix (or any other graphics software), solve the following problems.

1. A pet store sold only birds and cats. One day, the store owner asked his clerk to count how many animals there were in the store. The clerk counted 12 legs. How many cats and birds might there have been?
2. Julie, a pet store owner, sold birds and another type of animal with three legs. She counted 21 legs among the animals sold. If she sold three birds, how many animals with three legs did she sell?
3. Martin, a pet store owner, sold two types of animals on Monday. Three of them were cats and two of them were some other type of animal. He counted 22 legs among the animals sold. How many legs did the other animal have?
4. Mary, a pet store clerk, sold five trimps and two grimps, which have the total of 19 legs. Joshua, another clerk, sold four trimps and two grimps, which have the total of 18 legs. How many legs does a trimp have and how many legs does a grimp have?
5. Jack, a pet store clerk, sold four trigs and three grigs, which have the total of 20 legs. Robin, another clerk, sold three trigs and two grigs,

which have the total of 14 legs. How many legs does a trig have and how many legs does a grig have?

6. A bike store owner sells only bicycles and tricycles. One day, she asked her clerk to count how many vehicles there were in the store. Instead of counting vehicles, the clerk counted wheels and reported the total of 16 wheels. How many bicycles and tricycles might there have been?

7. A bike store owner sells only bicycles and tricycles. One day, she asked her clerk to count how many vehicles there were in the store. Instead of counting vehicles, the clerk counted wheels and reported the total of 19 wheels. How many bicycles and tricycles might there have been?

8. A pet store sold birds, starfish, and eight-leg spiders only. One Friday afternoon, the store owner asked her clerk to count how many species were left in the store. Instead of counting species, the clerk counted legs and reported the total of 15 legs. How many different combinations of the species could have been left in the store?

CHAPTER 4

HIDDEN MATHEMATICS OF THE MULTIPLICATION TABLE

The old, the near, the accustomed, is not that to which but that with which we attend;
it does not furnish the material of a problem, but of its solution.

—John Dewey (1910, p. 222)

1. INTRODUCTION

One of three major themes within the mathematics curriculum for grades 3–5 in North America is multiplicative reasoning (National Council of Teachers of Mathematics, 2000). The basic topic here is the multiplication of whole numbers. Typically, the study of this topic converges to the memorization of basic multiplication facts presented in the form of what is commonly referred to as the multiplication table. Many teachers enter teacher education programs having a very traditional (and often frustrating) experience with the table, as they recall long hours spent on memorizing multiplication facts without paying any attention to the table's rich conceptual structure. The Conference Board of the Mathematical Sciences (2001) argued for the importance of learning environments for teachers that enable them "to create meaning for what many had only committed to memory but never really understood" (p. 18). The learning environment of the multiplication table represents a large source of conceptually rich

Topics in Mathematics for Elementary Teachers, pages 51–68
Copyright © 2010 by Information Age Publishing

activities that can be used to enhance a conceptual component in the teaching of elementary school mathematics.

2. MOTIVATION

A Parade Problem: *How many ways can 24 cadets march in columns with the same number of cadets marching in each of the columns?*

Recommended as an activity that motivates and provides context for multiplication, the parade problem can be extended to motivate the development of the multiplication table itself. To this end, let us draw several diagrams representing a solution to the problem (Figure 4.1). Each diagram represents an arrangement of 24 people (modeled by blocks) into rectangular arrays (marching squads), thereby enabling the representation of 24 as a repeated sum of equal numbers. Each representation of that kind can be associated with two numbers: the number of repetitions and the repeated number. The summation of several *equal* numbers can be replaced by a new operation on the two numbers only. As is well known, this new operation is called *multiplication.*

By multiplying two numbers (called factors), one creates their product. The diagram of Figure 4.1 also shows that the product of two factors does not depend on their order. This feature is called the commutative property of multiplication. In terms of the parade problem, where each block represents a marching individual, 24 people can march in columns in eight different ways (depending on who marches in the first row).

Like many other integers, the number 24 can be represented as the product of two positive integers in more than one way. Yet, the product of any two numbers has the unique value. This relationship between representing a number as the product of two factors, perhaps in more than one way, and multiplying the factors to get the number is similar to having multiple possibilities to partition the number into two summands and then adding the

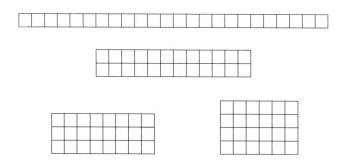

Figure 4.1 Solution to the manipulative task.

summands to get the unique sum. Just as the properties of addition can be introduced through the partition of a set of objects into two groups, the arrangement of a set of objects into a rectangular shape enables one to interpret such an arrangement as multiplication (alternatively, repeated addition). Furthermore, just like the addition table can be developed through counting, the multiplication table can be developed through the meaning of multiplication as repeated addition.

3. DEVELOPING THE MULTIPLICATION TABLE THROUGH REPEATED ADDITION

One way in which the multiplication table can be developed is to start with an empty chart (like the one shown in Figure 4.2) with factors (inputs) x and y in the range $[1, 10]$. Then, one can be asked to find products $x \times y$ by using the meanings of each such product (output) as the total number of objects comprising x groups with y objects in each group. In doing so, a student of mathematics (typically a third-grader) can use their knowledge of counting by one, two, three, five, ten to develop the cases of $y = 1, 2, 3, 5, 10$. The knowledge of doubles can be used in developing the cases of $y = 4, 6, 8$. For example, as shown in Figures 4.3–4.5, respectively, three groups of four circles is the double of three groups of two circles; four groups of six circles is the double of four groups of three circles, and two groups of eight circles is the double of two groups of four circles. Finally, the cases $y = 7$ and $y = 9$ can be developed, respectively, through straightforward addition and finger multiplication.

Numerically, the multiplication table consists of the products of two positive integers, each of which varies over a given range. Geometrically, the multiplication table represents a square (or rectangular) grid. As will be

Figure 4.2 A chart to be developed into the 10×10 multiplication table.

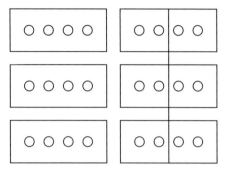

Figure 4.3   Representing 3×4 as $2 \times (3 \times 2)$.

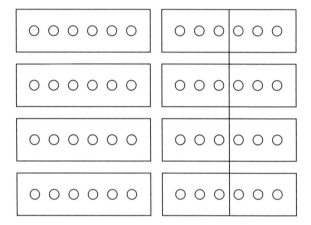

Figure 4.4   Representing 4×6 as $2 \times (4 \times 3)$.

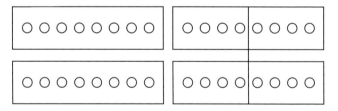

Figure 4.5   Representing 2×8 as $2 \times (2 \times 4)$.

shown in Chapter 9, each number (product) in the table can be associated with a set of identical rectangles that can be found in the grid. It is mainly through a geometrization that the multiplication table can become a tool for one's conceptual development, rather than be used as a learning environment focusing on pure memorization.

4. THE COMMUTATIVE LAW

Many mathematical concepts taught at the elementary level and beyond can be introduced through a numerical approach by exploring the multiplication table. The commutative law of multiplication is such a concept. One can take a square-shaped printout of the multiplication table, fold it along the main (top-left/bottom-right) diagonal, with the numbers facing outward, and, using a paper clip or sharpened pencil, poke a hole at any cell of the table all the way through. Unfolding the table leads naturally to the following observation: The two numbers marked by this hole are equal to each other. The geometric interpretation of this phenomenon is that x groups of y objects, when arranged in a rectangular array, are structurally identical to the arrangement of y groups of x objects (see also Figure 4.1). In that way, the commutative law of multiplication can be first introduced informally through punching holes and then demonstrated more formally through geometrization.

5. THE DISTRIBUTIVE LAW

The distributive law of multiplication over addition can be discovered by recognizing that the sum of any two numbers chosen from the same row/column of the multiplication table belongs to this row/column. For example, the sum of the numbers 4 and 8 from row 2 is equal to 12, a number in the same row (see Figure 4.6). This observation can be given a geometric interpretation. The lengths of the three rectangles with the same width can be associated with their distances from the left border of the table. So, the fact that the length of the far-left rectangle in the diagram of Figure 4.7 is two, determines the difference in length between the other two rectan-

	1	2	3	4	5	6	7	8	9	10
1	1	2	3	4	5	6	7	8	9	10
2	2	4	6	8	10	12	14	16	18	20
3	3	6	9	12	15	18	21	24	27	30
4	4	8	12	16	20	24	28	32	36	40
5	5	10	15	20	25	30	35	40	45	50
6	6	12	18	24	30	36	42	48	54	60
7	7	14	21	28	35	42	49	56	63	70
8	8	16	24	32	40	48	56	64	72	80
9	9	18	27	36	45	54	63	72	81	90
10	10	20	30	40	50	60	70	80	90	100

Figure 4.6 The 10×10 multiplication table.

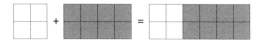

Figure 4.7 Distributive property of multiplication over addition: $2 \times 2 + 2 \times 4 = 2 \times (2 + 4)$.

gles. Numerically, the addition fact $4 + 8 = 12$ is equivalent to the equality $2 \times 2 + 2 \times 4 = 2 \times 6$, in which $6 - 4 = 2$ (or $6 = 4 + 2$) and 2 is the common coefficient in 2 and 4.

We can formulate this geometric interpretation of the relationship among triples of numbers that belong to the same row of the multiplication table in the following general form: Whichever two numbers in the same row of the multiplication table one chooses, their sum can be found in the same row. Furthermore, the distance from this sum to the largest addend is equal to the distance from the smallest addend to the left border of the multiplication table. Algebraically, this can be written in the form $n \times m + n \times p = n \times (m + p)$, a relation that describes the distributive property of multiplication over addition (see Figure 4.7 for $n = 2$, $m = 2$, $p = 4$).

Another interesting pattern that can be discovered in a square-shaped multiplication table (Figure 4.6) is that the sum of numbers in the same row/column that are equidistant from its borders (either left and right or top and bottom) has a constant value for this row/column that is a multiple of the size of the table plus one. For example, in row 2, one has $2 + 20 = 22$, $4 + 18 = 22$, and $22 = 2 \times 11$. Once again, we can see that this phenomenon is due to the distributive law of multiplication over addition. Numerically, this can be described as follows: $2 + 20 = 2 \times 1 + 2 \times 10 = 2 \times (10 + 1)$, $4 + 18 = 2 \times 2 + 2 \times 9 = 2 \times (2 + 9) = 2 \times (10 + 1)$.

We see that in any row of the multiplication table, the pairs of numbers equidistant from the borders of the table have equal sums. Geometrically, this can be explained through the diagram of Figure 4.8, in which 11 pairs of blocks are re-arranged differently. It is important to emphasize that the so discovered phenomenon is a simple consequence of partitioning a number (which is one greater than the size of the table) in two summands.

This property can also be described in the following algebraic form: $n \times p + n \times (m - p + 1) = n(m + 1)$, where m is the size of the table, n is the column/row number, and p is the rank of the product $n \times p$ in the column/row.

6. DEVELOPING THE MULTIPLICATION TABLE THROUGH RECURSIVE DEFINITION

As was shown in the previous section, the multiplication table provides a learning environment through which teachers can appreciate algebra

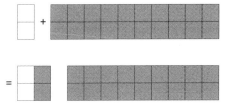

Figure 4.8 Geometrizing the identity $2 \times (1 + 10) = 2 \times (2 + 9)$.

and its notation—"an efficient means for representing properties of operations and relations among them" (Conference Board of the Mathematical Sciences, 2001, p. 20). Numerical patterns of the multiplication table discussed in the previous section can be used to introduce the concept of recursion, one of the basic representational tools in mathematics (see Chapter 1). For example, one can observe (Figure 4.6) that each number in the table, beginning from its second column, is equal to the number immediately to the left plus the number in the first column of the table (in the case of the second column, the sum consists of equal addends). Alternatively, each number in the table, beginning from its second row, is equal to the number immediately above plus the number in the first row of the table. In other words, each number in the multiplication table, being the product of two factors, develops by iterating one of its factors. As the Conference Board of the Mathematical Sciences (2001) put it, "If . . . prospective teachers are offered a course that helps them make sense of number and operations . . . then they are prepared to learn to use algebraic notation to express relationships that have meaning for them" (p 74). The multiplication table is a rich learning environment for the teachers within which algebraic skills can be effectively developed through a numerical approach.

For example, in the table of Figure 4.6, the number 30 appears four times and, thereby, it can be expressed in four different ways:

$$30 = 5 \times 6 = (5 - 1) \times 6 + 6,$$

$$30 = 6 \times 5 = (6 - 1) \times 5 + 5,$$

$$30 = 3 \times 10 = (3 - 1) \times 10 + 10,$$

$$30 = 10 \times 3 = (10 - 1) \times 3 + 3.$$

One can see that 30 can be reached within the table by iterating any one of the factors 3, 5, 6, or 10. These numerical relationships can be generalized to the algebraic identities $xy = (x - 1)y + y$ and $xy = x(y - 1) + x$, where x and y are positive integers (see Figure 4.9 for $x = 3$, $y = 4$). In a more formal-

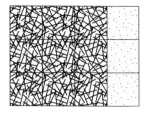

Figure 4.9 Geometrizing the identity $3 \times 4 = 2 \times 4 + 4$ (left), $3 \times 4 = 3 \times 3 + 3$ (right).

ized notation, setting $P(x, y) = xy$, these two identities can be expressed in the form of the following recursive definitions:

$$P(x, y) = P(x - 1, y) + y, P(1, y) = y \tag{1}$$

$$P(x, y) = P(x, y - 1) + x, P(x, 1) = x \tag{2}$$

These definitions (sometimes referred to by mathematicians as partial difference equations) can be used to interpret the development of the multiplication table, starting from one of its boundaries (as suggested in section 3). Indeed, the boundary condition $P(1, y) = y$ means that one group of y objects contains y objects; the boundary condition $P(x, 1) = x$ means that x groups of single objects contain x objects. Repeatedly adding a group of y objects to have x such groups—in other words, by iterating y until the product $P(x, y)$ defined by Formula (1) is reached—the multiplication table can be developed. Likewise, repeatedly adding a group of x objects to have y such groups can be interpreted as the iteration of x until the product $P(x, y)$, defined by Formula (2), is reached. In other words, counting by y's is an iteration by y, and counting by x's is an iteration by x. Figure 4.10 shows how adding a group of three counters to have four such groups and adding a group of four counters to have three such groups yield the same number of counters.

Let us prove that $P(x, y + m) = P(x, y) + mx$. Indeed, by definition,

$$P(x, y + m) = x(y + m).$$

Due to the distributive law of multiplication over addition,

$$x(y + m) = xy + xm = P(x, y) + mx.$$

In much the same way, one can prove the following three identities:

$$P(x + m, y) = P(x, y) + my$$
$$P(x, y + m) = P(x, y) + P(x, m)$$
$$P(x + m, y) = P(x, y) + P(m, y).$$

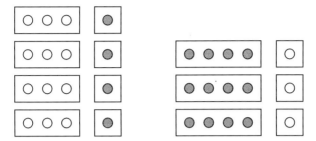

Figure 4.10 Iterating the number 3 four times and the number 4 three times.

7. DISCOVERING CLASSIC ALGEBRAIC IDENTITIES IN THE MULTIPLICATION TABLE

Another interesting pattern that can be observed in the 10×10 multiplication table of Figure 4.6 concerns the sequence of numbers 1, 4, 9, 16, ... that belong to the main (top left–bottom right) diagonal of the table, thereby representing the products of two equal numbers. This pattern can be described as follows: The difference between any two consecutive products of that kind is an odd number. In other words, each number in the main diagonal is the sum of the previous number and the corresponding odd number. Indeed, $4 = 1 + 3$; $9 = 4 + 5$; $16 = 9 + 7$; and so on. Numerically, whereas $3 = 2 \times 1 + 1$, $5 = 2 \times 2 + 1$, and $7 = 2 \times 3 + 1$, the factors 1, 2, and 3 can be interpreted as positional ranks of the numbers 1, 4, and 9 in the main diagonal.

This phenomenon has a lucid geometric interpretation shown in Figure 4.11 for the case $16 = 9 + 7$. The meaning of the number 9 in the main diagonal of the multiplication table is that it describes quantitatively 3 groups of 3 objects—they are represented by a 3×3 square in Figure 4.11. The meaning of the number 16 in the main diagonal of the multiplication table is that it describes 4 groups of 4 objects—they are represented by a 4×4 square in Figure 4.11.

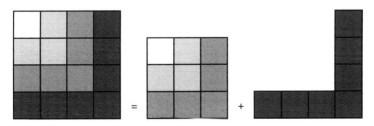

Figure 4.11 Visualizing the relationships $1 + 3 + 5 + 7 = 4 \times 4 = 3 \times 3 + 7$.

One can see that the transition from the smaller square to the larger square requires augmentation by a structure (sometimes referred to as *gnomon*), which can be described as a "double plus one" (see the far-right part of Figure 4.11). This geometric observation can be generalized to the form $(n+1)^2 = n^2 + 2n + 1$ (Figure 4.12, $n = 3$), one of the basic identities in algebra. Likewise, as shown in Figure 4.13 (where $n = 4$), the identity $(n-1)^2 = n^2 - 2n + 1$ can be introduced. Finally, the formulas $(n+m)^2 = n^2 + 2nm + m$ and $(n-m)^2 = n^2 - 2nm + m^2$ can be introduced through geometrization as shown in Figures 4.14 and 4.15.

Another famous identity,

$$\frac{n(n-1)}{2} + \frac{n(n+1)}{2} = n^2, \tag{3}$$

implicitly present in the multiplication table, is known as the Theon theorem.[1] It can be discovered by representing the relationship among three

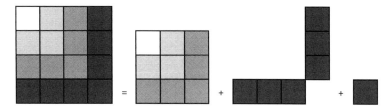

Figure 4.12   Squaring $n + 1$ (here $n = 3$).

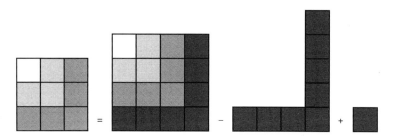

Figure 4.13   Squaring $n - 1$ (here $n = 4$).

$n \times n$	$n \times m$
$m \times n$	$m \times m$

Figure 4.14   Squaring the sum $m + n$.

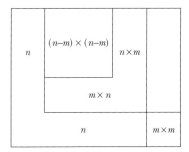

Figure 4.15 Squaring the difference $m - n$.

consecutive products, $(n - 1)n$, n^2, and $n(n + 1)$, in the multiplication table as $n^2 - (n - 1)n = (n + 1)n - n^2$, whence $(n - 1)n + (n + 1)n = 2n^2$. Dividing both sides of the last inequality by 2 yields Identity (3). In terms of polygonal numbers (discussed in detail in Chapter 8), the Theon theorem states that the square number of rank n is the sum of two triangular numbers of ranks n and $n - 1$ respectively. This approach of the geometrization of the multiplication table appears to be "particularly instructive . . . , illustrating how algebraic strategies mirror the actions modeled by other methods" (Conference Board of the Mathematical Sciences, 2001, p. 20).

8. COUNTING EVEN PRODUCTS IN THE MULTIPLICATION TABLE

In this section, we will explore several divisibility properties of numbers in the $n \times n$ multiplication table. To this end, we will start with exploring how many numbers in the 10×10 multiplication table are divisible by 2, 3, 4, etc. This exploration can be supported by the spreadsheet of Figure 4.16 that displays all even products appearing in the multiplication table of size ten and shows that the total number of such products is 75. In other words, for every odd product (a shaded cell in Figure 4.16), there are three even products (forming a flipped letter L). Mathematical visualization made possible by spreadsheet modeling clarifies the meaning of the number 75. Indeed, among the factors 1 through 10, there are five even and five odd numbers. Therefore, there exists one chance out of four to get an odd product when multiplying two numbers from this range (see the tree diagram of Figure 4.17). Consequently, there are three chances out of four to get an even product when multiplying any two numbers from this range. In other words, three-fourth (or 75%) of the products in the 10×10 multiplication table are divisible by two, that is, 75 products out of 100 are even numbers.

	A	B	C	D	E	F	G	H	I	J	K
1	SIZE			DIVISIBLE			2		75		
2	10	← ▦ →				← ▮ →			COUNT		
3		1	2	3	4	5	6	7	8	9	10
4	1		2		4		6		8		10
5	2	2	4	6	8	10	12	14	16	18	20
6	3		6		12		18		24		30
7	4	4	8	12	16	20	24	28	32	36	40
8	5		10		20		30		40		50
9	6	6	12	18	24	30	36	42	48	54	60
10	7		14		28		42		56		70
11	8	8	16	24	32	40	48	56	64	72	80
12	9		18		36		54		72		90
13	10	10	20	30	40	50	60	70	80	90	100

Figure 4.16 An even-size multiplication table.

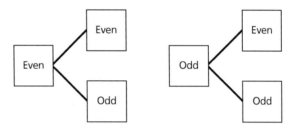

Figure 4.17 An even number has three chances out of four to appear in the $2k \times 2k$ table.

The use of the dynamic feature of a spreadsheet makes it possible to explore whether the percentage of even numbers in the multiplication table depends on the size of the table. Changing the size of the table from ten to nine yields 56 even numbers out of 81 total (Figure 4.18). That is, less than 70% of all numbers in the table are even numbers. In the 8×8 multiplication table, there are 48 even numbers, which are exactly 75% of the 64 numbers in the entire table. One can extend the spreadsheet to include a chart that shows how the percentage of even numbers in a square-shaped multiplication table depends on the size of the table. Such a spreadsheet (the programming of which is discussed in Chapter 13) is shown in Figure 4.19. The chart in the bottom part of the spreadsheet shows that each even-size table has products of which 75% are even. However, as the size of the table increases, the percentage of even numbers in an odd-size table increases also. This numerical approach can motivate its algebraic formalization concerning the dependence on n of the percentage of even numbers among all numbers in the $n \times n$ multiplication table.

	A	B	C	D	E	F	G	H	I	J
1		SIZE			DIVISIBLE		2		56	
2	9	←	→				←	▤ →	COUNT	
3		1	2	3	4	5	6	7	8	9
4	1		2		4		6		8	
5	2	2	4	6	8	10	12	14	16	18
6	3		6		12		18		24	
7	4	4	8	12	16	20	24	28	32	36
8	5		10		20		30		40	
9	6	6	12	18	24	30	36	42	48	54
10	7		14		28		42		56	
11	8	8	16	24	32	40	48	56	64	72
12	9		18		36		54		72	

Figure 4.18   An odd-size multiplication table.

	A	B	C	D	E	F	G	H	I	J	K	L	M
1		SIZE			DIVISIBLE BY		2		108				
2	12	←	→				←	▤ →	COUNT				
3		1	2	3	4	5	6	7	8	9	10	11	12
4	1		2		4		6		8		10		12
5	2	2	4	6	8	10	12	14	16	18	20	22	24
6	3		6		12		18		24		30		36
7	4	4	8	12	16	20	24	28	32	36	40	44	48
8	5		10		20		30		40		50		60
9	6	6	12	18	24	30	36	42	48	54	60	66	72
10	7		14		28		42		56		70		84
11	8	8	16	24	32	40	48	56	64	72	80	88	96
12	9		18		36		54		72		90		108
13	10	10	20	30	40	50	60	70	80	90	100	110	120
14	11		22		44		66		88		110		132
15	12	12	24	36	48	60	72	84	96	108	120	132	144
16													
22		n	2	3	4	5	6	7	8	9	10	11	12
23		%	75%	56%	75%	64%	75%	67%	75%	69%	75%	70%	75%

Figure 4.19   Calculating the percentage of even numbers in a square-shaped table.

Toward this end, one can use the following indirect counting technique through which, instead of counting even numbers, one counts odd numbers in the table. Consider the $2k \times 2k$ multiplication table. In the range 1 through $2k$, there are k odd numbers. Therefore, there are k^2 odd products and $3k^2$ ($= 4k^2 - k^2$) even products in such a table. Now, consider the $(2k - 1) \times (2k - 1)$ multiplication table. In the range 1 through $2k - 1$ there are k odd numbers

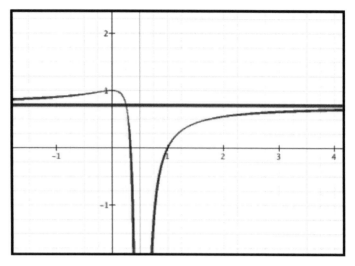

Figure 4.20   Graphs representing the fraction of even numbers in a square-shaped table.

as well. Therefore, there are k^2 odd products and $3k^2 - 4k + 1$ ($= (2k-1)^2 - k^2$) even products in the $(2k-1) \times (2k-1)$ table. In other words, in an even-size multiplication table, the percentage of even numbers does not depend on the table's size. On the other hand, in an odd-size multiplication table, such a percentage is described by the fraction $(3k^2 - 4k + 1)/(2k-1)^2$, which tends to $3/4$ as k grows larger. Figure 4.20 shows the limiting relationship

$$\lim_{k \to \infty} \frac{3k^2 - 4k + 1}{4k^2 - 4k + 1} = \frac{3}{4}$$

in a graphic form.

One can see that the larger the table of an odd size, the larger the percentage of even numbers in it. Note that $3k^2 - 4k + 1 = (3k-1)(k-1)$. Thus, it appears that the number of even products in an odd-size $(2k-1) \times (2k-1)$ multiplication table can be counted as $(3k-1)(k-1)$. An interesting exercise is to give a qualitative interpretation to this fact. Likewise, the meaning of the trinomial $3k^2 - 4k + 1$ can be expressed in terms of the rule of counting even numbers in the table.

9. COUNTING PRODUCTS DIVISIBLE BY THREE

A more difficult task is to explain the experimental finding of having in the 10×10 multiplication table 51 products divisible by three. To this end, note that if at least one of two factors is a multiple of three, then the product is divisible by three. There are three rows and three columns in the table (each containing ten products) with at least one factor being a multiple of three (Figure 4.21). This results in 60 products. However, by counting products in three intersecting rows and columns, one counts nine products twice. Therefore, the total number of products in the 10×10 multiplication table that are multiples of three is 51 ($= 6 \times 10 - 9$).

Now, consider the general case of the $n \times n$ multiplication table. A computational experiment using the spreadsheet shows that not only the number of multiples of three changes along with the size of the table, but also the geometric arrangement of the multiples depends on the size of the table. Analyzing such an arrangement in Figures 4.21–4.23 indicates that three cases need to be considered: $n = 3k - 1$, $n = 3k + 1$, and $n = 3k$. Once

	1	2	3	4	5	6	7	8	9	10
1			3			6			9	
2			6			12			18	
3	3	6	9	12	15	18	21	24	27	30
4			12			24			36	
5			15			30			45	
6	6	12	18	24	30	36	42	48	54	60
7			21			42			63	
8			24			48			72	
9	9	18	27	36	45	54	63	72	81	90
10			30			60			90	

Figure 4.21 Six lines with multiples of three have nine intersections.

	1	2	3	4	5	6	7	8	9	10	11
1			3			6			9		
2			6			12			18		
3	3	6	9	12	15	18	21	24	27	30	33
4			12			24			36		
5			15			30			45		
6	6	12	18	24	30	36	42	48	54	60	66
7			21			42			63		
8			24			48			72		
9	9	18	27	36	45	54	63	72	81	90	99
10			30			60			90		
11			33			66			99		

Figure 4.22 Each row and column gains an extra element with the change of the table's size.

	A	B	C	D	E	F	G	H	I	J	K	L	M
1	SIZE			DIVISIBLE BY			3		80				
2	12	←	→			←		→	COUNT				
3		1	2	3	4	5	6	7	8	9	10	11	12
4	1			3			6			9			12
5	2			6			12			18			24
6	3	3	6	9	12	15	18	21	24	27	30	33	36
7	4			12			24			36			48
8	5			15			30			45			60
9	6	6	12	18	24	30	36	42	48	54	60	66	72
10	7			21			42			63			84
11	8			24			48			72			96
12	9	9	18	27	36	45	54	63	72	81	90	99	108
13	10			30			60			90			120
14	11			33			66			99			132
15	12	12	24	36	48	60	72	84	96	108	120	132	144
16													
17		*n*	2	3	4	5	6	7	8	9	10	11	12
18	non-multiples of 3		4	4	9	16	16	25	36	36	49	64	64

Figure 4.23 Counting non-multiples of three.

again, one can use an indirect counting approach to count non-multiples of three. Similar to the development of the chart in the spreadsheet of Figure 4.19, one can develop a chart that relates the size of the multiplication table to the number of non-multiples of three in the table (Figure 4.23).

Analyzing the chart at the bottom of Figure 4.23, one can come up with the following three propositions.

- **Proposition 1**: In the table of size $n = 3k + 1$, there are $(2k + 1)^2$ products that are not divisible by three; therefore, the number of products divisible by three is equal to $(3k + 1)^2 - (2k + 1)^2 = (3k + 1 - 2k + 1)(3k + 1 + 2k + 1) = k(5k + 2)$. For example, the case $n = 10$ implies $k = 3$; therefore, $2k + 1 = 7$ and $(3k + 1)^2 - (2k + 1)^2 = 51$.
- **Proposition 2**: In the table of size $n = 3k$, there are $(2k)^2$ products that are not divisible by three; therefore, the number of products divisible by three is equal to $(3k)^2 - (2k)^2 = (3k - 2k)(3k + 2k) = 5k^2$. For example, the case $n = 12$ implies $k = 4$; therefore $2k^2 = 64$ and $(3k)^2 - (2k)^2 = 80$.
- **Proposition 3**: In the table of size $n = 3k - 1$, there are $(2k)^2$ products that are not divisible by three; therefore, the number of products divisible by three is equal to $(3k - 1)^2 - (2k)^2 = (3k - 1 - 2k)(3k - 1 + 2k) = (k - 1)(5k - 1)$. For example, the case $n = 11$ implies $k = 4$; therefore $(3k - 1)^2 - (2k)^2 = 57$.

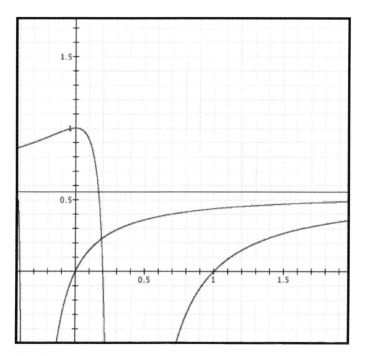

Figure 4.24   The fraction of the multiples of three in a square-shaped table.

Finally, one can find the end behavior of the expression $P(n, 3)$—the fraction of the multiples of three in the $n \times n$ multiplication table:

$$P(3k + 1, 3) = k(5k + 2) / (3k + 1)^2 \to 5/9 \text{ as } k \to \infty$$

$$P(3k, 3) = 5/9$$

$$P(3k - 1, 3) = (k - 1)(5k - 1) / (3k - 1)^2 \to 5/9 \text{ as } k \to \infty$$

The graphs of the functions $y = x(5x + 2) / (3x + 1)^2$, $y = 5/9$, and $y = (x - 1)(5x - 1)/(3x - 1)^2$ are shown in Figure 4.24. One can see that the end behavior of the three functions (as x grows) is identical.

10. ACTIVITY SET

1. How many products in the 10×10 multiplication table are divisible by four?
2. How many products in the 10×10 multiplication table are divisible by five?

3. How many products in the 10×10 multiplication table are divisible by six?
4. How many products in the 10×10 multiplication table are divisible by seven?
5. How many products in the 10×10 multiplication table are divisible by eight?
6. How many products in the 10×10 multiplication table are divisible by nine?
7. How many products in the 9×9 multiplication table are divisible by four?
8. How many products in the 9×9 multiplication table are divisible by nine?
9. How many products in the $n \times n$ multiplication table are divisible by four?
10. Explore the behavior of the function $P(n, 4)$—the fraction of the multiples of four in the $n \times n$ multiplication table.

NOTE

1. Theon is the 4th century A. D. Greek mathematician who lived in Alexandria, Egypt.

CHAPTER 5

APPLICATION
OF UNIT FRACTIONS
TO TESSELATIONS

High quality teaching requires that teachers have a deep knowledge of subject matter.
For this there is no substitute.

—The Glenn Commission (U.S. Department of Education, 2000, p. 22)

1. INTRODUCTION

Connections is one of the five process standards of the *Principles and Stan dards for School Mathematics*. This standard emphasizes the importance for all students to "recognize and use connections among mathematical ideas ... [and] understand how [they] interconnect and build on one another to produce a coherent whole" (National Council of Teachers of Mathematics, 2000, p. 64). In turn, the Conference Board of the Mathematical Sciences (2001) recommended that "teachers should learn mathematics in a coherent fashion that emphasizes the interconnections among theory, procedures, and applications" (p. 8), and that they should "see the links between different mathematical topics and make their students aware of them" (p. 13). In particular, "Making connections between geometry and other areas within mathematics is an important aspect of preparing teachers to teach mathematics" (ibid, p. 33). Engaging teachers in connecting

Topics in Mathematics for Elementary Teachers, pages 69–90
Copyright © 2010 by Information Age Publishing

ideas of arithmetic and geometry makes it possible to address both standards for teaching and recommendations for teachers.

This chapter will explore connections that exist between the arithmetic of unit fractions and the geometry of tessellations. It will be demonstrated how unit fractions can be used in geometric applications (Abramovich, 2010). These connections and applications will be based on the concept of isomorphism, applied "when two complex structures can be mapped onto each other, in such a way that to each part of one structure there is a corresponding part in the other structure" (Hofstadter, 1999, p. 49).

2. MOTIVATION

Manipulative Task (New York State Education Department, 1998): *Using pattern blocks such as green (equilateral) triangles, blue rhombuses, red (isosceles) trapezoids, and yellow (regular) hexagons, have students discover the quantity of triangles needed to cover the blue rhombus, the red trapezoid, and the yellow hexagon.*

Recommended as a geometric activity appropriate for grades 1 or 2, this manipulative task has a hidden meaning. It enables rather sophisticated mathematical concepts (that teachers need to know) to be gradually developed. In that way, the task can motivate various mathematical activities. For example, Figure 5.1 may be interpreted as covering the space around a point, with no gaps or overlaps, using six identical equilateral triangles. This construction can then be extended to the whole plane by covering, step by step, the space around any point with the triangles. In much the same way, one can cover the whole plane with trapezoids (not necessarily isosceles) and rhombuses. Such geometric activities are commonly referred to as tessellations. In this regard, a few definitions should be introduced.

- Definition 1: A *tessellation* of the plane is a collection of plane figures that fills the plane with no gaps or overlaps.
- Definition 2: A *regular tessellation* is a tessellation made up of congruent regular polygons. (One can say that Figure 5.1 represents a

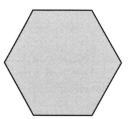 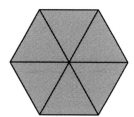

Figure 5.1 Six triangles cover a hexagon.

fragment of a regular tessellation with equilateral triangles. In what follows, a polygon with *n* sides will be referred to as an *n*-gon.)

- Definition 3: A *semi-regular tessellation* is a tessellation with different regular polygons in which the arrangement of polygons at every vertex is identical. (For example, Figure 5.2 shows a fragment of tessellation with three different polygons mentioned in the above manipulative task. This tessellation is not a semi-regular one because the rhombus and trapezoid are not regular polygons.)
- Definition 4: An *edge-to-edge tessellation* with regular polygons is a tessellation in which adjacent polygons share full sides having the same endpoint. (An example of edge-to-edge tessellation with regular polygons is shown in Figure 5.3. One can see that an equilateral tri-

Figure 5.2 Is this a fragment of a semi-regular tessellation?

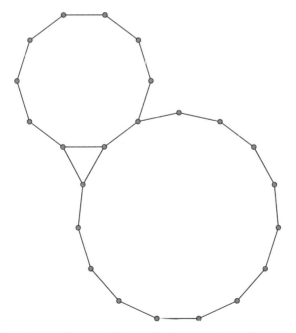

Figure 5.3 An edge-to-edge tessellation with three regular polygons.

angle, regular 10-gon, and regular 15-gon share full sides and cover completely the space around the only point they have in common.)

3. EXPERIENTIAL APPROACH TO FINDING THE SUM OF ANGLES IN A TRIANGLE

To begin the introduction of ideas associated with tessellations, recall that one of the recommendations of the Conference Board of the Mathematical Sciences (2001) for elementary teacher preparation includes the need for teachers to understand "that the measures of the angles of a triangle sum to 180 degrees (a straight angle); and be able to prove that the measures of the angles of an *n*-gon sum to $180(n-2)$" (p. 22). The formula for the sum of angles in a triangle can be discovered experientially by demonstrating that any triangle can tessellate the plane. Note that the use of the word *any* is not rigorous and, thereby, can be associated with the notion of *informal deduction*—one of the levels of geometric thinking (Van Hiele, 1986). Using a sextuple of identical (scalene) triangles, one can cover the space around a point with no gaps or overlaps.

In order to demonstrate this phenomenon, one can use either paper manipulatives or the *Geometer's Sketchpad* (*GSP*). Figure 5.4 shows how three identical triangles make up a straight angle with the vertex at the point *C*. By differently shading the angles *A*, *B*, and *C* in the original triangle, one can see that the straight angle is comprised of their sum, $\angle A + \angle B + \angle C$. Within the *GSP* environment, the arrangement of the three triangles shown in Figure 5.4 can be carried out in two steps: (1) rotate triangle *ABC* around the midpoint *M* of side *BC* by 180° to get △*CBA'*, and (2) rotate △*CBA'* around the midpoint *N* of side *CA'* by 180° to get △*CA'B'*. This experiential approach enables one to conclude that the sum of three angles in any triangle is 180°. Of course, the generality of this conclusion is limited to the number of successful experiments with triangles; that is, the conclusion

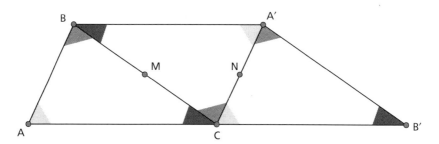

Figure 5.4 Experiential derivation of the formula $S(3) = 180°$.

about the possibility of tessellation with triangles is understood in terms of informal deduction. Setting $S(3)$ to denote the sum of angles in a triangle yields the formula $S(3) = 180°$.

One can use this result to find a formula for $S(n)$—the sum of angles in a polygon with n sides. This can be done in at least two ways. As shown in Figure 5.5 (where $n = 7$), by choosing an arbitrary point O within a polygon and connecting the point to all the vertexes, one gets as many triangles as the vertexes. The sum of angles in all so constructed triangles is equal to $180°n$ (1260° in Figure 5.5). However, this sum includes the angles built around the point O. Therefore, one has to subtract 360° from $180°n$. This yields the formula

$$S(n) = 180°(n - 2) \tag{1}$$

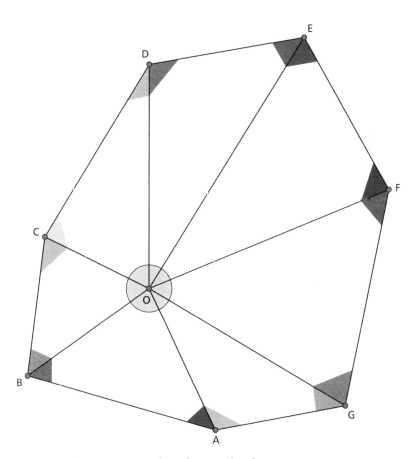

Figure 5.5 A heptagon as a union of seven triangles.

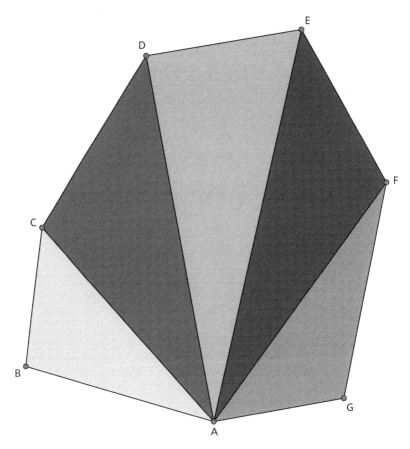

Figure 5.6 A heptagon as a union of five triangles.

One can also derive Formula (1) by using the sketch of Figure 5.6 that shows a heptagon divided into five triangles. In other words, the number of triangles is equal to the number of the sides of the heptagon diminished by two. One can see that all angles of the heptagon are comprised of the angles of the triangles. Therefore, using Formula (1), one has $S(7) = 180°(7 - 2)$. Generalizing the last relation to a polygon with n sides results in Formula (1). Note that such a generalization is justified by the generality of triangulation shown in Figure 5.6.

4. CONNECTING FRACTIONS TO TESSELLATIONS

Hereafter in this chapter, only edge-to-edge tessellations with regular polygons will be considered. Figure 5.7 shows a fragment of an edge-to-edge

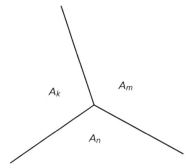

Figure 5.7 An edge-to-edge tessellation.

tessellation with three regular polygons (a k-gon, an m-gon, and an n-gon), the angles of which are A_k, A_m, and A_n, respectively. The question to be answered is: What are the possible values of k, m, and n? To this end, some uncomplicated algebraic transformations will be used below.

To begin, note that the edge-to-edge tessellation (Figure 5.7) implies the relation

$$\angle A_k + \angle A_m + \angle A_n = 360°. \tag{2}$$

From Formula (1) it follows that

$$\angle A_k = \frac{180°(k-2)}{k}, \ \angle A_m = \frac{180°(m-2)}{m}, \ \angle A_k = \frac{180°(n-2)}{n}.$$

Therefore, substituting the three fractional expressions for the angles A_k, A_m, and A_n in Equation (2) yields

$$\frac{180°(k-2)}{k} + \frac{180°(m-2)}{m} + \frac{180°(n-2)}{n} = 360°.$$

Canceling out the common factor $(180°)$ in both sides of the last equality yields the equation

$$\frac{k-2}{k} + \frac{m-2}{m} + \frac{n-2}{n} = 2,$$

which, in turn, can be replaced by

$$3 - 2(\frac{1}{k} + \frac{1}{m} + \frac{1}{n}) = 2.$$

Finally, the last equation can be simplified to the form

$$\frac{1}{k} + \frac{1}{m} + \frac{1}{n} = \frac{1}{2}. \tag{3}$$

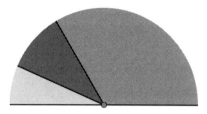

Figure 5.8   An edge-to-edge tessellation presented through its isomorphic model.

Equation (3) establishes an isomorphism between the domain of regular polygons and the domain of fraction circles. A triple of polygons that allows for an edge-to-edge tessellation can be mapped onto the triple of fraction circles that jointly make up a semi-circle. Just as the triple of polygons covers the space around a point with no gaps or overlaps, the isomorphic triple of fraction circles completely covers a semicircle.

For example, the edge-to-edge tessellation shown in Figure 5.3 is isomorphic to the representation of the fraction circle one-half as a sum of three fraction circles shown in Figure 5.8. The reason for establishing an isomorphism between the domain of regular polygons and the domain of fraction circles is that in the latter world, one can use a system in partitioning a unit fraction into three like fractions (see the next section), whereas the development of such a system in the domain of regular polygons is more complex.

5. REPRESENTING ONE–HALF AS A SUM OF THREE UNIT FRACTIONS

In this section, the partitioning of one-half into a sum of three unit fractions will be reformulated in terms of angular relations, and, thereby, used as a tool in the context of tessellations. This, perhaps unexpected, connection between two areas of elementary school mathematics—arithmetic and geometry—further reveals the meaning and importance of the *Connections* standard and *Technology* principle (National Council of Teachers of Mathematics, 2000). As in the previous chapters, connections between arithmetic and geometry have been established through the modeling of one class of problems (and associated concepts) in terms of another class of problems and concepts.

In order to find all edge-to-edge tessellations with three regular polygons, one has to find all ways to represent the fraction one-half as a sum of three unit fractions. These representations can be found in a number of ways. The first approach is based on the use of a spreadsheet as a three-dimensional modeling tool. Figure 5.9 shows the spreadsheet that displays *ten* representations of one-half as a sum of three unit fractions. For example,

	A	B	C	D	E	F	G
1	2		←	▓▓ →			
2			3	4	5	**6**	
3		**5**		20	10		
4		**6**		12		**6**	
5		7	42				
6		8	24	8			
7		9	18				
8		10	15				
9		11					
10		12	12				

Figure 5.9 A three-dimensional partitioner.

the triple $(k, m, n) = (6, 6, 6)$, displayed in bold, indicates that three regular hexagons enable an edge-to-edge tessellation.

To list all the representations, one can divide them into three groups. The first group is comprised of six representations using three *different* unit fractions:

$$\frac{1}{2} = \frac{1}{4} + \frac{1}{6} + \frac{1}{12}, \quad \frac{1}{2} = \frac{1}{4} + \frac{1}{5} + \frac{1}{20}, \quad \frac{1}{2} = \frac{1}{3} + \frac{1}{7} + \frac{1}{42},$$

$$\frac{1}{2} = \frac{1}{3} + \frac{1}{8} + \frac{1}{24}, \quad \frac{1}{2} = \frac{1}{3} + \frac{1}{9} + \frac{1}{18}, \quad \frac{1}{2} = \frac{1}{3} + \frac{1}{10} + \frac{1}{15}.$$

The second group includes three representations using two identical unit fractions:

$$\frac{1}{2} = \frac{1}{4} + \frac{1}{8} + \frac{1}{8}, \quad \frac{1}{2} = \frac{1}{3} + \frac{1}{12} + \frac{1}{12}, \quad \frac{1}{2} = \frac{1}{5} + \frac{1}{5} + \frac{1}{10}.$$

Finally, the third group consists of a single representation using three identical unit fractions:

$$\frac{1}{2} = \frac{1}{6} + \frac{1}{6} + \frac{1}{6}.$$

Another way of finding all the representations of one-half is to use the equalities

$$\frac{1}{2} = \frac{1}{4} + \frac{1}{4} \text{ and } \frac{1}{2} = \frac{1}{3} + \frac{1}{6},$$

followed by partitioning each of the fractions 1/4, 1/3, and 1/6 into a sum of two unit fractions. This approach is similar to partitioning, say, 5 into a sum of three integers in two steps: Start with the equalities $5 = 2 + 3$ and $5 = 1 + 4$, and then use the equalities $2 = 1 + 1$, $3 = 1 + 2$, $4 = 1 + 3$, and $4 = 2 + 2$ to partition each of the summands 2, 3, and 4. Note that some of the partitions obtained in that way would be identical. Applying this two-step approach, one can recall that there are three such representations of $1/4$ as a sum of two unit fractions, namely,

$$\frac{1}{4} = \frac{1}{8} + \frac{1}{8}, \quad \frac{1}{4} = \frac{1}{6} + \frac{1}{12}, \quad \frac{1}{4} = \frac{1}{5} + \frac{1}{20}.$$

Therefore, the equality

$$\frac{1}{2} = \frac{1}{4} + \frac{1}{4}$$

yields

$$\frac{1}{2} = \frac{1}{4} + \frac{1}{8} + \frac{1}{8}, \quad \frac{1}{2} = \frac{1}{4} + \frac{1}{6} + \frac{1}{12}, \quad \frac{1}{2} = \frac{1}{4} + \frac{1}{5} + \frac{1}{20}.$$

Applying the relationships

$$\frac{1}{3} = \frac{1}{6} + \frac{1}{6} \text{ and } \frac{1}{3} = \frac{1}{4} + \frac{1}{12}$$

to the equality

$$\frac{1}{2} = \frac{1}{3} + \frac{1}{6}$$

yields

$$\frac{1}{2} = \frac{1}{6} + \frac{1}{6} + \frac{1}{6} \text{ and } \frac{1}{2} = \frac{1}{4} + \frac{1}{12} + \frac{1}{6}.$$

One can note that the last representation has already been found.

Finally, one has to use the following five representations of $1/6$ as a sum of two unit fractions:

$$\frac{1}{6} = \frac{1}{12} + \frac{1}{12}, \quad \frac{1}{6} = \frac{1}{10} + \frac{1}{15}, \quad \frac{1}{6} = \frac{1}{9} + \frac{1}{18}, \quad \frac{1}{6} = \frac{1}{8} + \frac{1}{24}, \quad \frac{1}{6} = \frac{1}{7} + \frac{1}{42}.$$

These yield

$$\frac{1}{2} = \frac{1}{3} + \frac{1}{12} + \frac{1}{12}, \quad \frac{1}{2} = \frac{1}{3} + \frac{1}{10} + \frac{1}{15}, \quad \frac{1}{2} = \frac{1}{3} + \frac{1}{9} + \frac{1}{18},$$

$$\frac{1}{2} = \frac{1}{3} + \frac{1}{8} + \frac{1}{24}, \quad \frac{1}{2} = \frac{1}{3} + \frac{1}{7} + \frac{1}{24}.$$

In that way, all representations, except

$$\frac{1}{2} = \frac{1}{5} + \frac{1}{5} + \frac{1}{10},$$

generated by the spreadsheet can be confirmed through a non-computational approach. One may wonder: What is special about this missing representation? To answer this question, consider the equality

$$\frac{1}{2} = \frac{1}{4} + \frac{1}{5} + \frac{1}{20},$$

which can be further transformed to the following representation of one-half as the sum of four unit fractions:

$$\frac{1}{2} = \frac{1}{5} + \frac{1}{20} + \frac{1}{5} + \frac{1}{20}.$$

Due to the equality

$$\frac{1}{20} + \frac{1}{20} = \frac{1}{10},$$

in which two unit fractions convolute into one, the missing representation

$$\frac{1}{2} = \frac{1}{5} + \frac{1}{5} + \frac{1}{10}$$

found through spreadsheet modeling has been discovered.

This case of the missing representation merits special consideration. It appears that the non-computational approach described above is flawed and cannot be trusted. Without using technology, in order to overcome a possible deficiency of paper and pencil calculations, one has to continue partitioning fractions into the sums of four unit fractions to see if other cases in which a sum of two unit fractions convolutes into one such fraction can be found. This demonstrates the didactical significance of the unity of computational and theoretical approaches in exploring mathematical ideas. Whereas one needs a theory in order to make sense of a computational experiment, one also can benefit from the use of technology as a means of the validation of theoretically developed results.

6. EDGE-TO-EDGE TESSELLATION WITH THREE DIFFERENT POLYGONS

In this section, edge-to-edge tessellations with three different regular polygons will be considered. To this end, solutions to Equation (3) will be used to find all the tessellations. As the first example, consider the equality

$$\frac{1}{2} = \frac{1}{4} + \frac{1}{6} + \frac{1}{12}.$$

Due to an isomorphism established between Angular Equation (2) and Fractional Equation (3), one can conclude that square, hexagon, and dodecagon (see the glossary of terms in section 9) allow for an edge-to-edge tessellation. Formula (1) can be used to confirm this statement by finding an internal angle for each of the polygons. Indeed, when $n = 4$, one gets $S(4)/4 = 360°/4 = 90°$, $S(6)/6 = 720°/6 = 120°$, and $S(12)/12 = 1800°/12 = 150°$. The three angles satisfy the angular relation $90° + 120° + 150° = 360°$, thereby confirming the possibility of edge-to-edge tessellation with square, hexagon, and dodecagon.

In much the same way, other triples of regular polygons can be shown to enable edge-to-edge tessellation. Figure 5.10 shows a table developed by using Formula (1) in computing internal angles of regular polygons that allow for an edge-to-edge tessellation. In that way, the following six pairs of mutually isomorphic fractional and angular relations can be interpreted in terms of an edge-to-edge tessellation with three different regular polygons.

n	$S(n) = 180°(n-2)$	$S(n)/n = 180°(n-2)/n$
3	180°	60°
4	360°	90°
5	540°	108°
6	720°	120°
7	900°	128.57°
8	1080°	135°
9	1260°	140°
10	1440°	144°
12	1800°	150°
15	2340°	156°
18	2880°	160°
20	3240°	162°
24	3960°	165°
42	7200°	171.43°

Figure 5.10 Internal angles of regular polygons.

1. $\frac{1}{4} + \frac{1}{5} + \frac{1}{20} = \frac{1}{2} \Leftrightarrow 90° + 108° + 162° = 360°$ (edge-to-edge tessellation with square, pentagon, and icosagon)

2. $\frac{1}{4} + \frac{1}{6} + \frac{1}{12} = \frac{1}{2} \Leftrightarrow 90° + 120° + 150° = 360°$ (edge-to-edge tessellation with square, hexagon, and dodecagon)

3. $\frac{1}{3} + \frac{1}{7} + \frac{1}{42} = \frac{1}{2} \Leftrightarrow 60° + 128.57° + 171.43° = 360°$ (edge-to-edge tessellation with triangle, heptagon, and tetracontadigon)

4. $\frac{1}{3} + \frac{1}{8} + \frac{1}{24} = \frac{1}{2} \Leftrightarrow 60° + 135° + 165° = 360°$ (edge-to-edge tessellation with triangle, octagon, and icosotetragon)

5. $\frac{1}{3} + \frac{1}{9} + \frac{1}{18} = \frac{1}{2} \Leftrightarrow 60° + 140° + 160° = 360°$ (edge-to-edge tessellation with triangle, nonagon, and octadecagon)

6. $\frac{1}{3} + \frac{1}{10} + \frac{1}{15} = \frac{1}{2} \Leftrightarrow 60° + 144° + 156° = 360°$ (edge-to-edge tessellation with triangle, decagon, and pentadecagon)

7. CONSTRUCTING REGULAR POLYGONS USING THE GSP

7.1. Constructing an Equilateral Triangle

The use of the *GSP* (or any similar dynamic geometry program) allows one to rotate a point around another point by the given angle. This dynamic feature of the *GSP* makes it possible, given two vertices of an equilateral triangle, to construct its third vertex. To this end, one can use a radius of a circle as a side of the equilateral triangle and then rotate a point of the circle about its center by 60°. This construction is shown in Figure 5.11. By connecting the points A, B, and O with line segments, one gets an isosceles triangle ($OB = OA$) with $\angle AOB = 60°$. Therefore, the other two angles of $\triangle AOB$ are 60° as well. This implies $AB = OA = OB$.

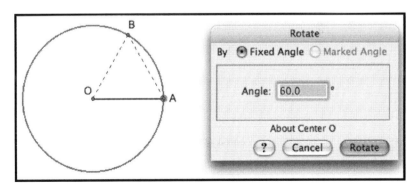

Figure 5.11 Constructing an equilateral triangle.

7.2. Constructing a Square

Just as in the case of an equilateral triangle, a square can be constructed through rotating points by 90°. To this end, one can use a radius of a circle as a side of the square and then rotate a point of the circle about its center by 90°. In that way, as Figure 5.12 shows, the point *A* can be transformed into the point *B* so that $BO \perp AO$ (Figure 5.13). The fourth vertex, *C*, can be constructed by rotating the point *O* around the point *B* by 90°.

7.3. Constructing a Regular Pentagon

The same rotating technique can be used to construct a regular pentagon. First, let the radius *OA* serve as a side of the pentagon (Figure 5.14). By

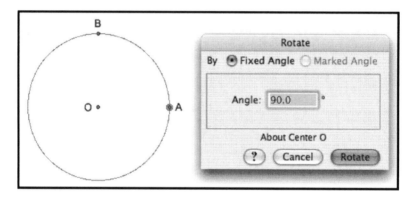

Figure 5.12 Constructing a square (step 1).

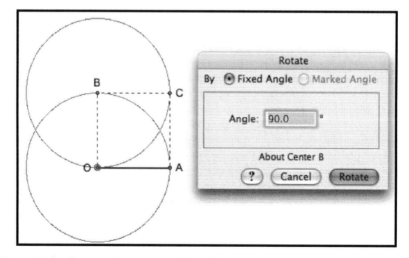

Figure 5.13 Constructing a square (step 2).

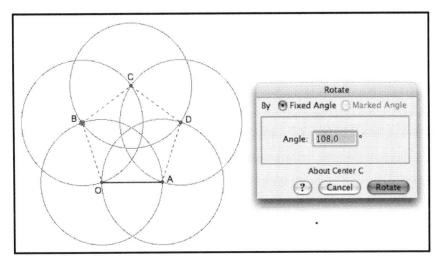

Figure 5.14   Constructing regular pentagon.

choosing O as the center, rotate the point A around O by 108°. This yields $\angle AOB = 108°$. Then, choosing the point B as a new center, rotate the point O around B by 108°. Now, $\angle CBO = 108°$. Choosing the point C as a new center, rotate the point B around C by 108°. In doing so, one gets $\angle BCD = 108°$. Finally, choosing the point D as a new center, rotate the point C around D by 108° to get $\angle CDA = 108°$. This completes the construction of a regular pentagon. One can be asked to prove that $\angle OAD = 108°$ as well.

7.4. Construction of a Regular Polygon as an Iterative Process

One may note that the construction of regular polygons depends on two parameters only—the length of a side of an n-gon and the value of $180°(n-2)/n$. For example, by choosing OA as a side of a pentagon $(n = 5)$, and its left endpoint O as the center of rotation, one rotates the right endpoint A by 108° (in general, by $180°(n-2)/n$) to get the point B, connects O and B so that the segment BO becomes a side of the n-gon adjacent to OA from the left. Mapping the point O onto the point B (a new center) and the point A onto the point O (the new point to be rotated), and then iterating the process 3 times (in general, $n-2$ times) yields the full construction of a pentagon (in general, an n-gon).

8. USING THE GSP IN CONSTRUCTING EDGE-TO-EDGE TESSELLATIONS

Geometric ideas introduced in the previous section, can be applied to the construction of ten edge-to-edge tessellations with three regular polygons found by spreadsheet modeling. These constructions may be a combination of the step-by-step rotation and iterative rotation techniques. In making such constructions, the use of data presented in Figure 5.10 is essential. Figures 5.15 through 5.24 show ten solutions to Equation (3) presented in a geometric form.

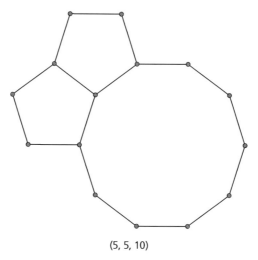

(5, 5, 10)

Figure 5.15   Edge-to-edge tessellation with two pentagons and one decagon.

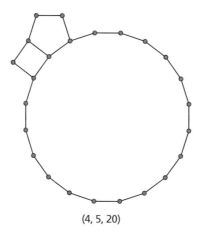

(4, 5, 20)

Figure 5.16   Edge-to-edge tessellation with a square, a pentagon, and an icosagon.

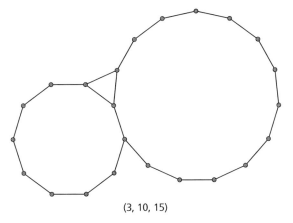

(3, 10, 15)

Figure 5.17   Edge-to-edge tessellation with a triangle, a decagon, and a pentadecagon.

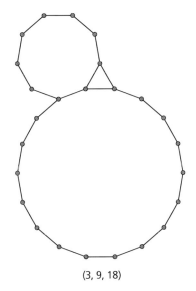

(3, 9, 18)

Figure 5.18   Edge-to-edge tessellation with a triangle, a nonagon, and an octadecagon.

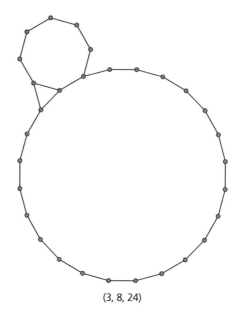

(3, 8, 24)

Figure 5.19 Edge-to-edge tessellation with a triangle, an octagon, and an icositetragon.

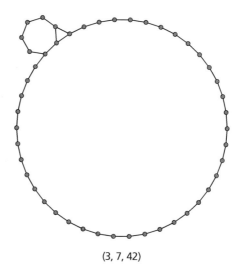

(3, 7, 42)

Figure 5.20 Edge-to-edge tessellation with a triangle, a heptagon, and a tetracontadigon.

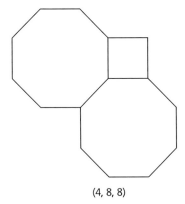

(4, 8, 8)

Figure 5.21   Edge-to-edge tessellation with one square and two octagons.

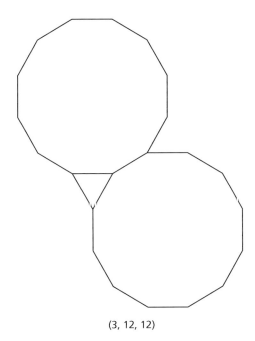

(3, 12, 12)

Figure 5.22   Edge-to-edge tessellation with one triangle and two dodecagons.

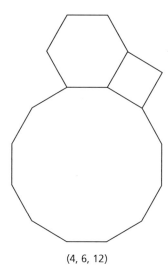

(4, 6, 12)

Figure 5.23 Edge-to-edge tessellation with a square, a hexagon, and a dodecagon.

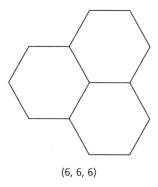

(6, 6, 6)

Figure 5.24 Edge-to-edge tessellation with three hexagons.

9. GLOSSARY

- equilateral triangle: a regular polygon with *three* sides
- square: a regular polygon with *four* sides
- regular pentagon: a regular polygon with *five* sides
- regular hexagon: a regular polygon with *six* sides
- regular heptagon: a regular polygon with *seven* sides
- regular octagon: a regular polygon with *eight* sides
- regular nonagon: a regular polygon with *nine* sides
- regular decagon: a regular polygon with *ten* sides
- regular dodecagon: a regular polygon with *twelve* sides

- regular pentadecagon: a regular polygon with *fifteen* sides
- regular hexadecagon: a regular polygon with *sixteen* sides
- regular octadecagon: a regular polygon with *eighteen* sides
- regular icosagon: a regular polygon with *twenty* sides
- regular icositetragon: a regular polygon with *twenty-four* sides
- regular tricontagon: a regular polygon with *thirty* sides
- regular tetracontadigon: a regular polygon with *forty-two* sides

10. ACTIVITY SET

1. Find a relationship between an angle of a regular *n*-gon and the corresponding fraction circle.
2. Construct an edge-to-edge tessellation with a triangle, a decagon, and a pentadecagon. Is it possible to continue such a tessellation to have the full petal around the pentadecagon? Is it possible to continue such a tessellation to have the full petal around the decagon? Is it possible to continue such a tessellation to have the full petal around the triangle? Describe what you have found.
3. Construct an edge-to-edge tessellation with a square, a hexagon, and a dodecagon. Is it possible to continue such a tessellation to have the full petal around the dodecagon? Is it possible to continue such a tessellation to have the full petal around the hexagon? Is it possible to continue such a tessellation to have the full petal around the square? Describe what you have found.
4. Construct an edge-to-edge tessellation with a square, a pentagon, and an icosagon. Is it possible to continue such a tessellation to have the full petal around the icosagon? Is it possible to continue such a tessellation to have the full petal around the pentagon? Is it possible to continue such a tessellation to have the full petal around the square? Describe what you have found.
5. Construct an edge-to-edge tessellation with a triangle, an octagon, and an icositetragon. Is it possible to continue such a tessellation to have the full petal around the icositetragon? Is it possible to continue such a tessellation to have the full petal around the octagon? Is it possible to continue such a tessellation to have the full petal around the triangle? Describe what you have found.
6. Construct an edge-to-edge tessellation with a triangle, a nonagon, and an octadecagon. Is it possible to continue such a tessellation to have the full petal around the octadecagon? Is it possible to continue such a tessellation to have the full petal around the nonagon? Is it

possible to continue such a tessellation to have the full petal around the triangle? Describe what you have found.

7. Construct an edge-to-edge tessellation with a triangle, a heptagon, and a tetracontadigon. Is it possible to continue such a tessellation to have the full petal around the tetracontadigon? Is it possible to continue such a tessellation to have the full petal around the heptagon? Is it possible to continue such a tessellation to have the full petal around the triangle? Describe what you have found.

8. Find all edge-to-edge tessellations with four regular polygons.

9. Find all edge-to-edge tessellations with five regular polygons.

10. Is it possible to find edge-to edge tessellations with more than five different regular polygons? Why or why not?

CHAPTER 6

DIVISIBILITY AND
PRIME NUMBERS

The elementary theory of numbers should be one of the very best subjects
for early mathematical instruction. It demands very little previous knowledge,
its subject matter is tangible and familiar; the processes of reasoning which it employs
are simple, general and few, and it is unique among the mathematical sciences
in its appeal to natural human curiosity.

—G. H. Hardy (1929, p. 818)

1. INTRODUCTION

Several topics listed in the *Algebra* standard of the *Principles and Standards for School Mathematics* belong to number theory. A reference to one such topic is an expectation that "upper elementary students [can] conjecture that the sum of the first n odd numbers is n^2" (National Council of Teachers of Mathematics, 2000, p. 39). Once the students have a conjecture, they might be wondering whether it is true or not. This implies that in order to be able to "appreciate and nurture the creative suggestions of talented students" (Conference Board of the Mathematical Sciences, 2001, p. 13), the teachers should have experience with mathematics that goes beyond one's informal conjecturing.

Topics in Mathematics for Elementary Teachers, pages 91–112
Copyright © 2010 by Information Age Publishing
All rights of reproduction in any form reserved.

Number theory is a natural extension of arithmetic in which properties of numbers discovered through operations on them are put in a theoretical perspective. That is why number theory provides many opportunities for fostering teachers' mathematical experience. Many properties of numbers were already discussed in Chapter 4 in connection with the multiplication table. By exploring a new set of questions, other properties of numbers can be discovered: *Why do some numbers appear more often than others in the multiplication table? Why are some numbers absent from the multiplication table?* These questions are connected to the concept of divisibility. In what follows, this concept will be explored using concrete materials and spreadsheets.

2. MOTIVATION

Tutoring Problem: *You would really like to have that car you saw for sale last week. To earn some extra money, you ask your school counselor about different jobs. She informs you that you could earn $10 per hour tutoring three middle school students, named Alan, Beth, and Chuck. You will tutor Alan every second day, Beth every third day, and Chuck every fifth day. On which days would you tutor no students? How often would you have two days off (tutor no students) during any three-day period? On which days would you tutor all three students? And most importantly, how much money would you expect to make over a month (31 days) by taking this job?*

The chart pictured in Figure 6.1 can be used to support an inquiry into the tutoring problem. In this chart, an asterisk in the row for Alan (Beth or Chuck) means that the tutoring of Alan (Beth or Chuck) is scheduled on the corresponding day. The absence of asterisks on any particular day is the indication of a day off. By observing the chart, one can develop the list of days off: 1, 7, 11, 13, 17, 19, 23, 29, 31.

What is special about these nine numbers, mathematically? One can observe that these are odd numbers—a typical answer one would hear in the classroom of pre-service elementary teachers. Yet, many odd numbers in the range 1 through 31 are absent from the list. This prompts one to look for another, more specific property that characterizes the numbers. The following commonality can be observed: *Each number in the list is divisible by one and itself only.* This observation may be prompted by a method used to

Day	1	2	3	4	5	6	7	8	9	10	11	12	13	14	15	16	17	18	19	20	21	22	23	24	25	26	27	28	29	30	31
Alan		*		*		*		*		*		*		*		*		*		*		*		*		*		*		*	
Beth			*			*			*			*			*			*			*			*			*			*	
Chuck					*					*					*					*					*					*	

Figure 6.1 A chart in support of inquiry into the tutoring situation.

generate the asterisks in the chart: One puts an asterisk in the row for Alan, Beth, or Chuck if the day number is, respectively, a multiple of two, three, or five. Any number not greater than 31 that is not a multiple of 2, 3, or 5 can be divided by one and itself only. One can say that all numbers in the list of days off, except the first one, have exactly two *different* divisors. This enables the introduction of Definition 1: *Counting numbers with exactly two different divisors are called prime numbers.*

Note that there are prime numbers smaller than seven that are absent from the list. These numbers are 2, 3, and 5. As was mentioned above, these three numbers were used to develop the chart by marking with an asterisk any day number that is divisible by one of them, thereby leaving without asterisks only days off. In that way, there exist eleven prime numbers not greater than the number 31. These are 2, 3, 5, 7, 11, 13, 17, 19, 23, 29, and 31. By definition, prime numbers may only be located in the first row/column of the multiplication table. That is why, whereas each of the numbers 2, 3, 5, and 7 appears only twice in the 10×10 table, the other prime numbers are absent from this table. On the other hand, no composite number (a number with more than two different divisors) appears more than four times in this table.

Next, observing the chart of Figure 6.1, one can identify three pairs of numbers that represent two days off during a three-day period: (11, 13), (17, 19), and (29, 31). Besides being prime numbers, the elements of these pairs differ by two. A mathematical significance of this property is reflected in Definition 2: *A prime number that differs from another prime number by two is called a twin prime. A pair of prime numbers with difference two is called a prime twin.*

In answering the third question of the tutoring problem, one can see that on the 30th day, for the first time, all three students are scheduled for tutoring. The way the asterisks appear in the chart suggests that the number 30 is divisible by 2, 3, and 5. In other words, the number 30 is a common multiple of 2, 3, and 5. Furthermore, it is the least common multiple of the three numbers. If only Alan and Beth were tutored, the first day when they both would be tutored would be day 6, as it is the least common multiple of 2 and 3.

Definition 3: *The smallest number that is divisible by a and b is called the least common multiple of a and b, and is denoted by the symbol LCM(a, b).*

The concept of the least common multiple can be extended to more than two numbers. For example, $LCM(2, 3, 5) = 30$. One can recall the application of the concept of the *LCM* to the addition and subtraction of fractions with different denominators: The least common denominator of two or more fractions is the least common multiple of their denominators. In some cases, $LCM(a,b) = a \cdot b$, in other cases, $LCM(a,b) < a \cdot b$. The former relationship indicates the absence of common divisors between a and b. The latter relationship suggests that a and b have common divisors. For example, the *LCM* of two consecutive integers is equal to their product. This fact was used in Chapter 5 in connection with the identity

$$\frac{1}{n} - \frac{1}{n+1} = \frac{1}{n(n+1)},$$

which gives a remarkably simple formula for finding the difference between two consecutive unit fractions. As will be shown in Chapter 10, when n is a prime number, the unit fraction $1/n$ has only two representations as a sum of two unit fractions.

Tutoring Problem Extended: Dealing with Possible Students' Observations

An interesting didactic situation may occur in connection with answering the last question of the tutoring problem: How much money would the tutor expect to make over a month? First, one can observe that the total number of asterisks in the chart of Figure 6.1 is 31. Therefore, the total earnings over one month would be $310. Apparently, already on the 30th day, the tutor shall make $310. One may wonder: *Would this pattern continue, that is, would every 31 days of tutoring bring $310?* Secondly, one can observe that Alan would take 15 lessons, Beth, 10 lessons, and Chuck, 6 lessons. But the last three numbers are consecutive triangular numbers! Another question might be raised: *Is this a coincidence or a mathematically explainable phenomenon?*

Finally, one can observe that, whereas 31 is a prime number, the relationship $31 = 15 + 10 + 6$ holds. This observation can motivate yet another question: *Is any prime number a sum of three triangular numbers?* These are kinds of questions that curious students might be raising in a mathematics classroom already at the upper elementary level. How can a teacher respond to such questions?

It is not so much the teacher's answers to the emerging mathematical curiosity of students that matter, but, rather, the development of the environment that motivates unexpected questions by the students. A teacher should be prepared to naturally say, "Good question, let us think together," and then use their own excitement about the question raised by a student in order to encourage curiosity and drive for further learning. As Pólya (1981) put it: "The ideas should be born in students' minds and the teacher should act only as midwife" (p. 104). In the particular case of the extension of the tutoring problem, one can use a spreadsheet to investigate how much money one could make over the period of 300, 500, 1000, and so on days. For example, as a practice in computational problem solving (see Chapter 11), one can demonstrate that over the 1,000-day period, the amount of $10,330 would be earned. This sum is approximately $3 less than one can find through proportional reasoning under the assumption that the answer to the first question posed in this section is positive.

An answer to the second question regarding the number of lessons taken by each student being a triangular number depends on the interpretation of the numbers 2, 3, and 5. If we interpret them as prime numbers, consider the next two primes, 7 and 11. Tutoring a student every seventh day brings about four lessons over a 31-day period; in the case of eleven, there will be two lessons over a 31-day period. Neither 4 nor 2 is a triangular number. Next, one can interpret 2, 3, and 5 as the first three terms of the sequence 2, 3, 5, 9, 17,... with a power of two being a difference between two consecutive terms (indeed, $3 - 2 = 1$, $5 - 3 = 2$, $9 - 5 = 4$, $17 - 9 = 8$). Tutoring a student every 9 days brings about 3 lessons over a 31-day period. Tutoring a student every 17 days brings about 1 lesson over that period. In that way, the numbers 2, 3, 5, 9, 17 can be associated with the triangular numbers 15, 10, 6, 3, 1, respectively. This raises another inquiry: *Can this phenomenon be observed over the period of two months?*

As to the third question concerning the representation of a prime number as a sum of three triangular numbers, this relationship holds true not only for any prime number but also for any counting number. Indeed, according to Fermat,[1] *Every counting number is the sum of, at most, three triangular numbers.* So, such a simply formulated theorem by one of the founders of modern mathematics shows how mathematical discoveries can be made through observations. On the other hand, one can show that the above association of the numbers 2, 3, 5, 9, and 17 with triangular numbers cannot be confirmed for the period of two months and, thereby, observations, while being important means of mathematical discovery, might or might not lead to a general statement, be it a theorem or conjecture. As Euler[2] noted:

> Therefore, we should take great care not to accept as true such properties of numbers which we have discovered by observation and which are supported by induction alone. Indeed, we should use such a discovery as an opportunity to investigate more exactly the properties discovered and to prove or disprove them; in both cases we may learn something useful. (translated from the Latin by Pólya, 1981, p. 3)

This is exactly what we did (and students of mathematics can do) when investigating questions about the properties of numbers motivated by observations.

3. THE SIEVE OF ERATOSTHENES

Consider another three questions that can be posed as an extension of the tutoring problem:

- If the tutoring schedule were extended to two months (61 days), what is the smallest number representing a day off that is not a prime number?
- How many prime numbers not greater than 61 are there?
- Given a two-digit number, how does one decide if this number is a prime or not?

To answer these new questions, a tool for identifying prime numbers among counting numbers can be introduced. Such a tool, known for more than two thousand years and called the sieve of Eratosthenes, is due to the 3rd century B.C. Greek scholar Eratosthenes, who designed a simple method of finding prime numbers among counting numbers. This method allows one to obtain all the prime numbers less than any given integer N by crossing out from the set of all counting numbers less than N the multiples of each of the primes up to the $INT(\sqrt{N})$, where $INT(x)$ is the largest integer smaller than x. All numbers that remain undeleted are the primes sought. This process was, in fact, implemented in the chart of Figure 6.1, where prime numbers were obtained by eliminating all multiples of 2, 3, and 5 in the range 1 through 31 (note, $INT(\sqrt{31}) = 5$). To start the process, one needs to know the smallest prime number, that is, the smallest integer with exactly two different divisors. The number 2 is such an integer. After eliminating all multiples of 2 from a given list of consecutive counting numbers, one concludes that the smallest number to survive this process is 3, which, thereby, has only two different divisors (see the second line in the charts of Figure 6.2).

	A	B	C	D	E	F	G	H	I	J	K	L	M	N	O	P	Q	R	S	T	U	V	W	X	Y	Z	AA	AB	AC	AD	AE
1																															
2		2	3	4	5	6	7	8	9	10	11	12	13	14	15	16	17	18	19	20	21	22	23	24	25	26	27	28	29	30	31
3																															
4		2	3		5		7		9		11		13		15		17		19		21		23		25		27		29		31
5																															
6		2	3		5		7				11		13				17		19				23		25				29		31
7																															
8		2	3		5		7				11		13				17		19				23						29		31
9																															
10		2	3		5		7				11		13				17		19				23						29		31
11																															
12																															
13																															
14																															
15		32	33	34	35	36	37	38	39	40	41	42	43	44	45	46	47	48	**49**	50	51	52	53	54	55	56	57	58	59	60	61
16																															
17			33		35		37		39		41		43		45		47		**49**		51		53		55		57		59		61
18																															
19					35		37				41		43				47		**49**				53		55				59		61
20																															
21							37				41		43				47		**49**				53						59		61
22																															
23							37				41		43				47						53						59		61

Figure 6.2 Generating prime numbers not greater than 61.

Next, by eliminating all multiples of 3 from the list (some of which were already eliminated as the multiples of 2), one can conclude that the smallest number to survive this process is the number 5 (see the third line in the upper chart of Figure 6.2), which, thereby, has exactly two different divisors. Now, all multiples of 5 have to be eliminated. The result is presented in the fourth line of each chart that includes numbers not divisible by 2, 3, and 5. Yet, we have not eliminated those multiples of 7 that are not divisible by 2, 3, and 5. The smallest multiple of 7 not divisible by 2, 3, and 5 is $7 \cdot 7 = 49$. So, by interpreting the sieve of Eratosthenes developed at the third step (after eliminating all multiples of 5) as a tutoring schedule, one would consider the 49th day as a day off, which, however, has three divisors (1, 7, and 49) and, thereby, 49 is not a prime number. The fifth line in each chart includes prime numbers only. Extending the search for primes to the range 32 through 61 resulted in seven new prime numbers: 37, 41, 43, 47, 53, 59, and 61. Therefore, there are 18 prime numbers not greater than 61.

The development of the sieve of Eratosthenes shows that in order to decide if a number N is a prime number or not, one has to test whether N is divided by any of the prime numbers not greater than $INT(\sqrt{N})$. If none of those primes divides N, then N is a prime number, as it has exactly two different divisors (the numbers 1 and N). In particular, in order to decide if a two-digit number is a prime or not, one has to perform, at most, four divisions. Indeed, as 99 is the largest two-digit number and $INT(\sqrt{99}) = 9$, only 2, 3, 5, and 7 are the prime numbers smaller than 9. Sometimes, carrying out divisions is not necessary. Instead, the so-called tests of divisibility can be used. Some such tests are not difficult, yet some tests are very complicated, and, in the age of computing technology, have little practical value. In the next section, the most commonly known and easily applicable tests of divisibility by 2, 3, 5, 9, and 11 will be discussed.

4. DIVISIBILITY TESTS

What does it mean for a number to divide another number? To answer this question, consider two models for division—partition model and measurement model—that can be introduced through the following two problems.

Problem 1 (Partition Model for Division): *Andy had ten marbles. He put them evenly in two boxes. How many marbles are in each box?*

Problem 2 (Measurement Model for Division): *Andy had ten marbles. He put them in boxes designed for five marbles each. How many boxes did he need?*

Figure 6.3 represents a solution for each of the two problems. Yet, the answer for each problem is different. For Problem 1, the answer is five marbles; for Problem 2, the answer is two boxes. We solved Problem 1 by dividing two into ten using the partition model, something that conceptualizes division as fair sharing. We solved Problem 2 by dividing five into ten using the measurement model, something that conceptualizes division as repeated subtraction. One can see that the partition model with respect to divisibility of ten by two is equivalent to the measurement model with respect to divisibility of ten by five.

By the same token, as shown in Figure 6.4, the partition model with respect to divisibility of ten by five (arranging ten marbles in five groups) is equivalent to the measurement model with respect to divisibility of ten by two (arranging ten marbles in groups of two).

In that way, at a physical level, the statement "n divides N" means that N objects can either be put in n groups of N/n objects in each, or in N/n groups of n objects in each. Figures 6.3 and 6.4 show two meanings of the statement "5 divides 10": there are either 5 groups of 2 objects in each (partition model), or there are 2 groups of 5 objects in each (measurement model). By the same token, these diagrams show two meanings of the statement "2 divides 10": there are either 2 groups of 5 objects in each (partition model) or 5 groups can be created by pairing 10 objects (measurement model).

Proposition 1: *All powers (or, more generally, multiples) of 10 are divisible by 2, 5, and 10.*

Proof. The fact that the number 10 is divisible by 2, 5, and 10 implies that any multiple of ten is divisible by 2, 5, and 10. Indeed, within the partition model, any k-multiple of ten objects can be placed in either five or two boxes; however, the number of objects in each box would increase k-fold. For example, as Figure 6.3 indicates, increasing the amount of marbles in each box by the factor 4 would yield 40 marbles and $40 = 4 \cdot 10$. Within the measurement model, for any k-multiple of ten objects, there will be either five or two objects in each box; yet, this

Figure 6.3 Partition model for $10 \div 2 = 5$ and measurement model for $10 \div 5 = 2$.

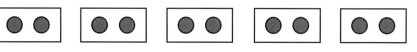

Figure 6.4 Partition model for $10 \div 5 = 2$ and measurement model for $10 \div 2 = 5$.

time, the number of boxes would increase *k*-fold. For example, increasing the number of boxes shown in Figure 6.4 by the factor 4, once again, would yield 40 marbles.

Proposition 2 (Test of Divisibility by 2): *If the last digit of an integer is an even number, the integer is divisible by 2.*

Proof. Because the number 2 is divisible by 2, any multiple of 2, as Figure 6.5 shows, is divisible by 2. At the same time, any multiple of 2 can be reached through counting by twos, thus having numbers with an even last digit (note: zero is considered an even number).

Proposition 3 (Test of Divisibility by 5): *If the last digit of an integer is either 0 or 5, the integer is divisible by 5.*

Proof. Because the number 5 is divisible by 5, any multiple of 5 is divisible by 5. At the same time, any multiple of 5 can be reached through counting by fives, thus having numbers with the last digit either 0 or 5.

Proposition 4: *The number 9 is divisible by 3.*

Proof. As shown in Figure 6.6, both the measurement and the partition models show that 3 divides 9.

Proposition 5: *If a number N has no digits other than 9, then it is divisible both by 3 and 9.*

Proof. Let $N = \underbrace{99\ldots99}_{k-nines}$.

Then, representing N as the sum of products of its face values (digits) and the corresponding place values (powers of 10) yields

$$N = 10^k \times 9 + 10^{k-1} \times 9 + \ldots + 10 \times 9 + 9.$$

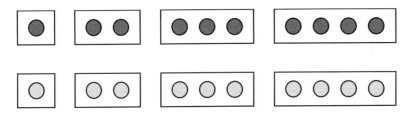

Figure 6.5 Pairing two counters implies pairing any multiple of the two counters.

Figure 6.6 Illustration to Proposition 4.

Due to the distributive property of multiplication over addition (Chapter 4), the number 9 is a factor of N. Therefore, N is divisible by 3 and 9.

Proposition 6 (Test of Divisibility by 3): *A number is divisible by 3 if the sum of its digits is divisible by 3.*

Proof. Consider a k-digit number $N = a_1 10^{k-1} + a_2 10^{k-2} + \ldots + a_{k-1} 10 + a_k$ and its equivalent representation:

$$N = a_1(10^{k-1} - 1) + a_2(10^{k-2} - 1) + \ldots + a_{k-1}(10 - 1) + a_1 + a_2 + \ldots + a_{k-1} + a_k$$
$$= [a_1 \cdot \underbrace{99\ldots9}_{(k-1)-nines} + a_2 \cdot \underbrace{99\ldots9}_{(k-2)-nines} + \ldots + a_{k-1} \cdot 9] + [a_1 + a_2 + \ldots + a_{k-1} + a_k].$$

According to Proposition 5, the sum in the first pair of brackets is divisible by 3. Therefore, N is divisible by 3 if the sum in the second pair of brackets is divisible by 3. Noting that the latter sum is the sum of the digits of N completes the proof.

Proposition 7 (Test of Divisibility by 9): *A number is divisible by 9 if the sum of its digits is divisible by 9.*

Proof. Consider a k-digit number $N = a_1 10^{k-1} + a_2 10^{k-2} + \ldots + a_{k-1} 10 + a_k$ and its equivalent representation:

$$N = a_1(10^{k-1} - 1) + a_2(10^{k-2} - 1) + \ldots + a_{k-1}(10 - 1) + a_1 + a_2 + \ldots + a_{k-1} + a_k$$
$$= [a_1 \cdot \underbrace{99\ldots9}_{(k-1)-nines} + a_2 \cdot \underbrace{99\ldots9}_{(k-2)-nines} + \ldots + a_{k-1} \cdot 9] + [a_1 + a_2 + \ldots + a_{k-1} + a_k].$$

Once again, reference to Proposition 5 completes the proof.

Proposition 8: *Any integer with an even number of identical digits is divisible by 11.*

Proof. Without loss of generality, one may consider an integer of the form

$$\underbrace{1111\ldots11}_{even\ number\ of\ ones}.$$

For example, $1{,}111 = 11 \times 10^2 + 11$; adding another pair of ones yields $111{,}111 = 11 \times 10^4 + 11 \times 10^2 + 11$. In general, if the number

$$\underbrace{111\ldots111}_{2k-\ ones}$$

is divisible by 11, then

$$\underbrace{111\ldots111}_{(2k+2)-\ ones} = 11 \cdot 10^{2k-2} + \underbrace{11\ldots11}_{2k-\ ones}$$

is divisible by 11.

Proposition 9: *Any number of the form* $\underbrace{100\ldots001}_{\text{even number of zeros}}$ *is divisible by 11.*

Proof. It follows from Proposition 8 that any number of the form

$$\underbrace{9999\ldots990}_{\text{even number of nines}} = 9\times 10\times \underbrace{1111\ldots11}_{\text{even number of ones}}$$

is divisible by 11. Therefore, the sum

$$\underbrace{99\ldots990}_{\text{even number of nines}} + 11 = \underbrace{100\ldots001}_{\text{even number of zeros}}$$

is divisible by 11. One can see that each of the numbers

$$11, 1001, 100001, \ldots, \underbrace{100\ldots001}_{\text{even number of zeros}}, \ldots$$

is divisible by 11. Note that a number $100\ldots001$ with an even number of zeros has an even number of digits also.

Proposition 10 (Test of Divisibility by 11): *Take the sum of every other digit beginning from the last one and subtract from it the sum of the remaining digits. If the difference is divisible by 11, so is the original number.*

Proof. Note that the closest number to 10^{2k} divisible by 11 is

$$\underbrace{99\ldots99}_{\text{even number of nines}} .$$

The closest number to 10^{2k+1} divisible by 11 is

$$\underbrace{100\ldots001}_{\text{even number of zeros}} .$$

For example, 356,279 is divisible by 11 because

$$356,279 = 3\times 10^5 + 5\times 10^4 + 6\times 10^3 + 2\times 10^2 + 7\times 10 + 1$$
$$= 3\times (100,001-1) + 5\times (9,999+1) + 6\times (1,001-1) + 2\times (99+1) + 7\times (11-1) + 9$$
$$= \underbrace{(3\times 100,001 + 5\times 9,999 + 6\times 1,001 + 2\times 99 + 7\times 11)}_{\text{divisible by 11}} + \underbrace{(-3+5-6+2-7+9)}_{=0-\text{divisible by 11}}.$$

Now, consider a $2k$-digit number[3] $N = a_1 10^{2k-1} + a_2 10^{2k-2} + a_3 10^{2k-3} \ldots + a_{2k-2} 10^2 + a_{2k-1} 10 + a_{2k}$ and its equivalent representation

$$N = a_{2k} + a_{2k-1}(10+1) - a_{2k-1} + a_{2k-2}(10^2 - 1) + a_{2k-2} + \dots$$

$$+ a_3(10^{2k-3} + 1) - a_3 + a_2(10^{2k-2} - 1) + a_2 + a_1(10^{2k-1} + 1) - a_1$$

$$= \left[a_{2k-1} \cdot 11 + a_{2k-2} \cdot 99 + \dots + a_3 \cdot \underbrace{100\dots01}_{(2k-4)-zeros} + a_2 \cdot \underbrace{99\dots9}_{(2k-2)-nines} + a_1 \cdot \underbrace{100\dots01}_{(2k-2)-zeros} \right]$$

$$+ \left[a_{2k} + a_{2k-2} + \dots + a_2 - a_{2k-1} - a_{2k-3} - \dots - a_1 \right].$$

According to Proposition 9, each term in the first pair of brackets is divisible by 11. Therefore, N is divisible by 11 if the sum in the second pair of brackets is divisible by 11. This completes the proof.

Example. Consider the number **1,325,929**. Calculating the difference between the sums of bold and non-bold digits yields $(9 + 9 + 2 + 1) - (2 + 5 + 3) = 21 - 10 = 11$. Therefore, 11 divides 1,325,929. One can use a calculator to check that $1,325,929 \div 11 = 120,539$.

To conclude this section, note that tests of divisibility do not produce quotients. These kinds of tests guarantee only that the corresponding quotients are whole numbers. A similar situation was encountered in Chapters 1 and 2 when the questions *How many?* were answered theoretically, rather than through the development of an organized list.

5. EXPLORATIONS WITH PRIME NUMBERS AND INDUCTIVE REASONING

Euclid, the most prominent Greek mathematician of the 3rd century B.C., commonly known for his work on the axiomatization of geometry (as it is taught currently in the schools), also made several important contributions to the foundations of number theory. In particular, Euclid proved that the number of primes is infinite. His proof is a classic example of a proof by contradiction. Euclid made an assumption that there exists the largest prime number p, and then constructed another prime number $q > p$, thereby, running into a contradiction with the assumption made.

As it turned out, a situation with twin primes is much more complicated. The problem of the infinitude of twin primes (or prime twins) is still an open problem in mathematics. The twin prime conjecture states that there are infinitely many prime numbers p, such that $p + 2$ is also a prime number. Our inability to prove such a simply formulated statement points at the inherent complexity of the ideas associated with the distribution of prime numbers among counting numbers. In fact, no formula exists that generates prime numbers only.

A classic example of the difficulty in developing such a formula is due to Fermat, who conjectured that for all $n = 0, 1, 2, \ldots$ the expression $2^{2^n} + 1$ yields prime numbers only. Fermat based his conjecture on inductive reasoning, as the cases $n = 0, 1, 2, 3$, and 4, indeed, produce, respectively, prime numbers 3, 5, 17, 257, and 65537. However, as was proved later by Euler, the case $n = 5$ produces a composite number $4{,}294{,}967{,}297 = 641 \cdot 6{,}700{,}417$.

Euler, however, found a function, $f(x) = x^2 - x + 41$, of integer variable x that produces different prime numbers only (although not consecutive ones) for any *successive* value of x from quite a large range, $1 \le x \le 40$. (The same primes, $41, 43, 47, 53, 61, \ldots, 1523, 1601$, can be generated for $-39 \le x \le 0$). One can see that $f(41) = 41^2$ is a composite number. What is also interesting about $f(x)$ is that the difference between successive primes in this list of forty primes forms an arithmetic progression $2, 4, 6, \ldots, 78$. Furthermore, as x increases, $f(x)$ continues generating mostly prime numbers. For example, in the range $41 \le x \le 120$, the function $f(x)$ generates 62 primes out of 80 values (more than 75%). One can use a spreadsheet to carry out the exploration of the function $f(x)$ found by Euler. Once again, we can recall Euler's remark (section 2) that knowledge supported by observations (that is, reasoning by induction) should not be confused with truth.

Another example of the deficiency of reasoning by induction that leads to incorrect generalization deals with twin primes. In what follows, the tests of divisibility established above will be applied to the investigation of patterns among twin primes. Toward this end, note that one can organize all twin primes into three groups depending on their last digits. The prime twins $(11, 13)$, $(17, 19)$, and $(29, 31)$ are the smallest representatives of each of the three groups. Below, the case of the first group will be explored as a way of demonstrating the complexity of the distribution of prime numbers among counting numbers.

Twin Primes Activity: *Find four consecutive pairs of twin primes with the endings 1 and 3, starting from the pair (11, 13). Guess the fifth pair in this sequence. Describe what you have found.*

Description: In the first two columns of the chart pictured in Figure 6.7, numbers that differ by 2 and have the last digit either 1 or 3 are presented. These numbers are not divisible by either 2 or 5 because their endings do not match the corresponding divisibility tests. However, they might be divisible by 3, 7, and 11. Numbers smaller than 49 should be tested by three only, numbers smaller than 121 (but greater than 49) should be tested by 3 and 7 only, and numbers greater that 121 (but smaller than 169) should be tested by 3, 7, and 11. (Recall that $49 = 7^2$, $121 = 11^2$, and $169 = 13^2$). This exploration shows that the first four pairs of twin primes with the endings

11	13		twin primes
21	23	21 is divisible by 3	reject
31	33	23 is divisible by 3	reject
41	43	neither is divisible by 3	twin primes
51	53	51 is divisible by 3	reject
61	63	63 is divisible by 3	reject
71	73	neither is divisible by 3 or 7	twin primes
81	83	81 is divisible by 3	reject
91	93	93 is divisible by 3	reject
101	103	neither is divisible by 3 or 7	twin primes
111	113	111 is divisible by 3	reject
121	123	123 is divisible by 3	reject
131	133	$133 = 140 - 7 = 20 \times 7 - 7 = 19 \times 7$	reject

Figure 6.7 Exploring divisibility properties of integers with the endings 1 and 3.

1 and 3 are (11, 13), (41, 43), (71, 73), and (101, 103). One can see that the corresponding elements of two consecutive prime twins differ from each other by 30.

Using inductive reasoning, that is, making a generalization based on a number of observed instances, one can reasonably conjecture that the numbers 131 and 133 are twin primes (the author observed many teachers who, by making this conjecture, appeared quite proud of their ability to recognize a pattern). This, however, is not true, as $133 = 140 - 7 = 20 \times 7 - 7 = 19 \times 7$; that is, the number 133 has more than two different divisors. Once again, we learned that inductive reasoning is not rigorous.

In order to find the fifth pair of twin primes with the endings 1 and 3, the chart of Figure 6.8 should be extended, and larger pairs of numbers with these endings should be explored. Each of the numbers 141, 153, and 183 is divisible by 3 (indeed, $1 + 4 + 1 = 6$, $1 + 5 + 3 = 9$, and $1 + 8 + 3 = 12$), and the number 161 is divisible by 7 ($161 = 140 + 21$). This leaves us with the numbers 191 and 193 that have to be tested by the prime numbers 3, 7, 11, and 13 only (as $13^2 < 191$ and $17^2 > 193$).

First, $191 \xrightarrow{\div 3} 1 + 9 + 1 = 11$ and $193 \xrightarrow{\div 3} 1 + 9 + 3 = 13$; in both cases, the sums of digits are not divisible by 3. Next, the equalities $191 = 189 + 2 = 7 \cdot 27 + 2$ and $193 = 189 + 4 = 7 \cdot 27 + 4$, as well as $191 = 195 - 4 = 13 \cdot 15 - 4$ and $193 = 195 - 2 = 13 \cdot 15 - 2$ defy divisibility by 7 and 13. Similarly, the testing of $191 \xrightarrow{\div 11} 1 + 1 - 9 = -7$ and $193 \xrightarrow{\div 11} 3 + 1 - 9 = -5$ shows that both numbers are not divisible by 11. Therefore, the pair (191, 193) is the fifth prime twin with the endings 1 and 3.

To conclude this section, note that the sequence of five consecutive prime twins (11, 13), (41, 43), (71, 73), (101, 103), and (191, 193) with the endings 1 and 3 does not suggest any pattern. The only observation that one can make is that the average of the twin primes is always a multiple of six; that is, the twin primes are separated by the multiples of six. Whereas not all multiples of six have twin primes as immediate neighbors on the (whole) number line, one may wonder if all twin primes are separated by a multiple of six. For more information on this topic, a book by Loweke (1982) can be recommended.

5. THE GREATEST COMMON DIVISOR

Problem 3: *Two cohorts of cadets are to be combined to march in a parade. A 30-cadet cohort will march behind a 24-cadet cohort. The combined cohorts must have the same number of columns. What is the greatest number of columns in which they can march?*

Solution: Figure 6.8 shows a manipulative-based solution to this problem. First, we attempted to put a 24-cadet cohort in three rows, thereby creating eight columns. In doing so, we applied the partition model for division by dividing 3 into 24 to get 8 (columns). Alternatively, we divided 8 into 24 using the measurement model for division to get 3 (rows). Likewise, dividing 6 into 30 using the partition model yields 5 (columns). Alternatively, dividing 5 into 30 using the measurement model yields 6 (rows). The numbers 3 and 5 are divisors of 24 and 30, respectively; yet, they are not common divisors. So, we have to find all integers (greater than one) that divide both 24 and 30, and then select the largest such integer. The latter is called the greatest common divisor of 24 and 30. Below, the notation *GCD*(*a*, *b*) will be used to refer to the greatest common divisor of *a* and *b*.

As shown in Figure 6.8, the number 2 is a common divisor of 24 and 30. Are there other common divisors? Divisibility tests can be applied to find that both 3 and 6 are common divisors of 24 and 30. One can see

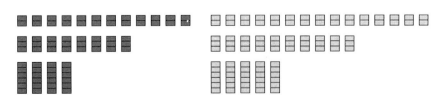

Figure 6.8   Arranging the bands into groups of two, three, and six.

that $GCD(24, 30) = 6$. That is, 6 is the largest number of columns in which the cadets can march. This fact was established experimentally by using concrete objects (e.g., square tiles). The question remains as to how one can find the greatest common divisor of two numbers other than through manipulating tiles. With this in mind, consider

> **Problem 4:** *Two cohorts of cadets are to be combined to march in a parade. A 282-cadet cohort will march behind a 136-cadet cohort. The combined cohorts must have the same number of columns. What is the greatest number of columns in which they can march?*

Solution: Apparently, the numbers 282 and 136 are too large to allow for a manipulative solution. This requires one to find all divisors of the two numbers in a numeric way. Let us divide the numbers as follows:

$$282 \xrightarrow{\div 2} 141 \xrightarrow{\div 3} 47 \xrightarrow{\div 47} 1;$$
$$136 \xrightarrow{\div 2} 68 \xrightarrow{\div 2} 34 \xrightarrow{\div 2} 17 \xrightarrow{\div 17} 1.$$

Divisors of 282 and 136 are, respectively, (2, 3, 6, 47, 94, 141, 282) and (2, 4, 8, 17, 34, 68, 136). The number 2 is the only divisor that belongs to both sets of divisors. Therefore, $GCD(282, 136) = 2$.

One may wonder if there exists a more effective way of finding the GCD of any two sufficiently large integers. A positive answer to this question has been known for more than 2,000 years, due to Euclid, who developed a method commonly referred to as the Euclidean algorithm.

7. THE EUCLIDEAN ALGORITHM

The Euclidean algorithm of finding the $GCD(a, b)$ of two whole numbers a and b is a recursive procedure of successive divisions based on the relation of fundamental importance in number theory—the remainder (R) equals the dividend (D) minus the divisor (d) times the quotient (Q). That is, $R = D - dQ$. Setting two whole numbers a and b as a dividend and a divisor, one can find their remainder, which (if greater than zero) becomes a new divisor, whereas the old divisor becomes a new dividend. This process of calculating remainders continues until a zero remainder is reached. According to Euclid, the last non-zero remainder represents the $GCD(a, b)$.

To clarify, consider a numeric example of dividing 5 into 13 using long division. In the diagram of Figure 6.9, the following four numbers can be identified: 13 is the dividend, 5 is the divisor, 2 is the quotient, and 3 is the remainder. Moreover, the four numbers satisfy the equality $13 = 2 \times 5 + 3$, whence $3 = 13 - 2 \times 5$. In other words, the remainder 3 is equal to the divi-

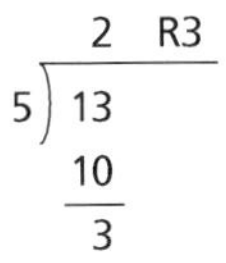

$$\begin{array}{r} 2 \quad R3 \\ 5\overline{)\,13} \\ 10 \\ \hline 3 \end{array}$$

Figure 6.9 Dividing 5 into 13 using long division.

dend 13 minus the product of the quotient 2 and the divisor 5. This definition of remainder is integrated into the $MOD(a, b)$ function that returns the remainder of a divided by b.

Problem 5: *Find the GCD(54, 21) using the Euclidean algorithm.*

Solution: We separate a solution into steps required to reach a zero remainder.

Step 1. Divide 21 into 54 and find the remainder R_1: $R_1 = 54 - 2 \times 21 = 12$. Using the MOD notation, $R_1 = MOD(54, 21) = 12$.

Step 2. Divide R_1 into 21 and find the remainder R_2: $R_2 = 21 - 1 \times 12 = 9$. Alternatively, $R_2 = MOD(21, 12) = 9$.

Step 3. Divide R_2 into 12 and find the remainder R_3: $R_3 = 12 - 1 \times 9 = 3$. Alternatively, $R_3 = MOD(12, 9) = 3$.

Step 4. Divide R_3 into 9 and find the remainder R_4: $R_4 = 9 - 3 \times 3 = 0$. Alternatively, $R_4 = MOD(9, 3) = 0$.

The process terminates when a zero remainder has been reached, as one may not divide by zero. The sequence of remainders generated through the above four steps is $R_1 = 12$, $R_2 = 9$, $R_3 = 3$, $R_4 = 0$. According to Euclid, the last non-zero remainder (R_3) in this sequence is $GCD(54, 21)$. Indeed, as $GCD(12, 9) = 3$ (according to the expression for R_3), it follows that 3 is a divisor of 12 and 21 (according to the expression for R_2), and, therefore, 3 is a divisor of 21 and 54 (according to the expression for R_1). If there exists a number $n > 3$ that divides both 54 and 21, this value of n divides 12, as well (according to the expression for R_1). Therefore, n divides 9 (according to the expression for R_2). Finally, the expression for R_3 implies n divides 3. The latter implication contradicts the assumption $n > 3$. Therefore, no number greater than 3 divides both 54 and 21, that is, $GCD(54, 21) = 3$.

Problem 6: *Find the GCD(282, 136) through the Euclidean algorithm.*

Solution: Using the *MOD* notation, one has $MOD(282, 136) = 10$, $MOD(136, 10) = 6$, $MOD(10, 6) = 4$, $MOD(6, 4) = 2$, and, finally, $MOD(4, 2) = 0$. Therefore, $GCD(282, 136) = 2$.

	A	B	C	D	E
1	Euclidean Algorithm				
2		282			377
3		136			233
4		10			144
5		6			89
6		4			55
7	GCD=	2			34
8					21
9					13
10					8
11					5
12					3
13					2
14				GCD=	1

Figure 6.10 Euclidean algorithm and Fibonacci numbers.

The spreadsheet pictured in Figure 6.10 is designed to calculate the *GCD* of two numbers through the use of the *MOD* function—one of the spreadsheet-based functions. In particular, it shows that *GCD*(377, 233) = 1. Note that the numbers a and b are called relatively prime if $GCD(a, b) = 1$. One can also note that, along with 377 and 233, all remainders in the process of finding the *GCD*(377, 233) are consecutive Fibonacci numbers (studied in the next chapter). Using this spreadsheet, one can investigate if there exists another pair of whole numbers in the range 1 through 400 for which the Euclidean algorithm requires exactly 12 steps to reach a zero remainder. This investigation would show that no pair with such a property other that 377 and 233 exists. It turns out that the Euclidean algorithm follows the rule of Fibonacci recursion in the case of the unit quotient.

8. CONNECTION BETWEEN LCM AND GCD

An interesting relationship between the least common multiple and greatest common divisor can be formulated.

Proposition 10: *For any two positive integers a and b,* $GCD(a, b) \cdot LCM(a, b) = a \cdot b$.

Proof. The numbers a and b can be represented as $a = GCD(a, b) \cdot s$ and $b = GCD(a, b) \cdot r$, where $GCD(r, s) = 1$. Then, by definition, $LCM(a, b) = a \cdot s = b \cdot r$. Therefore,

$$a \cdot b = GCD(a,b) \cdot GCD(a,b) \cdot r \cdot s = GCD(a,b) \cdot a \cdot s = GCD(a,b) \cdot LCM(a,b).$$

Problem 7: *Find LCM(568, 168).*

Solution: Implementing the Euclidean algorithm, one has $MOD(568, 168) = 64$, $MOD(168, 64) = 40$, $MOD(64, 40) = 24$, $MOD(40, 24) = 16$, $MOD(24, 16) = 8$, and $MOD(16, 8) = 0$. Therefore,

$$LCM(568, 168) = \frac{568 \cdot 168}{GCD(568, 168)} = \frac{95,424}{8} = 11,928.$$

The last example can also be used to clarify the proof of Proposition 10. Indeed, $568 = 8 \cdot 71$, $168 = 8 \cdot 21$, and $GCD(71, 21) = 1$. Therefore, $LCM(568, 168) = 8 \cdot 71 \cdot 21 = 11,928$. Finally,

$$568 \cdot 168 = 8 \cdot 8 \cdot 71 \cdot 21 = GCD(568, 168) \cdot LCM(568, 168).$$

9. TECHNOLOGY AS AN AGENT OF MATHEMATICAL ACTIVITY: AN EXAMPLE

Problem-solving activities and concepts presented in this section emerged from the construction of an electronic manipulative environment for exploring percentage problems in the elementary classroom. The environment in question utilizes a spreadsheet's capacity to be used as a manipulative with a hot link to numeric notation. In such an environment, a student is presented with a rectangular grid that contains less than 100 cells. On this grid, a number of cells are shaded (Figure 6.11), so that the shaded part constitutes a whole number percentage of the entire grid. A task for a student (at the upper elementary level) is to evaluate what percent of the grid is shaded and enter this percentage number into the cell of the spreadsheet designated as an answer box. If the student's answer is incorrect, a computer-generated message suggests to continue the task on an, otherwise hidden, identical adjacent non-shaded grid. The objective of this new task is to give a student an opportunity to use an incorrect answer as a thinking device and, in doing so, to shade a region on the adjacent grid (the spreadsheet is programmed in such a way as to enable an interactive

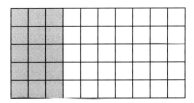

Figure 6.11   What percent of the grid is shaded?

evaluation of the shaded part in numeric form) that does correspond to this answer. That is, if the right answer is $p\%$ and a student's answer is $q\%$ ($q \neq p$), the task is to shade $q\%$ of the adjacent grid and, by seeing the self-created representation of $q\%$, to reconsider the original evaluation.

Technically, however, the idea of turning a negative evaluation into a generator of new meanings cannot be implemented in this environment without restrictions, because not every whole number percentage can be represented by a shaded part of a grid with less than 100 cells. For example, if a student evaluates the shaded part of a 50-cell grid (Figure 6.11) as 25%, the task of shading 25% of an adjacent 50-cell grid would be impossible. In such a way, the tension between a non-authoritative pedagogy and the semiotic structure of the task has led to the idea to restrict a student's possible guessing by offering a choice of selecting answers from a set of percentage numbers including the correct answer. This, in turn, yielded the question: *Given a rectangular grid, what is the total number of choices available on this grid?* Mathematically, this question can be formulated in the form of

Problem 8: *On an n-cell grid, $0 < n \leq 100$, k cells are shaded. In how many ways can one shade k cells on an n-cell grid, $0 < n \leq 100$, in a whole number percentage, provided that shape and location of the cells is not important? In other words, given a positive integer n, in how many ways can one choose a positive integer $k \leq n$, such that $100k/n$ is a positive integer also?*

Solution: One can first approach the problem computationally. To this end, one can use a spreadsheet (Figure 6.12) that generates the values of the expression $100k/n$ for different k and n.

Figure 6.12 shows a fragment of a template with percentage numbers generated in the k-range from 1 to 100, and in the n-range from 1 to 100. To clarify, note that the number 25 in cell J4 means that two (cell B4) is 25% of eight (cell J2); blank cell J5 indicates that three (cell B5) is not a whole number percentage of eight (cell J2); the number four in cell J1 means that there exist four ways of shading an eight-cell grid in a whole number percentage. Numerical evidence of whole number percentages provided by spreadsheet modeling can lead to the following conjecture: *The number of cells that result in whole number percentages is equal to the GCD(n, 100).* Indeed, the numbers in row 1 of the spreadsheet are the *GCD*s between 100 and the corresponding number in row 2.

The availability of a plausible conjecture can mediate its formal proof. To this end, let $n = r \cdot s$ and $100 = m \cdot s$, where $GCD(r, m) = 1$ and $s = GCD(n, 100)$. It follows that

$$\frac{k}{n} \cdot 100 = \frac{k \cdot m \cdot s}{r \cdot s} = \frac{k \cdot m}{r}.$$

	A	B	C	D	E	F	G	H	I	J	K	L	M	N	O	P	Q	R
1	← →		1	2	1	4	5	2	1	4	1	10	1	4	1	2	5	4
2	100	k\n	1	2	3	4	5	6	7	8	9	10	11	12	13	14	15	16
3		1	100	50		25	20					10						
4		2		100		50	40			25		20						
5		3			100	75	60	50				30		25			20	
6		4				100	80			50		40						25
7		5					100					50						
8		6						100		75		60		50			40	
9		7							100			70			50			
10		8								100		80						50
11		9									100	90		75			60	

Figure 6.12 Spreadsheet solution to Problem 8.

One can see that the following s values of $k \in \{r, 2r, 3r, \ldots, s \cdot r\}$ make the ratio

$$\frac{k \cdot m}{r}$$

a whole number. The list of such values of k indeed ends with $k = s \cdot r$, because $k \le n = s \cdot r$. Therefore, the number of the values of k sought is equal to the $GCD(n, 100)$. This completes the solution to Problem 8, thereby, demonstrating how the concept of the greatest common divisor can be used as a problem-solving tool.

10. ACTIVITY SET

1. Find three consecutive pairs of twin primes with the endings 9 and 11, starting from the pair $(29, 31)$. Guess the fourth pair in this sequence using inductive reasoning. Describe what you have found.
2. Find three consecutive pairs of twin primes with the endings 7 and 9, starting from the pair $(17, 19)$. Guess the fourth pair in this sequence using inductive reasoning. Describe what you have found.
3. A cousin prime is a prime number that differs from another prime number by four. Starting from 7 and 11, find four consecutive pairs of cousin primes with the endings 7 and 1. Using inductive reasoning, guess the next two pairs in this sequence. Describe what you have found.
4. Find ways to make the number 135,896 divisible by 11 by swapping some of its digits.
5. Find ways to make the number 479,123 divisible by 11 by swapping some of its digits.

6. Find ways to make the number 270,709 divisible by 11 by swapping some of its digits.
7. Find the *LCM* (76, 144).
8. Find the *LCM* (129, 87).
9. Find the *GCD* (610, 377).

NOTES

1. Fermat, a French mathematician of the 17th century who is considered one of the founders of modern number theory, only conjectured this remarkable theorem. Cauchy, a French mathematician of the 19th century who introduced rigor to all branches of mathematics, including number theory, proved that, in general, every counting number is the sum of, at most, *m* polygonal numbers of side *m* (see Chapter 8).
2. Leonhard Euler, a Swiss mathematician of the 18th century, the father of all modern mathematics, including number theory.
3. A similar proof can be carried out in the case of an odd number of digits.

CHAPTER 7

FIBONACCI NUMBERS AND THE GOLDEN RATIO

In our classroom investigation it was very surprising to find the appearance of the Fibonacci sequence. Wow! The wonder of Fibonacci numbers . . . they pop up everywhere . . . and what does it mean?

—Dolores, a pre-service elementary teacher

1. INTRODUCTION

In this chapter, the sequence of numbers 1, 1, 2, 3, 5, 8, 13, . . . will be studied. This celebrated number sequence, introduced to Western European mathematics by an Italian mathematician Fibonacci (1170–1250), is commonly referred to as Fibonacci numbers. A rule through which the sequence develops can be described recursively: *The first two Fibonacci numbers are equal to one, and each number, beginning from the third, is the sum of the previous two numbers.* One may wonder if this kind of recursive relationship exists in the life around us? In what follows, several concrete activities through which Fibonacci numbers can be introduced to teachers and their students alike will be presented. The first activity is based on the use of two-sided counters, thereby demonstrating how concrete objects can be utilized in the teaching of rather advanced mathematical concepts. The second activity is also of a hands-on nature. The third activity is of special importance because of its direct connection to a real-life problem studied by Fibonacci himself.

Topics in Mathematics for Elementary Teachers, pages 113–133

113

2. ACTIVITIES LEADING TO FIBONACCI NUMBERS

Activity 1: *Determine the number of different arrangements of one, two, three, four, and so on two-sided (red/yellow) counters in which no two red counters appear in a row.*

By using two-sided (red/yellow) counters, one can discover (Figure 7.1) that one counter can be arranged in two ways (red or yellow), two counters in three ways (red–yellow, yellow–red, or yellow–yellow), three counters in five ways (red–yellow–red, red–yellow–yellow, yellow–red–yellow, yellow–yellow–red, or yellow–yellow–yellow).

The following classroom episode is worth noting. Proceeding from the above discovery, a teacher developed the chart shown in Figure 7.2, in which the first three numbers in the second row (2, 3, and 5) reflected data shown in Figure 7.1, whereas the rest of the numbers in that row (8, 12, 17, 23, and 30) were found by inductive reasoning. The teacher explained that she recognized the following pattern among the numbers in the first three columns of the chart: The sum of the number of counters and the number of their arrangements is equal to the next number in the second row (3 = 1 + 2 and 5 = 2 + 3). Based on this observation, she continued as follows: 8 = 3 + 5, 12 = 4 + 8, 17 = 5 + 12, 23 = 6 + 17, and 30 = 7 + 23. However, she could not explain the meaning of the observed pattern. This was not surprising, as the pattern was confirmed by very limited experiential evidence and, thereby, led to an incorrect generalization (see Chapters 6 and 10 for more examples of that kind). Indeed, using the counters, one can show that, although the number 8 does show the correct number of the corresponding arrangements (see Figure 7.3), already the number 12 does not.

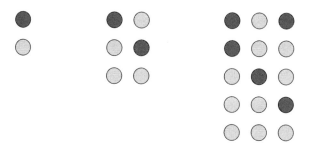

Figure 7.1   Arrangements of one, two, and three counters.

counters	1	2	3	4	5	6	7	8
arrangements	2	3	5	8	12	17	23	30

Figure 7.2   Inductive reasoning yields an erroneous guess.

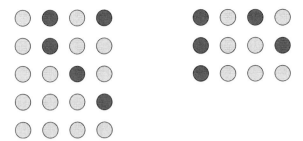

Figure 7.3 Pictorial representation of Fibonacci recursion $A(4) = A(3) + A(2)$.

The above reflection on the author's teaching experience supports an argument in favor of introducing teachers to formal mathematical reasoning. With this in mind, in the case of four counters, the following method of reduction to a simpler problem can be employed. All possible arrangements of four counters can be put in two groups, depending on the color of the first (far-left) counter. Let the first counter in each arrangement in the first group be yellow. Then, the second counter may be either yellow or red, as between the first two counters no two red ones would appear in a row. This implies that the total number of arrangements in the first group is equal to the number of arrangements of three counters where no two red counters appear in a row. As was already found, this can be done in five ways. Therefore, the first group includes five different arrangements of counters (Figure 7.3).

Now, consider the second group, where the first counter in each arrangement is red. Consequently, the second counter must be yellow; otherwise, two red counters would appear in a row. In this case, one has to arrange only two remaining counters so that no two red counters appear in a row. Once again, as was already found, this can be done in three ways (Figure 7.3). Therefore, there exist eight ways of arranging four counters according to the rule of Activity 1 (Figure 7.3). In a numeric form, the diagram of Figure 7.3 can be expressed as $8 = 5 + 3$.

The method of reasoning used to count the number of arrangements of two-color counters is known as recursive reasoning—a method of reducing a problem of which the solution depends on the number of objects involved to an analogous problem involving a smaller number of objects. One may recall that this kind of reasoning was introduced earlier in Chapter 1. An important aspect of recursive reasoning is that, whereas the final solution of a problem does depend on the number of objects involved, the reasoning itself does not depend on this number. For example, regardless of the number of counters involved, they (counters) can always be put in two groups that differ in the color of the first (far-left) counter. Therefore, setting $A(n)$ to represent the total number of the arrangements of n counters yields the equation

$$A(n + 1) = A(n) + A(n - 1), \qquad (3)$$

where $A(1) = 2$ and $A(2) = 3$ are experientially established boundary conditions.

Equation (3) can generate the sequence of numbers 2, 3, 5, 8, 13,..., which differs from Fibonacci numbers by the absence of the first two terms only. Once can see that setting $A(0) = 1$ (indeed, zero counters can be arranged in one way only), the sequence can be extended to 1, 2, 3, 5, 8, 13,.... Now it is a question of agreement to add another unity to the sequence to match Fibonacci numbers exactly.

Activity 2: *Buildings of different number of stories are given and one has to paint them with a fixed color in such a way that no two consecutive stories are painted with it. How many ways of such painting of one-, two-, three-, four-, and so on storied buildings are possible? Note: Not painting building at all is considered a special case of painting, as, in that case, the condition of not having two consecutive stories painted is satisfied (see Figure 7.4).*

Once again, all n-storied buildings can be put in two groups, depending on whether the top story is painted or not. When the top story is painted, the penultimate story may not be painted and, therefore, the number of buildings with the painted top story is equal to the number of ways an $(n - 2)$-storied building can be painted. When the top story is not painted, then the penultimate story may be painted and, therefore, the number of buildings with the non-painted top story is equal to the number of ways an $(n - 1)$-storied building can be painted. In such a way, Equation (3) with the same boundary conditions can be developed through Activity 2. In turn, the sequence of Fibonacci numbers (starting from 2) can be generated.

The last activity leading to Fibonacci numbers is due to Fibonacci himself, who investigated the growth of the population of rabbits breeding in ideal circumstances (in the absence of a predator–prey system). This activity[1] can also be carried out in a hands-on format, although, due to lack of space, it will be discussed here in a more abstract form.

Figure 7.4 Painting one- and two-story buildings.

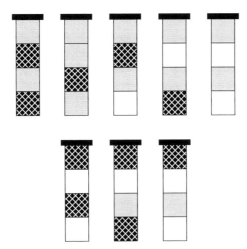

Figure 7.5 Painting through recursion.

Activity 3: *A just-born pair of rabbits is placed in a walled enclosure. During the first month of their life, the rabbits produce no offspring. They reproduce one new pair of rabbits at the age of one month, and another new pair of rabbits at the age of two months. If each new pair of rabbits reproduces in the same manner (and is capable of only two reproductions), how many pairs of rabbits (including the original pair) will be produced throughout one full year? (The production of offspring is pictured in Figure 7.6, where N and O stand, respectively, for a new pair and an old pair).*

Activity 3 can be accompanied by a chart (Figure 7.7), in which the number of pairs of rabbits produced at the end of each month is recorded.

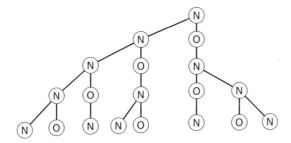

Figure 7.6 Production of offspring over the five-month span.

month	1	2	3	4	5	6	7	8	9	10	11	12
pairs	1	1	2	3	5	8	13	21	34	55	89	144

Figure 7.7 Chart representation of data generated through Activity 3.

The first five numbers in the bottom row of the chart are obtained experimentally (with the help of the diagram of Figure 7.6). The rest of the numbers, once again, can be found through recursive reasoning. To this end, consider the 6th month. One can put all possible pairs of rabbits born at the end of the 6th month in two groups, depending on the age of their parents. The first group includes pairs born from the one-month-old parents. The second group includes pairs born from the two-month-old parents. According to the diagram of Figure 7.7, in the first group, there are five pairs and in the second group, there are three pairs. Therefore, the total number of pairs born at the end of the 6th month can be found through a simple addition: $5 + 3 = 8$ (that is, adding N's and O's in the bottom row of the diagram of Figure 7.6). Once again, the method of recursive reasoning was used in finding the number of pairs born at the end of the 6th month. Continuing counting the pairs of rabbits in the same way, the bottom row of the chart of Figure 7.7 can be filled with numbers, each of which is the sum of the previous two numbers in that row.

Setting $R(n)$ to represent the number of pairs of rabbits born at the end of the nth month, the equation

$$R(n + 1) = R(n) + R(n - 1), \qquad (4)$$

in which $R(1) = R(2) = 1$, can be developed.

Proceeding from Equations (3) and (4), one can introduce the sequence F_n through the following definition:

$$F_{n+1} = F_n + F_{n-1} \qquad (5)$$

$$F_1 = 1, F_2 = 1 \qquad (6)$$

Formula (5), subject to initial conditions (6), is a recursive definition of Fibonacci numbers.

3. SUMMATION OF FIBONACCI NUMBERS

The partial sums of consecutive Fibonacci numbers $1, 1, 2, 3, 5, 8, 13, 21, \ldots$, starting from the first Fibonacci number, represent the following sequence of numbers: $F_1 = 1, F_1 + F_2 = 1 + 1 = 2, F_1 + F_2 + F_3 = 1 + 1 + 2 = 4, F_1 + F_2 + F_3 + F_4 = 1 + 1 + 2 + 3 = 7, F_1 + F_2 + F_3 + F_4 + F_5 = 1 + 1 + 2 + 3 + 5 = 12 \ldots$. One can note that the sequence of numbers $1, 2, 4, 7, 12, \ldots$ looks familiar: Each of the numbers in this sequence is one less than the corresponding Fibonacci number. Indeed, $1 = 2 - 1 = F_3 - 1$, $2 = 3 - 1 = F_4 - 1$, $4 = 5 - 1 = F_5 - 1$, $7 = 8 - 1 = F_6 - 1$, $12 = 13 - 1 = F_7 - 1, \ldots$. These relationships can be expressed in the following symbolic form:

$$F_1 + F_2 + \ldots + F_n = F_{n+2} - 1 \tag{7}$$

In order to explain Formula (7), one can add to Fibonacci numbers another unity to have the sequence $1, 1, 1, 2, 3, 5, 8, 13, 21, \ldots$, or $1, F_1, F_2, F_3, F_4, F_5, \ldots$, so that $1 + F_1 = F_3$, $1 + F_1 + F_2 = F_3 + F_2 = F_4$, $1 + F_1 + F_2 + F_3 = F_4 + F_3 = F_5, \ldots$.

That is, each Fibonacci number, beginning from the third one, is always one more than the corresponding sum of consecutive Fibonacci numbers, beginning from the first one.

If one adds every other Fibonacci number, beginning from the first one, the following sequence of numbers can be developed:

$$F_1 + F_3 = 1 + 2 = 3;$$

$$F_1 + F_3 + F_5 = 1 + 2 + 5 = 8;$$

$$F_1 + F_3 + F_5 + F_7 = 1 + 2 + 5 + 13 = 21;$$

$$F_1 + F_3 + F_5 + F_7 + F_9 = 1 + 2 + 5 + 13 + 34 = 55.$$

The numbers 3, 8, 21, and 55 look familiar as well: They are, respectively, Fibonacci numbers F_4, F_6, F_8, F_{10}. Using algebraic notation, one can write

$$F_1 + F_3 = F_4, F_1 + F_3 + F_5 = F_6, F_1 + F_3 + F_5 + F_7 = F_8, F_1 + F_3 + F_5 + F_7 + F_9 = F_{10}.$$

In general,

$$F_1 + F_3 + F_5 + \ldots + F_{2n-1} = F_{2n} \tag{8}$$

Combining (7) and (8), one can discover that the sums of every other Fibonacci number, beginning from the second number, have a simple representation:

$$F_2 + F_4 + F_6 + \ldots + F_{2n} = F_{2n+1} - 1 \tag{9}$$

Proofs of Formulas (7) and (8) by the method of mathematical induction is included in the activity set of Chapter 10.

4. CLOSED FORMULA FOR FIBONACCI NUMBERS AND THE GOLDEN RATIO

Although Fibonacci was probably not the first mathematician to consider Equation (5), which generates the number sequence 1, 1, 2, 3, 5, 8, 13, ..., these numbers, nevertheless, bear his name. In 1843 (five centuries after Fibonacci), a French mathematician, Jacques Binet, showed that Fibonacci numbers *Fn* have the following closed representation

$$F_n = \frac{1}{\sqrt{5}}[(\frac{1+\sqrt{5}}{2})^n - (\frac{1-\sqrt{5}}{2})^n], \; n = 1,2,3,... \tag{10}$$

Despite its rather complex form, Formula (10) generates integers only. A useful computational practice could be to find the first two numbers using Formula (10). This can be done either by pencil and paper or by using a calculator. For example,

$$F_1 = \frac{1}{\sqrt{5}}\left(\frac{1+\sqrt{5}}{2} - \frac{1-\sqrt{5}}{2}\right) = \frac{1+\sqrt{5}-1+\sqrt{5}}{2\sqrt{5}} = 1,$$

$$F_2 = \frac{1}{\sqrt{5}}\left[\left(\frac{1+\sqrt{5}}{2}\right)^2 - \left(\frac{1-\sqrt{5}}{2}\right)^2\right] = \frac{\left(1+\sqrt{5}-1+\sqrt{5}\right)\left(1+\sqrt{5}+1-\sqrt{5}\right)}{4\sqrt{5}} = 1.$$

As a technology-based alternative, one can use a spreadsheet to generate numbers F_n through Formula (10). Such a spreadsheet is shown in Figure 7.8. It also generates the ratios of two consecutive Fibonacci numbers and shows the behavior of the ratios in a graphic form.

The ratios of two consecutive Fibonacci numbers are special ones, for they exhibit an extremely interesting behavior: Every ratio is either smaller or bigger than each of the two ratios immediately above and below it (Figure 7.8). Odd ratios (generated in rows with even *n*'s) form a monotonically increasing sequence; even ratios (generated in rows with odd *n*'s) form a monotonically decreasing sequence. By exhibiting such a behavior, the ratios seem to approach (or converge to) the number 1.618... by oscillating about it.

A more detailed exploration of the behavior of the ratios F_{n+1}/F_n may involve finding the ratios of larger Fibonacci numbers computationally or using the theory of limits. A number to which the ratios of consecutive Fibonacci numbers converge is called the Golden Ratio, an irrational number of the form

$$\frac{1+\sqrt{5}}{2}$$

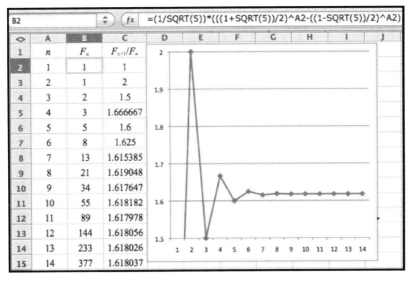

Figure 7.8 Fibonacci numbers (column B) and their ratios (column C).

known to mathematicians for about 2,500 years from various geometric investigations. Some of these investigations are considered below. The TI-83 calculator gives the value of the Golden Ratio with the following accuracy:

$$\frac{1+\sqrt{5}}{2} = 1.618033989.$$

In what follows, as a classic example of the interconnectedness of mathematical concepts, the appearance of the Golden Ratio in several, seemingly unrelated, mathematical contexts will be demonstrated.

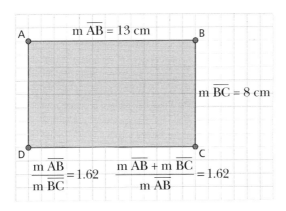

Figure 7.9 An approximation to the Golden Rectangle.

5. FIBONACCI NUMBERS AND THE GOLDEN RECTANGLE

In connection with the Golden Ratio, it is useful to give some meaning to the appearance of the fractions

$$\frac{1 \pm \sqrt{5}}{2}$$

in Formula (10). To this end, consider a rectangle in which length L and width W satisfy the equation

$$\frac{L}{W} = \frac{L+W}{L}. \tag{11}$$

A rectangle in which W and L satisfy Equation (11) to the accuracy of 0.01 is shown in Figure 7.9. One can see that $W = 8$ and $L = 13$ are, respectively, the 6th and 7th Fibonacci numbers.

Equation (11) is equivalent to the equation

$$\frac{L}{W} = \frac{L}{L} + \frac{W}{L}.$$

Substituting x for

$$\frac{L}{W}$$

yields

$$x = 1 + \frac{1}{x},$$

whence $x^2 - x - 1 = 0$. The last quadratic equation has two roots:

$$x_1 = \frac{1+\sqrt{5}}{2} > 0 \text{ and } x_2 = \frac{1-\sqrt{5}}{2} < 0.$$

Therefore, the ratio

$$\frac{L}{W} = \frac{1+\sqrt{5}}{2},$$

that is, the ratio of length to width of the rectangle, is the Golden Ratio. A rectangle the length and width of which satisfy Equation (11) is called the Golden Rectangle.

One can note that, whereas the recursive formula for Fibonacci numbers has an appeal of easiness, the closed formula is surprisingly complex, involving the powers of the Golden Ratio (the limiting value of the ratios of two consecutive Fibonacci numbers) and the negation of its reciprocal.

Yet, both formulas generate the same numbers. This indicates the intrinsic complexity of mathematical concepts, in general, and the importance of the Golden Ratio as a representational tool connecting geometry and discrete mathematics, in particular.

6. THE APPEARANCE OF THE GOLDEN RATIO IN A REGULAR PENTAGON

Identifying the Golden Ratio within other geometric contexts can further reveal its importance for mathematics. For example, by using the *GSP*, one can show that in a regular pentagon its diagonal and side form the Golden Ratio (Figure 7.10). To this end, using techniques described in Chapter 5, one can construct a regular pentagon and then find the above-mentioned ratio to the accuracy of 0.00001 to see that it coincides with the Golden Ratio to this accuracy. By changing the size of a pentagon, one can see that such a change does not alter the ratio. How can this phenomenon be explained?

To this end, a combination of different mathematical ideas taught at the pre-college level can be employed. Besides geometry, these include complex numbers, trigonometry, and algebra. To begin, let $d = $ BE and $a = $ AB, a diagonal and side of a regular pentagon, respectively (Figure 7.10). One can show that

$$\frac{d}{a} = \frac{1}{2\cos\dfrac{2\pi}{5}}.$$

Indeed, noting that

$$\cos\frac{3\pi}{5} = -\cos\frac{2\pi}{5}$$

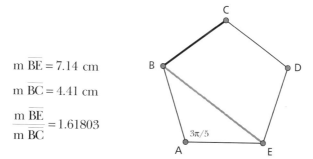

$$m\,\overline{BE} = 7.14 \text{ cm}$$

$$m\,\overline{BC} = 4.41 \text{ cm}$$

$$\frac{m\,\overline{BE}}{m\,\overline{BC}} = 1.61803$$

Figure 7.10   The Golden Ratio in a regular pentagon.

and applying the Law of Cosines (see Appendix, Formula [A25]) to triangle ABE yields

$$d^2 = 2a^2 - 2a^2 \cos \frac{3\pi}{5},$$

whence

$$\frac{d^2}{a^2} = 2\left(1 - \cos \frac{3\pi}{5}\right) = 2\left(1 + \cos \frac{2\pi}{5}\right) = 4\cos^2 \frac{\pi}{5}.$$

Continuously using the formula of double angle (see Appendix, Formula [A26]) and the relation

$$\sin \frac{\pi}{5} = \sin \frac{4\pi}{5},$$

one can complete the demonstration as follows:

$$\frac{d}{a} = 2\cos \frac{\pi}{5} = \frac{2\cos \frac{\pi}{5} \sin \frac{\pi}{5}}{\sin \frac{\pi}{5}} = \frac{\sin \frac{2\pi}{5}}{\sin \frac{\pi}{5}} = \frac{2\cos \frac{2\pi}{5} \sin \frac{2\pi}{5}}{2\cos \frac{2\pi}{5} \sin \frac{\pi}{5}}$$

$$= \frac{\sin \frac{4\pi}{5}}{2\cos \frac{2\pi}{5} \sin \frac{4\pi}{5}} = \frac{1}{2\cos \frac{2\pi}{5}}.$$

According to de Moivre's Formula (see Appendix, Formula [A27])

$$\left(\cos \frac{2\pi}{5} + i\sin \frac{2\pi}{5}\right)^5 = \cos 2\pi + i\sin 2\pi = 1.$$

Therefore,

$$\lambda = \cos \frac{2\pi}{5} + i\sin \frac{2\pi}{5}$$

satisfies the equation $\lambda^5 - 1 = 0$ or $(\lambda - 1)(\lambda^4 + \lambda^3 + \lambda^2 + \lambda + 1) = 0$, whence $\lambda^4 + \lambda^3 + \lambda^2 + \lambda + 1 = 0$ (note: $\lambda \neq 1$). Dividing the last equation by λ^2 yields

$$\lambda^2 + \lambda + 1 + \frac{1}{\lambda} + \frac{1}{\lambda^2} = 0,$$

whence

$$(\lambda + \frac{1}{\lambda})^2 + \lambda + \frac{1}{\lambda} - 1 = 0 \tag{12}$$

Once again, applying de Moivre's Formula yields

$$\lambda + \frac{1}{\lambda} = \cos\frac{2\pi}{5} + i\sin\frac{2\pi}{5} + \cos\frac{2\pi}{5} - i\sin\frac{2\pi}{5} = 2\cos\frac{2\pi}{5} > 0.$$

On the other hand, solving Equation (12) by substituting z for

$$\lambda + \frac{1}{\lambda}$$

yields $z^2 + z - 1 = 0$, whence

$$z_1 = \frac{-1+\sqrt{5}}{2} > 0 \text{ and } z_2 = \frac{-1-\sqrt{5}}{2} < 0.$$

Rejecting z_2 leaves us with

$$\lambda + \frac{1}{\lambda} = \frac{-1+\sqrt{5}}{2}.$$

Finally,

$$\frac{d}{a} = \frac{1}{2\cos\frac{2\pi}{5}} = \frac{1}{\lambda+\frac{1}{\lambda}} = \frac{1+\sqrt{5}}{2}.$$

That is, in a regular pentagon, the ratio of its diagonal to its side is the Golden Ratio.

7. THE APPEARANCE OF THE GOLDEN RATIO IN A REGULAR DECAGON

Similar explorations that combine a *GSP*-based computational experiment, the use of complex numbers, and trigonometry can demonstrate that in a regular decagon, the ratio of its radius[2] to its side is the Golden Ratio, as well. To this end, using techniques described in Chapter 5, one can construct a regular decagon (Figure 7.11) and then find the above-mentioned ratio to the accuracy of 0.00001 to see that it coincides with the Golden Ratio to this accuracy. By changing the size of the decagon, one can see that such a change does not alter the ratio.

To demonstrate the relation

$$\frac{BO}{AB} = \frac{1+\sqrt{5}}{2},$$

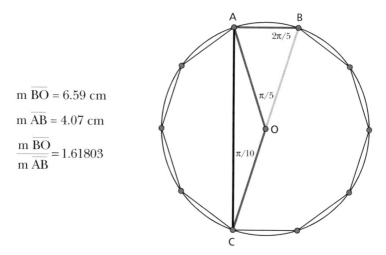

m $\overline{BO}$ = 6.59 cm

m $\overline{AB}$ = 4.07 cm

$\dfrac{m\ \overline{BO}}{m\ \overline{AB}}$ = 1.61803

Figure 7.11 The Golden Ratio in a regular decagon.

a different strategy will be used in this section. To this end, note that $\triangle ABC$ is a right triangle, as $\angle CAB$ is supported by the diameter BC. Furthermore, as

$$\angle AOB = \frac{2\pi}{10} = \frac{\pi}{5},$$

it follows that

$$\angle ACB = \frac{1}{2}\angle AOB = \frac{\pi}{10}.$$

Therefore,

$$\angle CBA = \frac{\pi}{2} - \frac{\pi}{10} = \frac{2\pi}{5}.$$

Next, in $\triangle ABC$, one has

$$AB = BC \cdot \cos(\angle ABC) = 2 \cdot BO \cdot \cos\frac{2\pi}{5}$$

whence

$$\frac{BO}{AB} = \frac{1}{2\cos\dfrac{2\pi}{5}}.$$

As was shown in section 6 of this chapter,

$$\frac{1}{2\cos\dfrac{2\pi}{5}} = \frac{1+\sqrt{5}}{2}.$$

This completes a formal demonstration that in a regular decagon, its radius and side form the Golden Ratio.

8. EXPLORING FIBONACCI-LIKE SEQUENCES

If we allow for the variation of the first two terms (initial conditions [6]) of the Fibonacci sequence, many other numerical sequences can be generated. For example, the case $F_1 = 2$ and $F_2 = 1$ yields the so-called Lucas numbers $2, 1, 3, 4, 7, 11, 18, \ldots$, named after the 19th-century French mathematician, Edouard Lucas, known also as an inventor of the Tower of Hanoi puzzle (Posamentier, Smith, & Stepelman, 2006). Lucas sequence, and any other similarly generated number sequence, will be referred to below as a Fibonacci-like sequence.

How do the ratios of two consecutive Lucas numbers behave? The spreadsheet pictured in Figure 7.12 shows that the Golden Ratio appears among Lucas numbers, as well. Furthermore, by altering the first two entries in the left column of the spreadsheet, one can discover that this phenomenon continues to hold for any Fibonacci-like sequence. In other words, there exist infinitely many number sequences within which the Golden Ratio occurs. Alternatively, there exist a multitude of rectangles with sides, although different from two consecutive Fibonacci numbers, having a ratio close to the Golden Ratio to any given accuracy. In order to explain this phenomenon, consider the sequence

$$x, y, x+y, x+2y, 2x+3y, 3x+5y, 5x+8y, 8x+13y, \ldots, \tag{13}$$

which develops from the first two terms x and y, through Fibonacci Recursion (5). Setting $f_8(x, y)$ to be the 8th term of Sequence (13), one can note that the coefficients in x and y are, respectively, the 6th and 7th Fibonacci numbers. Therefore, $f_8(x, y) = F_6 \cdot x + F_7 \cdot y$.

In general, $f_n(x, y) = F_{n-2} \cdot x + F_{n-1} \cdot y$ is the nth term of Sequence (13). Noting that

$$\frac{F_n}{F_{n-1}} \xrightarrow[n \to \infty]{} \frac{1+\sqrt{5}}{2},$$

2	
1	0.5
3	3
4	1.333333333
7	1.75
11	1.571428571
18	1.636363636
29	1.611111111
47	1.620689655
76	1.617021277
123	1.618421053
199	1.617886179
322	1.618090452
521	1.618012422
843	1.618042226
1364	1.618030842
2207	1.618035191
3571	1.61803353
5778	1.618034164
9349	1.618033922
15127	1.618034014
24476	1.618033979
39603	1.618033992
64079	1.618033987
103682	1.618033989
167761	1.618033989

Figure 7.12 The appearance of the Golden Ratio among Lucas numbers.

the ratio of two consecutive terms of Sequence (13) tends to the Golden Ratio, as well. Indeed,

$$\frac{F_{n-1} \cdot x + F_n \cdot y}{F_{n-2} \cdot x + F_{n-1} \cdot y} = \frac{F_{n-1} \cdot x \left(1 + \dfrac{F_n}{F_{n-1}} \cdot \dfrac{y}{x} \right)}{F_{n-1} \cdot x \left(\dfrac{F_{n-2}}{F_{n-1}} + \dfrac{y}{x} \right)} = \frac{1 + \dfrac{F_n}{F_{n-1}} \cdot \dfrac{y}{x}}{\dfrac{y}{x} + \dfrac{1}{\dfrac{F_{n-1}}{F_{n-2}}}} \xrightarrow{n \to \infty} \frac{1 + \dfrac{1+\sqrt{5}}{2} \cdot \dfrac{y}{x}}{\dfrac{y}{x} + \dfrac{2}{1+\sqrt{5}}}$$

$$= \frac{1+\sqrt{5}}{2} \cdot \frac{\dfrac{2}{1+\sqrt{5}} + \dfrac{y}{x}}{\dfrac{y}{x} + \dfrac{2}{1+\sqrt{5}}} = \frac{1+\sqrt{5}}{2}.$$

This explains that not only the ratios of two consecutive Lucas numbers converge to the Golden Ratio, but the ratios of two consecutive terms of any Fibonacci-like sequence converge to the Golden Ratio, as well.

9. EXTENDING FIBONACCI NUMBERS TO NON-POSITIVE SUBSCRIPTS

Can any integer N be the nth term of a Fibonacci-like sequence? In the case when N is the nth term of a Fibonacci-like sequence, does N uniquely determine such a sequence? The answer depends on the number of integer solutions of the equation $F_{n-2} \cdot x + F_{n-1} \cdot y = N$. For example, let $N = 20$ be the 5th term of Fibonacci-like Sequence (11). Then $20 = F_3 \cdot x + F_4 \cdot y = 2x + 3y$. How many solutions does the equation

$$2x + 3y = 20 \tag{14}$$

have? One may recall that in Chapter 3, the context of a pet store was used to find all integer solutions to equations of type (14). Here, a slight modification of the context is used to solve Equation (14).

A Bike Store Problem: *A bike store owner sells only bicycles and tricycles. One day, she asked her clerk to count how many vehicles there were in the store. The clerk counted 20 wheels. How many bicycles and tricycles might there have been?*

The chart pictured in Figure 7.13 gives all solutions to Equation (11). Now, using Sequence (13), one can write down all Fibonacci-like sequences with the number 20 as the 5th term:

$$1, 6, 7, 13, 20, 33, \ldots;$$

$$4, 4, 8, 12, 20, 32, \ldots;$$

$$7, 2, 9, 11, 20, 31, \ldots;$$

$$10, 0, 10, 10, 20, 30, \ldots.$$

The spreadsheet pictured in Figure 7.14 is designed to numerically model the problem of finding Fibonacci-like sequences having N as the nth term. In particular, the case $N = 20$ and $n = 5$ is presented within the spreadsheet. The graphical behavior of sequences generated thus is shown in Figure 7.15. The graphs demonstrate that after the Fibonacci-like sequences

x	y	2x + 3y
Bicycles	Tricycles	Wheels
1	6	20
4	4	20
7	2	20
10	0	20

Figure 7.13   There are four combinations of vehicles in the bike store.

◇	A	B	C	D	E	F	G	H	I	J
1										
2			◉◀▶		◉◀▶					
3		n	F_{n-2}	F_{n-1}	N	Total				
4		5	2	3	20	4				
5	x	y								
6	0									
7	1	6	7	13	20	33	53	86	139	225
8	2									
9	3									
10	4	4	8	12	20	32	52	84	136	220
11	5									
12	6									
13	7	2	9	11	20	31	51	82	133	215
14	8									
15	9									
16	10	0	10	10	20	30	50	80	130	210

Figure 7.14   Generating Fibonacci-like sequences with 20 as the 5th term.

pass over the fifth term, they continue growing large monotonically, yet their initial behavior was not necessarily monotonic.

Now, consider ten quadruples of like terms of Fibonacci-like numbers generated by the spreadsheet (located vertically within the first four rows of the chart in Figure 7.16). These quadruples form arithmetic sequences, the differences of which are displayed in the bottom row of the chart.

One can observe that to the right of the zero difference (that is, after all the four Fibonacci-like sequences met at the number 20), consecutive Fibonacci numbers appear. Furthermore, to the left of the zero difference (that is, before the sequences met), the absolute values of the differences are consecutive Fibonacci numbers, as well. This observation can motivate the idea of extending Fibonacci numbers F_n to $n \leq 0$ (non-positive subscripts) through the following definition:

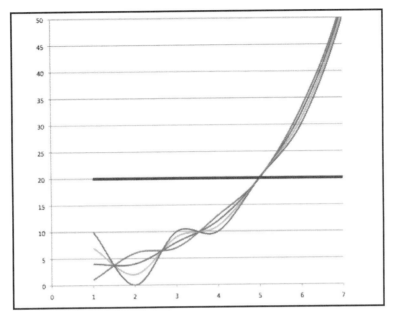

Figure 7.15 A graphic representation of Fibonacci-like sequences with 20 as the 5th term.

10	0	10	10	20	30	50	80	130	210
7	2	9	11	20	31	51	82	133	215
4	4	8	12	20	32	52	84	136	220
1	6	7	13	20	33	53	86	139	225
−3	**2**	**−1**	**1**	**0**	**1**	**1**	**2**	**3**	**5**

Figure 7.16 From the bike store problem to generalized Fibonacci numbers.

$$F_0 = 0, F_{-n} = (-1)^{n+1}F_n \tag{15}$$

One can see that to the right of zero, all Fibonacci numbers are positive, and to the left of zero, Fibonacci numbers alternate signs. In order to generate Fibonacci numbers in both directions, one has to have the triple of numbers $(1, 0, 1)$. Then, to the right of zero, the recursion $F_{n+1} = F_n + F_{n-1}$ should be used, and to the left of zero, the recursion $F_{n-1} = F_{n+1} - F_n$ should be used.

Combining Formulas (5) and (15), one has the following definition of numbers F_n for $n = 0, \pm1, \pm2, \ldots$: $F_{n+1} = F_n + F_{n-1}, F_0 = 0, F_{-1} = F_1 = 1$.

In that way, the unity of context, technology, and mathematics makes it possible to extend Fibonacci numbers to non-positive subscripts.

10. ACTIVITY SET

1. Find the length L of a rectangle with the width $W = 12$ cm, so that the equation

$$\frac{L}{W} = \frac{L+W}{W}$$

is satisfied to the accuracy of 0.0001.

2. Use a spreadsheet in order to find a rectangle with length and width satisfying Equation (4) to the accuracy of 0.00001.

3. Using the Graphing Calculator 3.5, construct the graph of the function

$$y = \frac{1}{\sqrt{5}}\left[\left(\frac{1+\sqrt{5}}{2}\right)^{n+1} - \left(\frac{1-\sqrt{5}}{2}\right)^{n+1}\right].$$

Using the slider of parameter n, explore for which values of n does the graph is represented by the lines $y = 5$, $y = 8$, and $y = 13$. Is there an integer value of n for which $y = 15$? Why or why not?

4. Using the Graphing Calculator 3.5, construct the graph of the equation

$$\frac{y}{x} = \frac{y+x}{x}.$$

Explain the meaning of the graph. Explore if the graph includes the points (5, 8), (8, 13), (13, 21). Explain your findings.

5. In a regular decagon (Figure 7.11), the points A and C are connected. What can be said about $\triangle ABC$? Verify your finding using other triangles within a regular decagon, two sides of which are a side and the corresponding diagonal that passes through the center of the decagon.

6. Show that the sum of any ten consecutive Fibonacci-like numbers is divisible by 11.

7. Show that the sum of any ten consecutive Fibonacci-like numbers is divisible by the 7th number of this sequence.

8. Using the Euclidean algorithm (Chapter 6), show that any two consecutive Fibonacci numbers are relatively prime numbers.

NOTES

1. The activity is a slightly modified version of Fibonacci's original investigation.
2. Recall that the radius of a regular polygon is a segment that connects the point of intersection of two of its diagonals with one of its vertices.

CHAPTER 8

FROM ARITHMETIC SEQUENCES TO POLYGONAL NUMBERS

Representing numbers with various physical materials should be a major part of mathematics instruction in the elementary grades.

—National Council of Teachers of Mathematics (2000, p. 33)

1. INTRODUCTION

A number sequence in which the difference between any two consecutive terms is a constant is called an *arithmetic sequence*. The simplest example of such a sequence is the sequence of counting numbers $1, 2, 3, 4, \ldots$, where the difference between any two consecutive terms is one. In much the same way, one can consider the sequence of consecutive odd $(1, 3, 5, 7, \ldots)$ or even $(2, 4, 6, 8, \ldots)$ numbers as arithmetic sequences with the difference two.

Many problems in mathematics lead to the summation of consecutive counting, odd, or even numbers. Finding such sums can be extended to the summation of other arithmetic sequences. Partial sums of arithmetic sequences (e.g., 1, $1 + 2 = 3$, $1 + 2 + 3 = 6$, $1 + 2 + 3 + 4 = 10$, etc.) form new number sequences known as polygonal numbers. In particular, these numbers, having strong connection to geometry, include triangular $(1, 3, 6, 10, \ldots)$ and square $(1, 4, 9, 16, \ldots)$ numbers, which can already be found in elementary

Topics in Mathematics for Elementary Teachers, pages 135–158
Copyright © 2010 by Information Age Publishing
All rights of reproduction in any form reserved.

school curricula as links between different mathematical concepts (e.g., New York State Education Department, 1996).

The study of arithmetic sequences and their sums lends itself to the use of context, concrete materials, and computing technology. It that way, in the context of arithmetic sequences, summation techniques can emerge from real-life situations, and can be introduced through experimentation with the tools of technology, both physical and digital. In this chapter, a number of such problem situations will be explored.

2. MOTIVATION

Brain Teaser: *Two players work together to fill a rectangular grid with counters and tiles by starting from diagonally opposite corners, placing one more counter/tile in the row below/above the previous row with each turn, moving towards each other (Figure 8.1). Assuming that the first player starts by placing a counter in the top left corner of the grid, help the second player determine the size of the grid by placing the first tile so that the game would continue until the grid is filled without any overlaps or gaps by counters and tiles. Is the solution unique?*

Whereas the reader may attempt to resolve the brain teaser by trial and error, our goal is to develop a method—"the attribute which distinguishes research activity from mere observation and speculation" (Shulman, 1997, p. 7)—through which a correct strategy can be found. To this end, we turn to the following.

Alternative Problem: *In order to motivate the study of a new mathematical concept, a teacher, Ms. Jones, initiates the following classroom activity. She*

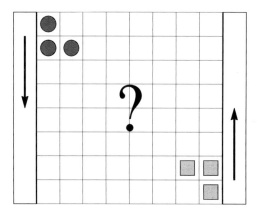

Figure 8.1 Is this a right strategy?

*claps one time and then a student, Andy, joins her. They both clap simultane-
ously one time each and then another student, Becky, joins in. The three clap
simultaneously one time each and invite Chuck to join them. Finally the four
clap simultaneously one time each. At that point, Ms. Jones asks the class:*

- *How many different claps took place?*
- *If this clapping activity were extended to ten people clapping, how many different claps would be counted among ten people?*

One way to answer these questions is to model the problem situation by
using multicolored counters (pictured below as patterned counters), and
assigning to each of the four people a particular color (pattern). Then,
counters representing individual claps can be counted. Although modeling
makes the situation more abstract, the availability of different colors (patterns) allows one to connect the physical model to the context it represents.
As shown in the diagram of Figure 8.2 (a physical model of the alternative
problem), the total number of claps among four people is ten. The arrangement of counters in the model suggests a method of counting claps,
something that could be used later in the counting of claps among a larger
number of people. Indeed, the sum $1 + 2 + 3 + 4$, consisting of four addends, each of which represents the number of claps made at each step of
the clapping activity, is equal to 10. Using the chart pictured in Figure 8.3, a
numerical pattern can be recognized and then used to represent the number of claps among ten people, without actually creating a physical model,
but rather by adding the numbers $1 + 2 + 3 + \ldots + 10$. Note that the last
sum is a special one, as *the first ten counting numbers* have been added. Once

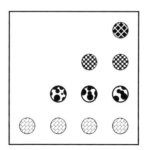

Figure 8.2   Modeling claps among four people.

Number of people	1	2	3	4
Number of claps	1	$1 + 2 = 3$	$1 + 2 + 3 = 6$	$1 + 2 + 3 + 4 = 10$

Figure 8.3   Counting claps among four people.

the pattern has been recognized, one may wonder: Is there a better way to find the sum of consecutive counting numbers other than adding numbers one by one? An answer to this question will be given in the next section.

3. SUMMATION OF CONSECUTIVE COUNTING NUMBERS

One may argue that the sum of the first ten counting numbers is not difficult to find through straightforward summation, let alone the sum of four such numbers. This kind of argument is not uncommon to be raised by teachers, and it stems from a lack of appreciation for the conceptual approach to mathematics. In order to motivate such an approach, one may be asked to find the number of claps among 100 people, that is, to find the sum $1 + 2 + 3 + \ldots + 100$, and then generalize the result to n people. As stressed by the Conference Board of the Mathematical Sciences (2001), the teachers "must come to recognize the centrality of generalization as a mathematical activity" (p. 20). Examples from the history of mathematics like the one that follows can play an important role in this regard.

The great Gauss at an early age was able to avoid the straightforward summation of 100 consecutive counting numbers—a task offered by his teacher—by recognizing a pattern that the numbers follow. According to a legend, young Gauss's insight was to pair numbers equidistant from the beginning and the end of the sum $1 + 2 + 3 + \ldots + 98 + 99 + 100$, because each such pair has the same sum, 101 (Figure 8.4). As the total number of pairs among 100 numbers is 50, Gauss, apparently, multiplied 50 by 101 to get 5050—the sum of the first 100 counting numbers.

In order to formalize and, thereby, generalize this summation method (referred to below as Gauss's method) to any number of summands, consider two simple examples supported by geometric representations. In finding the sum $1 + 2 + 3 + 4$, the addends can be paired, $1 + 4$ and $2 + 3$, each pair having the sum of 5, whence $1 + 2 + 3 + 4 = 2 \times 5 = 10$. However, in finding the sum $1 + 2 + 3 + 4 + 5$, the number 3 would be left without pair, and it may seem that the Gauss's method does not work in this case . . . unless one adds an extra 3 to the sum, arranges six numbers in the pairs $1 + 5$, $2 + 4$,

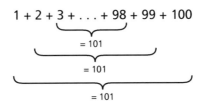

Figure 8.4 Young Gauss's insight.

and $3 + 3$, then multiplies 3 by 6, subtracts 3 from the product, and gets the sum, 15. Yet, in reality, we don't add/subtract the middle number to/from the sum with an odd number of summands. A geometric approach to the summation may clarify the situation.

Figures 8.5 and 8.6 show that each sum can be doubled by writing it twice—first forward and then backward—so that the pairing of the terms would not depend on their number. In each case, the circles and squares form a rectangle whose length is one more than its width. In order to find each sum, one has to divide the number of objects, that form the corresponding rectangle, by two. Numerically, this can be expressed as follows

$$1+2+3+4 = \frac{(1+2+3+4)+(4+3+2+1)}{2}$$

$$= \frac{(1+4)+(2+3)+(3+2)+(4+1)}{2}$$

$$= \frac{4 \cdot 5}{2}$$

$$= 10$$

and

$$1+2+3+4+5 = \frac{(1+2+3+4+5)+(5+4+3+2+1)}{2}$$

$$= \frac{(1+5)+(2+4)+(3+3)+(4+2)+(5+1)}{2}$$

$$= \frac{5 \cdot 6}{2}$$

$$= 15.$$

So, in the case of an odd number of summands, Gauss's method does not require adding another middle term as the whole sum is added twice and, as a result, divided by two. In that way,

$$1+2+3+\ldots+100 = \frac{(1+2+3+\ldots+100)+(100+99+98+\ldots+1)}{2}$$

$$= \frac{(1+100)+(2+99)+(3+98)+\ldots+(100+1)}{2}$$

$$= \frac{100 \cdot 101}{2}$$

$$= 5050.$$

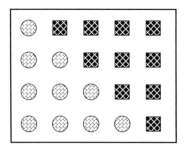

Figure 8.5   Finding the sum 1 + 2 + 3 + 4 by making a rectangle.

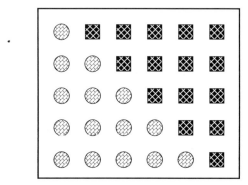

Figure 8.6   Finding the sum 1 + 2 + 3 + 4 + 5 by making a rectangle.

A transition to generalization (the development of algebraic expressions and formulas) requires that one recognize the meaning of each number in the fractions

$$\frac{4 \cdot 5}{2} \text{ and } \frac{5 \cdot 6}{2}.$$

In other words, the generalization requires that one understand which of the numbers varies and which does not as the number of terms in the sum changes. With this in mind, note that the number 2 in the denominator of each of the last two fractions reflects the counting strategy and should not change as the number of terms in a sum increases. The numbers 4 and 5 in the numerator of the first fraction stand, respectively, for the number of terms and the number of terms increased by one. The same relationship can be recognized between the numbers 5 and 6 in the numerator of the second fraction.

In general, proceeding from the above observation of special cases, the following summation formula can be conjectured

$$1+2+3+\ldots+n = \frac{n(n+1)}{2} \tag{1}$$

Geometrically, regardless of the number of terms in the sum, that is, regardless of whether n is even or odd, one side of the corresponding rectangle measures by an even number, thereby enabling the divisibility by two in the right-hand side of Formula (1). Using Formula (1), one can find that

$$1+2+3+\ldots+10 = \frac{10(10+1)}{2} = 55,$$

and then verify the result through straightforward summation. When $n = 100$, Formula (1) yields 5050, the number found by young Gauss. A formal proof of Formula (1) is discussed in Chapter 10.

4. TRIANGULAR NUMBERS

The sums of the first n counting numbers, that is, the sums of the form $1 + 2 + 3 + \ldots + n$, are called triangular numbers. The largest number in such a sum, n, is called the rank of the triangular number. Formula (1) can be used to generate the sequence of triangular numbers, 1, 3, 6, 10, 15, 21, 28, 36, ..., the first four of which have already appeared in the chart of Figure 8.3. Triangular numbers $t_n = 1 + 2 + 3 + \ldots + n$ can be defined using either the recursive formula

$$t_n = t_{n-1} + n, \tag{2}$$

where t_{n-1} is the triangular number of rank $n - 1$, or the closed formula

$$t_n = \frac{n(n+1)}{2}. \tag{3}$$

Formula (2) can be contextually interpreted in terms of the clapping problem: The total number of claps among n people is equal to the total number of claps among $n - 1$ people plus the number of claps when n people clap together one time each. By the same token, Formula (3) can be interpreted geometrically (with a reference to Gauss's method) as follows: A rectangle can be made out of two identical triangles. This geometric interpretation is of special importance and will be used below.

5. RESOLVING THE BRAIN TEASER

Now, we can return to the brain teaser that served as a motivation for the ideas of this chapter. While the reader could have found its several resolutions through trial and error, our goal, as mentioned above, is to demonstrate how one can use the concepts developed above to resolve the brain teaser through a method. The summation method, shown in Figures 8.5 and 8.6, resembles the game of filling a grid with counters and tiles, as introduced through the brain teaser. One can see that once the grid is filled completely with counters and tiles, its analysis yields the following strategy: Starting from the top-left corner, one has to create an $n \times (n + 1)$ grid and place the first tile in the bottom-right cell of such a grid. For example, Figure 8.7 shows that the second player chose $n = 10$ and measured ten cells down and eleven cells to the right. As n is a variable, it can be given any integer value and, therefore, the brain teaser has more than one correct solution (e.g., the cases $n = 5$ and $n = 4$ are shown in Figures 8.8 and 8.9 also). In particular, on the 10×11 grid there are nine successful strategies that can resolve the brain teaser (assuming that each player would make at least two turns).

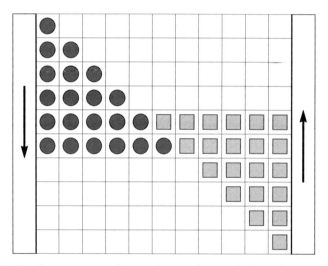

Figure 8.7   Moving to a successful conclusion of the task through a method.

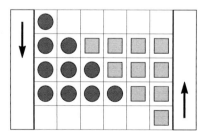

Figure 8.8   The case $n = 5$.

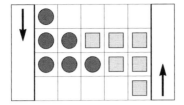

Figure 8.9   The case $n = 4$.

6. SUMMATION OF CONSECUTIVE ODD NUMBERS

As was mentioned at the beginning of this chapter, an arithmetic sequence is a series of numbers in which the difference between any two consecutive terms is constant. Triangular numbers t_n were introduced as (partial) sums of the sequence of counting numbers: $t_1 = 1$, $t_2 = 1 + 2$, $t_3 = 1 + 2 + 3, \ldots,$ $t_n = 1 + 2 + 3 + \ldots + n$. In order to open a window to the study of other arithmetic sequences, one can extend the clapping problem by making a change in its physical model (Figure 8.10). The new model describes an extended situation when, after four people clapped together (the far-right column of Figure 8.2 or the middle column of Figure 8.10), Chuck quit and then three people clapped, this followed by Becky quitting and only two people clapping. Finally, Ms. Jones concluded the activity with a single clap. A new inquiry into this extended situation is: *How many different claps took place now?*

The counters shown in Figure 8.10 (a visual representation of the claps) can be counted in several ways: (1) one by one (one, two, three, ..., sixteen); (2) adding separately counters representing the original situation and its extension ($10 + 6 = 16$); and (3) counting the claps of each individual ($1 + 3 + 5 + 7 = 16$). Whereas each counting strategy yields the same number, 16, the third way of counting introduces the sum of four consecutive odd

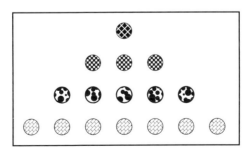

Figure 8.10   Geometrizing the sum $1 + 3 + 5 + 7$.

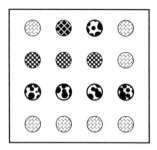

Figure 8.11   The sum $1 + 3 + 5 + 7$ as a square.

numbers, starting from one. This, together with rearranging the counters to form a square of size 4×4 (Figure 8.11), leads to the following proposition.

Proposition 1: *For all n = 1, 2, 3, . . . the formula*

$$1 + 3 + 5 + \ldots + 2n - 1 = n^2 \tag{4}$$

holds true. In other words, as was already mentioned in the introduction to Chapter 6, the sum of n consecutive odd numbers starting from one is equal to n^2.

This remarkably simple, yet rather unexpected summation formula can be found in many mathematics education curriculum documents (e.g., National Council of Teachers of Mathematics, 1989, p. 61; National Council of Teachers of Mathematics, 1991, p. 35; National Council of Teachers of Mathematics, 2000, p. 39; New York State Education Department, 1996, p. 26). The activity set of Chapter 10 includes the task of proving Formula (4) by the method of mathematical induction.

Consecutive odd numbers can be interpreted as an arithmetic sequence with the difference two: Each odd number, beginning from the number 3, is two more than the previous odd number. The summation of the arithmetic sequence with the first term one and difference two leads to the concept of square numbers. Ironically, although consecutive counting numbers is the simplest example of an arithmetic sequence, their summation required a more complicated counting strategy in comparison with the one used for the summation of odd numbers. As it turned out, the latter strategy did not require a change in the number of counters, but rather, this strategy was based on the rearrangement of counters only.

7. A GEOMETRIC APPROACH TO THE SUMMATION OF ARITHMETIC SEQUENCES

In this section, proceeding from an observation that a triangular array (Figure 8.10) can be rearranged into a square array (Figure 8.11), a method of summation of the sequence of odd numbers will be developed through a geometrization. This method will then be extended (or generalized) to any arithmetic sequence. As was shown through the diagrams of Figures 8.5 and 8.6, objects are easy to count when they are arranged in a rectangular array. In this regard, one may wonder if the sum of any arithmetic sequence with the first term one can be counted as a product of two numbers, one of which is the number of terms of the sequence. Indeed, comparing the arrangement of 16 counters shown in Figures 8.10–8.12, one can see that the same number of counters appears in each of the arrangements. Geometrically, the arrangement shown in Figure 8.12 is more specialized, for it indicates that at each step of the development of the sum of consecutive odd numbers, a new square is created. In finding this sum, that is, in counting objects arranged in a square, one can see one side of each of the 2×2, 3×3, and 4×4 squares as a clap repeated, respectively, 1, 2, and 3 times, and then augmented by one. Contextually, Figures 8.10 and 8.11 show two ways of counting claps in the extended situation: by adding four consecutive odd numbers and by multiplying equal numbers.

Numerically, the following three relationships can be developed from Figure 8.12:

$$1 + 3 = (1 \times 1 + 1) \times 2,$$

$$1 + 3 + 5 = (1 \times 2 + 1) \times 3,$$

$$1 + 3 + 5 + 7 = (1 \times 3 + 1) \times 4.$$

Generalizing from the three special cases yields the following variation of Formula (4): $1 + 3 + 5 + \ldots + 2n - 1 = (1 \times (n - 1) + 1) \times n$. Of course, different ways of counting objects, or, alternatively, finding the sum of the first n odd numbers, do result in the same sum.

An interesting observation about Formulas (1) and (4) can be made. The right-hand sides of the formulas are quadratic functions of n, the num-

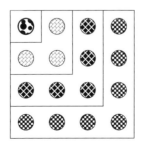

Figure 8.12 $1 + 3 + 5 + 7 = (1 \times 3 + 1) \times 4.$

ber of terms in each sum. Another observation is that the sum of the first n consecutive odd numbers is almost twice the sum of the first n consecutive counting numbers. Figure 8.10 can give a contextual explanation to the last observation: The larger the number of people clapping, the larger the difference between the number of claps made with and without the participation of the last person. Put another way,

$$1 + 3 + 5 + \ldots + 2n - 1 = (1 + 2 + 3 + \ldots + n) + (1 + 2 + 3 + \ldots + n - 1),$$

or

$$n^2 = t_n + t_{n-1} \tag{5}$$

Relation (5) states that a square number is the sum of two consecutive triangular numbers. It represents a remarkably profound, yet geometrically obvious connection that exists among different algebraic concepts. One can recognize in Formula (5) the Theon theorem discovered within the multiplication table in Chapter 4. It will be revisited again in Chapter 9.

In addition, in connection with a recommendation for the teacher preparation regarding the need to develop skills in reading and creating the graphs of functions (Conference Board of the Mathematical Sciences, 2001), the fact that a square number is the sum of two triangular numbers can be demonstrated graphically. The graphs in Figure 8.13 show that the

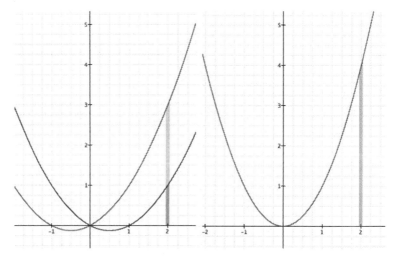

Figure 8.13 A graphic representation of Formula (5).

value of the function $f(x) = x^2$ at $x = 2$ is equal to the sum of the corresponding values of the functions

$$g(x) = \frac{x(x+1)}{2} \text{ and } h(x) = \frac{x(x-1)}{2}.$$

In that way, the same idea can be represented geometrically (Figures 8.10 and 8.11), algebraically (Formula [5]), and graphically (Figure 8.13). One's ability to represent connections between different mathematical concepts—in particular, between triangular and square numbers—using a multiple-representation environment is testament to one's conceptual understanding of mathematics, its ideas, and the tools of inquiry.

8. DEVELOPING GENERAL FORMULAS FOR ARITHMETIC SEQUENCES

Consider the problem of finding the sum of n odd numbers, starting from one, with the difference four between two consecutive numbers. The first four terms of this arithmetic sequence are 1, 5, 9, and 13. How can one express the nth term of this sequence? We will consider two strategies that can be used to answer this question.

The first strategy is based on exploring special cases. What do we know about the number 5 to suggest its representation that can then be extended to the numbers 9, 13, and, eventually, to any term of the sequence in question? We know that 5 is the 2nd term of the arithmetic sequence with the difference 4. How can 5 be expressed through 2 and 4? Several possibilities may be suggested, among them, $5 = 4 + 2 - 1$, $5 = 4 - 2 + 3$, or $5 = 4 \cdot 2 - 3$. Because 9 and 13 are, respectively, the 3rd and 4th terms of the arithmetic sequence, by analogy one can write $9 = 4 + 3 + 2$, $9 = 4 - 3 + 8$, or $9 = 4 \cdot 3 - 3$, and $13 = 4 + 4 + 5$, $13 = 4 - 4 + 13$, or $13 = 4 \cdot 4 - 3$.

Is there a pattern somewhere? One can see that the third representation (in italics) is consistent across the three special cases, and it holds true for the 1st term of the sequence, as well: $1 = 4 \cdot 1 - 3$. This suggests that the expression $4n - 3$ is likely to represent the nth term of the sequence 1, 5, 9, 13, ... (A useful practice in formal reasoning and proving could be to confirm this conjecture by the method of mathematical induction discussed in Chapter 10).

The "$4n - 3$ conjecture" can also be confirmed by proceeding from the recursive definition of the sequence 1, 5, 9, 13, ... Setting x_i to represent the *i*th term of this sequence, one has $x_i = x_{i-1} + 4$, $x_1 = 1$. When $i = 2, 3, 4, \ldots, n$, one can write

$$x_2 = x_1 + 4$$

$$x_3 = x_2 + 4$$

$$x_4 = x_3 + 4$$

. . . .

$$x_n = x_{n-1} + 4$$

Adding the above $n - 1$ equalities yields $x_2 + x_3 + x_4 + \ldots + x_n = x_1 + x_2 + x_3 + \ldots + x_{n-1} + 4(n-1)$. Cancelling out identical terms in both sides of the last equality results in $x_n = x_1 + 4(n-1)$ or $x_n = 1 + 4n - 4 = 4n - 3$. This confirms the "$4n - 3$ conjecture" regarding the closed formula for the *n*th term of the sequence $1, 5, 9, 13, \ldots$.

In general, for the arithmetic sequence with the first term x_1 and difference d, its *n*th term can be found through the following closed formula:

$$x_n = x_1 + d(n-1) \tag{6}$$

Indeed, as $x_2 = x_1 + d$, $x_3 = x_2 + d$, $x_4 = x_3 + d, \ldots, x_n = x_{n-1} + d$, one has

$$x_2 + x_3 + x_4 + \ldots + x_n = x_1 + x_2 + x_3 + \ldots x_{n-1} + d(n-1),$$

whence Formula (6).

Returning to our original summation problem, consider the sum $1 + 5 + 9 + 13 + \ldots + 4n - 3$. The sum of the first four terms, $1 + 5 + 9 + 13$, can be represented by the diagram of Figure 8.14. The counters in the diagram at each step make up a rectangular array. For example, the sum $1 + 5$ of the first two terms is represented by a 3×2 rectangle, where the first factor (the length) is the number of counters in the left column, and the second factor (the width) is the number of columns within the rectangle. The length can be represented as half the double of the top-left counter plus half the difference between 5 and 1. In other words,

$$1 + 5 = 3 \cdot 2 = \frac{2 \cdot 1 + 4 \cdot 1}{2} \cdot 2.$$

One can see that in the numerator of the last fraction, the first term, 1, of the sequence was doubled while the difference, 4, was taken one time.

Similarly, the sum $1 + 5 + 9$ of the first three terms is represented by a 5×3 rectangle, where, once again, the first factor (the length) is the num-

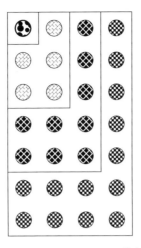

Figure 8.14 Visualizing the equality $1+5+9+13 = \dfrac{2 \cdot 1 + 4 \cdot 3}{2} \cdot 4$.

ber of counters in the left column and the second factor (the width) is the number of columns within the rectangle. In that way,

$$1+5+9 = 5 \cdot 3 = \frac{2 \cdot 1 + 4 \cdot 2}{2} \cdot 3.$$

This time, in the numerator of the last fraction, the first term of the sequence, 1, was doubled, whereas the difference, 4, was repeated two times.

Continuing in this vein, one can see (Figure 8.14) that the sum $1 + 5 + 9 + 13$ is represented by a 7×4 rectangle, where, once again, the first factor (the length) is the number of counters in the left column and the second factor (the width) is the number of columns within the rectangle. In that way,

$$1+5+9+13 = \frac{2 \cdot 1 + 4 \cdot 3}{2} \cdot 4.$$

Here, in the numerator of the last fraction, the first term of the sequence, 1, was doubled, whereas the difference, 4, was repeated three times.

Generalizing from the above three special cases yields

$$1+5+9+13+\ldots+4n-3 = \frac{2 \cdot 1 + 4 \cdot (n-1)}{2} \cdot n. \tag{7}$$

Alternatively,

$$1+5+9+13+\ldots+4n-3 = \frac{1 + (4n-3)}{2} \cdot n = (2n-1)n. \tag{8}$$

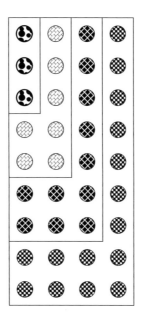

Figure 8.15 Visualizing the equality $3+7+11+15 = \dfrac{2\cdot 3 + 4\cdot 3}{2}\cdot 4$.

Similar formulas can be developed using the diagram of Figure 8.15 in finding the sum $3 + 7 + 11 + 15 + \ldots + 4n - 1$. Indeed,

$$3+7 = 5\cdot 2 = \frac{2\cdot 3 + 4\cdot 1}{2}\cdot 2$$

$$3+7+11 = 7\cdot 3 = \frac{2\cdot 3 + 4\cdot 2}{2}\cdot 3$$

$$3+7+11+15 = 9\cdot 4 = \frac{2\cdot 3 + 4\cdot 3}{2}\cdot 4$$

In general,

$$3+7+11+15+\ldots+4n-1 = \frac{2\cdot 3 + 4(n-1)}{2}\cdot n. \qquad (9)$$

Alternatively,

$$3+7+11+15+\ldots+4n-1 = \frac{3+4(n-1)}{2} \cdot n = (2n+1)n. \qquad (10)$$

A mathematical induction proof of Formulas (8) and (10) is included in the activity set of Chapter 10.

Formulas (8) and (10) can be given the following interpretation. In order to find the sum of n terms of an arithmetic sequence, one has to multiply the average of its first and last terms by n. Note that Formula (1) can be interpreted in like terms.

By the same token, the fraction in the right-hand side of Formula (7) can be interpreted as the average of twice the first term and the difference increased $(n-1)$-fold. The following two propositions introduce equivalent formulas for the sum of n terms of an arithmetic sequence.

Proposition 2: *The sum S_n of n terms of the arithmetic sequence x_1, $x_1 + d, \ldots,$ $x_1 + (n-1)d$ can be found by using the formula*

$$S_n = \frac{2x_1 + d(n-1)}{2} n. \qquad (11)$$

Applying Formula (6) to Formula (11) yields

Proposition 3: *The sum S_n of n terms of the arithmetic sequence x_1, $x_2, \ldots, x_n$ can be found by using the formula*

$$S_n = \frac{x_1 + x_n}{2} n. \qquad (12)$$

Activity: *Using Figure 8.16, find two ways of finding the sum of n terms of arithmetic sequence pictured at the diagram.*

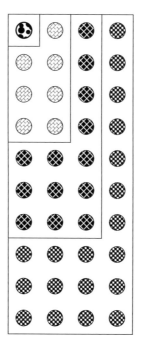

Figure 8.16 Visualizing the equality $1 + 7 + 13 + 19 = \dfrac{2 \cdot 1 + 3 \cdot 3}{2} \cdot 4$.

9. DIFFERENT WAYS OF INTRODUCING POLYGONAL NUMBERS

As was mentioned in section 1, polygonal numbers can be defined as partial sums of arithmetic sequences, the first terms of which are equal to one. The difference of such a sequence determines the type of polygonal numbers. For the differences $d = 1, 2, 3, 4$, we have, respectively, the sequences

$$1, 2, 3, \ldots n, \ldots;$$
$$1, 3, 5, \ldots, 2n - 1, \ldots;$$
$$1, 4, 7, \ldots, 3n - 2, \ldots;$$
$$1, 5, 9, \ldots, 4n - 3, \ldots;$$

and their partial sums

$$1 + 2 = 3, \; 1 + 2 + 3 = 6, \ldots, \; 1 + 2 + 3 + \ldots + n = \frac{n(n+1)}{2}, \ldots;$$

$$1, 1 + 3 = 4, 1 + 3 + 5 = 9, \ldots, 1 + 3 + 5 + \ldots + 2n - 1 = n^2, \ldots;$$

$$1, 1 + 4 = 5, 1 + 4 + 7 = 12, \ldots, 1 + 4 + 7 + \ldots + 3n - 2 = \frac{n(3n-1)}{2}, \ldots;$$

$$1, 1 + 5 = 6, 1 + 5 + 9 = 15, \ldots, 1 + 5 + 9 + \ldots + 4n - 3 = n(2n-1), \ldots.$$

Note that Formula (12) was used in finding the sums of the first n terms of each of the four sequences. These sums are called, respectively, triangular, square, pentagonal, and hexagonal numbers. In much the same way, polygonal numbers developed from arithmetic sequences with differences $d = 5, 6, 7$, and so on, can be introduced. Note that side s of a polygonal number (alternatively, s is the number of sides of the associated regular polygon) is two more than the difference d of the corresponding arithmetic sequence.

Now, consider the chart of Figure 8.17, in which the bottom and top rows are filled with counting and triangular numbers, respectively. For example, one can see that the numbers 5, 10, and 15 form an "L-flipped" shape within the chart. As $10 = 1 + 2 + 3 + 4$, the sum $1 + 2 + 3 + 4 + 5 = 15$ can be replaced by $15 = 10 + 5$ or $t_5 = t_4 + 5$, thereby confirming Formula (2) in the case $n = 5$. Likewise, other polygonal numbers can be generated through the "L-flipped" rule: square numbers (Figure 8.18), pentagonal numbers (Figure 8.19), and hexagonal numbers (Figure 8.20).

1	3	6	10	15	21	28	36	45	55
1	2	3	4	5	6	7	8	9	10

Figure 8.17 Generating triangular numbers using the "L-flipped" rule.

1	4	9	16	25	36	49	64	81	100
1	3	5	7	9	11	13	15	17	19

Figure 8.18 Generating square numbers through the "L-flipped" rule.

1	5	12	22	35	51	70	92	117	145
1	4	7	10	13	16	19	22	25	28

Figure 8.19 Generating pentagonal numbers through the "L-flipped" rule.

1	6	15	28	45	66	91	120	153	190
1	5	9	13	17	21	25	29	33	37

Figure 8.20 Generating hexagonal numbers through the "L-flipped" rule.

One can use a spreadsheet to computerize the process of generating polygonal numbers given the value of d, the difference of the corresponding arithmetic sequence. In particular, when $d = 5$, the spreadsheet shown in Figure 8.21 generates heptagonal numbers. The programming details of the spreadsheet are discussed in Chapter 13.

Alternatively, polygonal numbers can be developed from counting numbers through an action (process) that resembles the sieve of Eratosthenes. This process is shown in Figure 8.22 for triangular, square, pentagonal, and hexagonal numbers. To develop triangular numbers, one starts with 1, the first triangular number; skipping one number yields 3, the second triangular number; skipping two (consecutive) numbers yields 6, the third triangular number; skipping three (consecutive) numbers yields 10, the fourth triangular number; and so on. In terms of the operation of addition, skipping one number is equivalent to "adding two," skipping two consecutive numbers is equivalent to "adding three," and so on. In general, the move from t_{n-1} to t_n requires skipping $n-1$ consecutive natural numbers, or, in terms of addition, adding $(n-1)+1$ to t_{n-1}.

Similarly, the process of moving from the square number s_{n-1} to s_n results in skipping $2(n-1)$ numbers, or adding $2(n-1)+1$ to s_{n-1}; moving from the pentagonal number p_{n-1} to p_n results in skipping $3(n-1)$ numbers, or adding $3(n-1)+1$ to p_{n-1}; moving from the hexagonal number h_{n-1} to h_n results in skipping $4(n-1)$ numbers, or adding $4(n-1)+1$ to h_{n-1}. One can note that the coefficients in $(n-1)$ represent the number of sides in the corresponding polygon diminished by two, or, alternatively, the difference

	A	B	C	D	E	F	G	H	I	J	K
1											
2								Heptagonal numbers			
3		1	7	18	34	55	81	112	148	189	235
4		1	6	11	16	21	26	31	36	41	46
5	d = 5			←	→						

Figure 8.21 Generating heptagonal numbers through the "flipped-L" rule.

☐1☐ 2 ☐3☐ 4 5 ☐6☐ 7 8 9 ☐10☐ 11 12 13 14 ☐15☐ 16 17 18 19 20 ☐21☐ 22 23 24 25 26 27 ☐28☐ 29 30

☐1☐ 2 3 ☐4☐ 5 6 7 8 ☐9☐ 10 11 12 13 14 15 ☐16☐ 17 18 19 20 21 22 23 24 ☐25☐ 26 27 28 29 30

☐1☐ 2 3 4 ☐5☐ 6 7 8 9 10 11 ☐12☐ 13 14 15 16 17 18 19 20 21 ☐22☐ 23 24 25 26 27 28 29 30

☐1☐ 2 3 4 5 ☐6☐ 7 8 9 10 11 12 13 14 ☐15☐ 16 17 18 19 20 21 22 23 24 25 26 27 ☐28☐ 29 30

Figure 8.22 Developing polygonal numbers as a sieve process.

of the corresponding arithmetic sequence. Also, the above physical descriptions can be given geometric interpretations as one develops polygonal numbers using dot diagrams pictured in Figures 8.23–8.26. In particular,

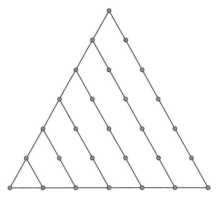

Figure 8.23 Dot diagrams for triangular numbers.

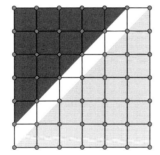

Figure 8.24 Dot diagrams for square numbers.

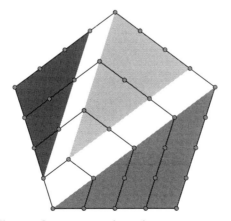

Figure 8.25 Dot diagram for pentagonal numbers.

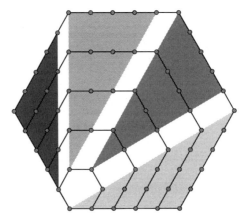

Figure 8.26 Dot diagram for hexagonal numbers.

the dot diagrams show that a square number is a sum of two triangular numbers (Theon theorem), a pentagonal number is a sum of three triangular numbers, and a hexagonal number is a sum of four triangular numbers. This is consistent with a simple geometric fact about dividing a polygon into triangles by connecting one of its vertices with all other vertices (see section 2 of Chapter 5).

10. SOME GENERAL FORMULAS FOR POLYGONAL NUMBERS

In general, by setting $P(m, n)$ to represent the nth polygonal number of side m (where $m \geq 3$, and $P(2, n) = n$) one can derive the recursive formula

$$P(m, n) = P(m, n - 1) + (m - 2)(n - 1) + 1, \tag{13}$$

where $P(m,1) = 1$, and the closed formula

$$P(m, n) = 0.5(m - 2)(n + 1)n - (m - 3). \tag{14}$$

From Formula (14), the sequences,

$$t_n = \frac{n(n+1)}{2}, \quad s_n = n^2, \quad p_n = \frac{n(3n-1)}{2}, \quad h_n = n(2n-1),$$

representing, respectively, triangular ($m = 3$), square ($m = 4$), pentagonal ($m = 5$), and hexagonal ($m = 6$) numbers results. From Formula (13), the formulas

$$t_n = t_{n-1} + n, \quad s_n = s_{n-1} + 2n - 1, \quad p_n = p_{n-1} + 3n - 2, \quad h_n = h_{n-1} + 4n - 3,$$

where

$$t_1 = s_1 = p_1 = h_1 = 1,$$

result.

Furthermore, using the identity

$$\frac{n(n-1)}{2}(m-2) + n = (m-2)\frac{n(n+1)}{2} - 2(m-3)n,$$

Formula (14) can be rewritten as

$$P(m,n) = \frac{n(n-1)}{2}(m-2) + n. \tag{15}$$

Formula (15) allows one to interpret a polygonal number of rank n as a linear function of its side m with the slope $n(n-1)/2$, the triangular number of rank $n-1$. Geometrically, assuming $m \geq 2$, Formula (15) defines in the plane (m, n) a family of rays (depending on n) with the initial point $(2, n)$ and slope t_{n-1}. Given n, each ray passes through the set of points with integer coordinates such that the difference between the vertical coordinates of two consecutive points is t_{n-1}. Analytically, this can be expressed through yet another formula, $P(m, n) = P(m-1, n) + t_{n-1}$, which emphasizes the meaning of a slope as the vertical increment (a rise) when the horizontal increment (a run) is equal to one.

11. ACTIVITY SET

1. Show that the number 2211 is a triangular number and find its rank.
2. Show that the number 2415 is a triangular number and find its rank.
3. Show that the number 4950 is a triangular number and find its rank.
4. Show that the number 5151 is a triangular number and find its rank.
5. Show that the number 2415 is a hexagonal number and find its rank.
6. Show that the number 4950 is a hexagonal number and find its rank.
7. Show that the number 5151 is a hexagonal number and find its rank.
8. Show that the number 1001 is a pentagonal number and find its rank.
9. Show that the number 1617 is a pentagonal number and find its rank.
10. Using a spreadsheet, generate consecutive triangular numbers, starting from one. Divide each triangular number by 11 and display only remainders. Do you see any pattern among the remainders? Describe the patterns found. Try other divisors.

11. Using a spreadsheet, generate consecutive pentagonal numbers, starting from one. Divide each pentagonal number by 11 and display only remainders. Do you see any pattern among the remainders? Describe the patterns found. Try other divisors.

CHAPTER 9

THE MULTIPLICATION TABLE REVISITED

The same ideas, one must believe, recur in men's minds not once or twice but again and again.

—Aristotle (Oxford Dictionary of Scientific Quotations, 2005, p. 19)

1. INTRODUCTION

In this chapter, the multiplication table will be revisited using tools developed in Chapter 8. To this end, summation formulas for triangular and square numbers will be utilized. In particular, the important role of triangular numbers as the building blocks of elementary number theory and polygonal numbers will be demonstrated. It will be shown how different summation formulas can be developed within the multiplication table and how these formulas can be interpreted in geometric terms. Recall that in Chapter 4, square numbers were observed as the elements of the main diagonal of the square-shaped multiplication table. Here, we begin with locating triangular numbers in the table and demonstrating the mutual arrangement of triangular and square numbers within the table.

Topics in Mathematics for Elementary Teachers, pages 159–169
Copyright © 2010 by Information Age Publishing

2. POLYGONAL NUMBERS IN THE MULTIPLICATION TABLE

Some polygonal numbers appear in the multiplication table in a regular pattern. As was discussed in Chapter 4, in the 10×10 multiplication table (Figure 9.1) square numbers 1, 4, 9, 16,... belong to the main (top left–bottom right) diagonal. This pattern can easily be explained, as the elements of the diagonal represent the products of equal numbers. The triangular numbers reside in pairs within the diverging rectangles located in odd rows/columns, as shown in Figure 9.1. One can also recognize that the sum of numbers in each such rectangle is equal to the corresponding number on the main diagonal. Furthermore, the distance from each such rectangle to the (left/top) border of the table is equal to its distance from the main diagonal.

This geometric "equal distance" phenomenon, occurring in odd rows/ columns of the multiplication table, can be explained algebraically if one recalls (Chapter 4, section 5) that the sum of any two numbers taken from any row of the multiplication table is equal to a number that belongs to the same row, and the distance from the sum to the largest addend is equal to the distance from the smallest addend to the left border of the table. For example, consider the case of row 9 in the table of Figure 9.1. We have $36 = 9 \times 4$, $45 = 9 \times 5$ and $36 + 45 = 9 \times (4 + 5) = 9 \times 9 = 9^2$. Furthermore, just as it takes four times to iterate 9 to reach 36 from 0 through addition, it also takes four times to iterate 9 to reach 81 from 45 through addition.

	A	B	C	D	E	F	G	H	I	J	K
1	×	1	2	3	4	5	6	7	8	9	10
2	1	1	2	3	4	5	6	7	8	9	10
3	2	2	4	6	8	10	12	14	16	18	20
4	3	3	6	9	12	15	18	21	24	27	30
5	4	4	8	12	16	20	24	28	32	36	40
6	5	5	10	15	20	25	30	35	40	45	50
7	6	6	12	18	24	30	36	42	48	54	60
8	7	7	14	21	28	35	42	49	56	63	70
9	8	8	16	24	32	40	48	56	64	72	80
10	9	9	18	27	36	45	54	63	72	81	90
11	10	10	20	30	40	50	60	70	80	90	100

Figure 9.1 Diverging pairs of triangular numbers.

Geometrically, three cells separate the shaded rectangle in row 9 from the border, as well as from the main diagonal.

In general, in order to reach the product mn from zero, one has to do m iterations of n; in order to reach n^2 from $nm + n$, one also has to do m iterations by adding n. The latter iterations result in the equation $(nm + n) + mn = n^2$. Solving this equation in n yields $n = 2m + 1$; that is, n is always an odd number whenever the "equal distance" phenomenon occurs. This confirms that the "equal distance" phenomenon can be observed only in the odd rows/columns of the multiplication table. In order to demonstrate that rectangles diverging from the main diagonal include triangular numbers only, one can write (noting that $n = [m - 1]/2$)

$$nm = n\frac{n-1}{2} = \frac{(n-1)n}{2} = t_{n-1}, \; nm + n = t_{n-1} + n = t_n,$$

$$\text{and } t_{n-1} + t_n = n^2. \tag{1}$$

Relation (1) is the Theon theorem mentioned earlier and derived in this section in terms of the multiplication table only by interpreting algebraically the "equal distance" phenomenon.

3. FINDING THE SUM OF ALL NUMBERS IN THE MULTIPLICATION TABLE

The next inquiry into the properties of numbers in the $n \times n$ multiplication table is to find the sum of all numbers in this table. This sum, for which the notation $S(n)$ will be used below, is a function of n. The sum $S(n)$ can be first found by using the spreadsheet shown in Figure 9.2. To begin, note that the case $n = 10$ returns the sum of 3025. How are the numbers 3025 and 10 related? In other words, what is the connection between the sum of all numbers in the table and its size? In order to explore this question, one can construct a tabular representation of the function $S(n)$. The programming of the corresponding spreadsheet is similar to other spreadsheets used in this chapter and is discussed in Chapter 13.

A two-column representation of the function $S(n)$, $1 \le n \le 10$ can be used to guess the formula for $S(n)$ prior to its formal demonstration. It appears that the first four values of $S(n)$ belong to the main diagonal of the 10×10 multiplication table; thus, they are square numbers. One can conjecture that all the values of $S(n)$ are square numbers (yet, the converse statement is untrue, as not all square numbers are the values of this function). Furthermore, one can check to see that the values of $S(n)$ are squares of the numbers 1, 3, 6, 10, 15, 21, 28, 36, 45, and 55. Surprise! The ten listed

	1	2	3	4	5	6	7	8	9	10				n	S(n)
1	1	2	3	4	5	6	7	8	9	10				1	1
2	2	4	6	8	10	12	14	16	18	20				2	9
3	3	6	9	12	15	18	21	24	27	30				3	36
4	4	8	12	16	20	24	28	32	36	40				4	100
5	5	10	15	20	25	30	35	40	45	50				5	225
6	6	12	18	24	30	36	42	48	54	60				6	441
7	7	14	21	28	35	42	49	56	63	70				7	784
8	8	16	24	32	40	48	56	64	72	80				8	1296
9	9	18	27	36	45	54	63	72	81	90				9	2025
10	10	20	30	40	50	60	70	80	90	100				10	3025

SIZE 10 SUM 3025

Figure 9.2 Finding $S(n)$ computationally.

numbers are triangular numbers. Furthermore, the ranks of the triangular numbers are the sizes of the corresponding multiplication tables.

This completes the inductive phase of finding the sum of all numbers in the $n \times n$ multiplication table, The following technology-motivated formula can be conjectured:

$$S(n) = \left(\frac{n(n+1)}{2} \right)^2 \tag{2}$$

Note that adding numbers in the first row (or column) of the $n \times n$ multiplication table yields

$$1 + 2 + 3 + \ldots + n = \frac{n(n+1)}{2},$$

a relation already discussed in Chapter 8. Therefore, Formula (2) has the following interpretation: The sum of all numbers in a square-shaped multiplication table is equal to the square of the sum of all the numbers in the first row (or column) of the table. Put another way, the sum of all numbers in the $n \times n$ multiplication table is equal to the square of the nth triangular number. A mathematical induction proof of Formula (2) is discussed in Chapter 10.

4. MAKING MATHEMATICAL CONNECTIONS

One can construct a simple spreadsheet to numerically model the sums of cubes of consecutive counting numbers, starting from 1. Data so developed enables one to conjecture the formula

$$1^3 + 2^3 + 3^3 + \ldots + n^3 = \left(\frac{n(n+1)}{2} \right)^2. \tag{3}$$

Comparing Formulas (2) and (3) reveals the fact that the sum of all numbers in the $n \times n$ multiplication table equals $1^3 + 2^3 + 3^3 + \ldots + n^3$. The latter can be shown to represent the sum of all cubes within a cube of side n. In other words, the number of rectangles within the $n \times n$ checkerboard equals to the number of cubes within the $n \times n \times n$ cube. In order to explain this unexpected connection, all cubes in the $n \times n \times n$ cube can be arranged into n groups, depending on the size of a cube. Then, each such group can be mapped on a gnomon (see Chapter 4) in one of the faces of the $n \times n \times n$ cube. By representing a face of the cube as the $n \times n$ multiplication table, one can show that the sum of all numbers in each gnomon is equal to the number of cubes in the corresponding group. Indeed, the sum of numbers in the kth gnomon, representing the total number of cubes of side $n - k + 1$, can be found as follows:

$$2\left(k + 2k + \ldots + (k-1)k \right) + k^2 = 2k\left(1 + 2 + \ldots + (k-1) \right) + k^2$$

$$= 2k \frac{(k-1)k}{2} + k^2 = k^2(k-1) + k^2 = k^2(k-1+1) = k^3.$$

Here, Formula (5) mentioned in Chapter 8 was used in the case $n = k - 1$.

As was shown above, the sum of numbers in all n gnomons is equal to the total number of rectangles within the $n \times n$ face of the $n \times n \times n$ cube. In that way, geometric structures of different dimensions (cubes and rectangles) can become connected through the use of hidden mathematics of the multiplication table.

5. PERCENTAGE OF SQUARES AMONG RECTANGLES ON THE N × N CHECKERBOARD

Finding the number of squares among all rectangles on the $n \times n$ checkerboard leads to the sum of squares of consecutive counting numbers, starting from one. The formula for this sum has the form (Pólya, 1954)

$$1^2 + 2^2 + 3^2 + \ldots + n^2 = \frac{n(n+1)(2n+1)}{6}. \tag{4}$$

One can use a spreadsheet to find the percentage of squares among rectangles on the $n \times n$ checkerboard for different values of n beginning from $n = 1$. Such a spreadsheet is shown in Figure 9.3. The chart embedded into it shows that percentage of squares among the rectangles monotonically decreases as n increases.

The programming of the spreadsheet of Figure 9.3 is based on Formulas (2) and (4). The monotonic decrease of the percentage of squares among the rectangles can also be demonstrated formally as follows:

$$\frac{n(n+1)(2n+1)/6}{\left(n(n+1)/2\right)^2} = \frac{4n(n+1)(2n+1)}{6n^2(n+1)^2} = \frac{2(2n+1)}{3n(n+1)} = \frac{2n(2+1/n)}{3n^2(1+1/n)} \xrightarrow{n \to \infty} 0.$$

Furthermore, one can be asked to find, both computationally and graphically (for the latter approach, some algebraic skills are required), the smallest value of n for which the percentage of squares among rectangles becomes smaller than, say, 10%.

A computational solution is shown in Figure 9.3. A graphical solution is shown in Figure 9.4, where the positive root $n \cong 12.9$ of the function $f(n) = 3n^2 - 37n - 20$ determines the solution to the inequality

$$\frac{2(2n+1)}{3n(n+1)} < \frac{1}{10}.$$

In other words, the 13×13 checkerboard is the smallest checkerboard within which the percentage of squares among rectangles is smaller than 10%.

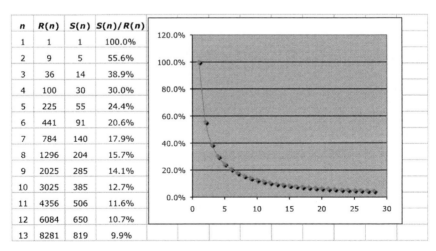

n	R(n)	S(n)	S(n)/R(n)
1	1	1	100.0%
2	9	5	55.6%
3	36	14	38.9%
4	100	30	30.0%
5	225	55	24.4%
6	441	91	20.6%
7	784	140	17.9%
8	1296	204	15.7%
9	2025	285	14.1%
10	3025	385	12.7%
11	4356	506	11.6%
12	6084	650	10.7%
13	8281	819	9.9%

Figure 9.3 Modeling the percentage of squares among rectangles function.

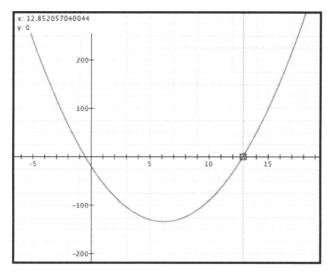

Figure 9.4   Finding the smallest checkerboard with less than 10% of squares.

6. FINDING THE SUM OF ODD NUMBERS IN THE MULTIPLICATION TABLE

Let $S_{odd}(n)$ be the sum of odd numbers in the $n \times n$ multiplication table. This sum can be found without difficulty if one observes (Figures 9.5 and 9.6) that $S_{odd}(n)$ is the same for $n = 2h - 1$ and $n = 2k$. Such an observation can be computationally confirmed by constructing a two-column representation of $S_{odd}(n)$ as a function of n. Furthermore, each of the k rows in a table of either size is a multiple of the first row; the sum of all numbers in the first row equals $1 + 3 + 5 + \ldots + 2k - 1 = k^2$. Here, Formula (4), mentioned in Chapter 8 (see also Appendix, Formula [A2]), was used. In such a way, we have

$$S_{odd}(n) = k^2(1 + 3 + 5 + \ldots + 2k - 1) = k^4,$$

where

$$k = \frac{n}{2} \text{ if } n \text{ is even and } k = \frac{n+1}{2} \text{ if } n \text{ is odd.}$$

For example, $n = 6$ yields $k = 3$, whence $S_{odd}(6) = 3^4 = 81$; $n = 7$ yields $k = 4$, whence $S_{odd}(7) = 4^4 = 256$.

| SIZE | 10 | | | | MODULO | | 2 | | | SUM | | 625 |

	1	2	3	4	5	6	7	8	9	10		n	$S_{odd}(n)$
1	1		3		5		7		9			1	1
2												2	1
3	3		9		15		21		27			3	16
4												4	16
5	5		15		25		35		45			5	81
6												6	81
7	7		21		35		49		63			7	256
8												8	256
9	9		27		45		63		81			9	625
10												10	625

Figure 9.5 The sum of odd numbers in an even size table.

| SIZE | 9 | | | | MODULO | | 2 | | | SUM | | 625 |

	1	2	3	4	5	6	7	8	9		n	$S_{odd}(n)$
1	1		3		5		7		9		1	1
2											2	1
3	3		9		15		21		27		3	16
4											4	16
5	5		15		25		35		45		5	81
6											6	81
7	7		21		35		49		63		7	256
8											8	256
9	9		27		45		63		81		9	625

Figure 9.6 The sum of odd numbers in an odd size table.

7. FINDING THE SUM OF EVEN NUMBERS IN THE MULTIPLICATION TABLE

Let $S_{even}(n)$ be the sum of even numbers in the $n \times n$ multiplication table. Whereas the sum of odd numbers in both the $(2k) \times (2k)$ table and $(2k-1) \times (2k-1)$ table equals k^4, the sum of even numbers changes as one moves from one table to another. Substituting $n = 2k$ in Formula (2) yields

$$\begin{aligned} S_{even}(2k) &= S(2k) - S_{odd}(2k) \\ &= k^2(2k+1)^2 - k^4 \\ &= k^2\left((2k+1)^2 - k^2\right) \\ &= k^2(k+1)(3k+1), \end{aligned}$$

that is,

$$S_{even}(2k) = k^2(k+1)(3k+1). \tag{5}$$

Substituting $n = 2k - 1$ in Formula (2) yields

$$\begin{aligned} S_{even}(2k-1) &= S(2k-1) - S_{odd}(2k-1) \\ &= k^2(2k-1)^2 - k^4 \\ &= k^2\left((2k-1)^2 - k^2\right) \\ &= k^2(k-1)(3k-1), \end{aligned}$$

that is,

$$S_{even}(2k-1) = k^2(k-1)(3k-1). \tag{6}$$

Formulas (5) and (6) can be computationally confirmed by using a spreadsheet (see Figures 9.7 and 9.8).

SIZE	10	MODULO	2	SUM	2400

	1	2	3	4	5	6	7	8	9	10		n	$S_{even}(n)$
1		2		4		6		8		10		1	0
2	2	4	6	8	10	12	14	16	18	20		2	8
3		6		12		18		24		30		3	20
4	4	8	12	16	20	24	28	32	36	40		4	84
5		10		20		30		40		50		5	144
6	6	12	18	24	30	36	42	48	54	60		6	360
7		14		28		42		56		70		7	528
8	8	16	24	32	40	48	56	64	72	80		8	1040
9		18		36		54		72		90		9	1400
10	10	20	30	40	50	60	70	80	90	100		10	2400

Figure 9.7 The $2 \cdot 5 \times 2 \cdot 5$ multiplication table.

	A	B	C	D	E	F	G	H	I	J	K	L	M	N	O	P
1																
2		SIZE		9				MODULO		2			SUM			1400
3				← ‖ →						← ▓ →						
4		1	2	3	4	5	6	7	8	9				n		$S_{even}(n)$
5	1		2		4		6		8					1		0
6	2	2	4	6	8	10	12	14	16	18				2		8
7	3		6		12		18		24					3		20
8	4	4	8	12	16	20	24	28	32	36				4		84
9	5		10		20		30		40					5		144
10	6	6	12	18	24	30	36	42	48	54				6		360
11	7		14		28		42		56					7		528
12	8	8	16	24	32	40	48	56	64	72				8		1040
13	9		18		36		54		72					9		1400
14																

Figure 9.8   The $2 \cdot 5 - 1 \times 2 \cdot 5 - 1$ multiplication table.

8. GEOMETRIC APPLICATIONS AND INTERPRETATIONS OF SUMMATION FORMULAS

Many algebraic results (summation formulas) found through the above explorations can be associated with integer-sided rectangles on a square-shaped checkerboard. For example, as is well known (National Council of Teachers of Mathematics, 2000), the total number of rectangles within the $n \times n$ checkerboard equals the sum of all numbers in the $n \times n$ multiplication table. By exploring the spreadsheet of Figure 9.7, one can see that the multiples of two in the $(2k) \times (2k)$ multiplication table can be associated with rectangles (on the related checkerboard) having at least one odd dimension; the same numbers in the $(2k - 1) \times (2k - 1)$ multiplication table can be associated with rectangles having at least one even dimension (Figure 9.8). Alternatively, one can see (Figure 9.5) that the odd numbers in the $(2k) \times (2k)$ multiplication table can be associated with rectangles having both dimensions measuring by even numbers. By the same token, in the $(2k - 1) \times (2k - 1)$ multiplication table, the odd numbers can be associated with rectangles having both dimensions measuring by odd numbers (Figure 9.6).

In that way, the use of spreadsheets allows one to enrich curriculum in the context of the multiplication table and to pose the following exploratory problems, the solutions of which are left to the reader.

- Exploration 1: On the $(2k-1) \times (2k-1)$ checkerboard, find the total number of rectangles of which at least one side is an even number. (*Hint:* The formula for $S_{odd}(n)$ found in section 6 can be used.)
- Exploration 2: On the $2k \times 2k$ checkerboard, find the total number of rectangles of which at least one side is an even number. (*Hint:* A slight modification of summation techniques demonstrated in sections 3 and 6 can be used.)
- Exploration 3: On the $2k \times 2k$ checkerboard, find the total number of rectangles of which at least one side is an odd number. (*Hint:* A combination of results found in sections 3 and 6 can be used.)
- Exploration 4: On the $(2k-1) \times (2k-1)$ checkerboard, find the total number of rectangles of which at least one side is an odd number. (*Hint:* A slight modification of summation techniques demonstrated in sections 3 and 7 can be used.)

CHAPTER 10

PROOF AND PROVING

When you have eliminated the impossible, whatever remains,
however improbable, must be the truth.

—Arthur Conan Doyle
(Oxford Dictionary of Scientific Quotations, 2005, p. 184)

1. INTRODUCTION

The *Reasoning and Proof* standard for grades pre-K through 2 (National Council of Teachers of Mathematics, 2000) sets an expectation for teachers to "help students understand the role of nonexamples as well as examples in informal proof" (p. 125) and "model ways that students can verify or disprove their conjectures" (p. 126). In grades 3 through 5, this standard plays an even greater role, as "posing conjectures and trying to justify them is an expected part of students' mathematical activity" (ibid, p. 191). In order to meet the expectations, teachers need to have experience with activities related to reasoning and proof. Situating mathematical ideas and formal reasoning in technologically and contextually supported learning environments makes it easier for the teachers to grasp the meaning of proof and understand the importance of transition from the reality of specific examples to the truth of their generalizations.

As was already mentioned above, the recommendations by the Conference Board of the Mathematical Sciences (2001) for the preparation of elementary teachers include the need for courses that demonstrate how mathematics can be approached, "at least initially, . . . from an experien-

Topics in Mathematics for Elementary Teachers, pages 171–193
Copyright © 2010 by Information Age Publishing

tially based direction, rather than an abstract/deductive one" (p. 96). The word "initially" implies that mathematical rigor is a reasonable expectation for any elementary mathematics teacher education program. In the words of a teacher who reflected on mathematical activities that were a combination of computational experiments and formal demonstration, "You must have theory in order to support the experiment that is being done. This is important because, in many cases, using experiential knowledge we can solve a math problem, but without knowing exactly how we solved it." The teacher's remark is due to her appreciation of the role that technology can play in developing a "deep understanding" of school mathematics through "giving meaning to the mathematical objects under study, only then moving on to higher orders of generality and rigor" (Conference Board of the Mathematical Sciences, 2001, p. 57).

Although the teaching of proofs is always a challenge, it can turn into a gratifying experience, as another teacher's comment indicates:

> My understanding of the meaning of mathematical proof is that it solidifies experiments and gives meaning to the experiment. What good is an experiment if we have no idea if it is in fact correct or not? It could appear as though it works visually, but could in fact be incorrect mathematically.

Providing teachers with experience in implementing the *Reasoning and Proof* standard can address the recommendation by Senk, Keller, and Ferrini-Mundy (2004) that "mathematics courses taken by prospective teachers should develop understanding of both mathematical content and mathematical processes such as defining, conjecturing and proving" (p. 148). These authors argue that pre-college mathematics textbooks for prospective teachers "do not emphasize reasoning and proof and as a result new materials . . . may need to be developed" (p. 151). The goal of the chapter is to demonstrate how this call can be addressed in the context of elementary teacher preparation.

2. EXAMINING AN ORGANIZED LIST

The following problem will be used to illustrate how the idea of mathematical proof can be introduced at a junior elementary level.

A Pet Store Problem: *A pet store sold only birds and cats. The store owner asked his clerk to count how many animals there were in the store. The clerk counted 18 legs. How many cats and birds might there have been?*

As discussed in detail in Chapter 3, one way to solve the pet store problem through modern didactics is to use the computer graphics software *Kid Pix*. In what follows, the proof aspect of the problem will be discussed. Figure 10.1 portrays a solution developed by a second grader using the earliest version of the software. In the chart of Figure 10.2, five combinations of animals found by trial and error are collected and arranged by the number of animals, from the smallest to the greatest number of cats (alternatively, from the greatest to the smallest number of birds). In that way, an organized list has been created.

By making use of the organized list, we have to prove that *all* combinations of animals were found and recorded in the chart of Figure 10.2. This proof may consist of three steps.

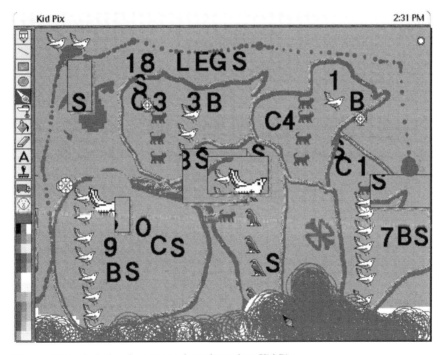

Figure 10.1 Solution by a second grader using *Kid Pix*.

Cats	0	1	2	3	4
Birds	9	7	5	3	1
Legs	18	18	18	18	18

Figure 10.2 Solutions to the pet store problem presented through an organized list.

- *Step 1*: Determine a range within which the number of cats varies. Obviously, there may be either no cats or four cats, at the most, as already five cats have more than 18 legs. Indeed, $4 + 4 + 4 + 4 + 4 = 20 > 18$.
- *Step 2*: Check that every whole number from the range zero through four is present in the chart. In other words, there may be no cats, one cat, two cats, three cats, or four cats.
- *Step 3*: Show that for each number of cats there exist a certain number of birds. Indeed, with no cats, we have nine birds; with one cat, seven birds; with two cats, five birds; with three cats, three birds; and with four cats, one bird. The correctness of the conclusions made at each step implies that, indeed, all combinations of animals jointly having 18 legs have been found by the second grader.

It should be noted that, rather than focusing on the range for the number of cats, one might consider the range within which the number of birds varies. The latter range includes all the odd numbers from one through nine (the largest possible number of birds), each number being paired with the corresponding number of cats. One can see that, unlike the case of the cats' range, not all integers in the range one through nine are present in the chart. Therefore, in addition, the following question has to be answered: *Could there be combinations of animals with an even number of birds in the store?*

To this end, one has to make an extra effort in demonstrating that whatever even number represents the number of birds, the remaining number of legs may not be assigned to cats. In doing so, one has to explore the numbers 0, 2, 4, 6, and 8 as possible candidates for the number of birds, and proceed with subtraction in completing the proof that focuses on the range within which the number of birds varies. For example, assuming that we have four birds, the following arithmetical computations should be carried out: $2 + 2 + 2 + 2 = 8$ (the number of legs among four birds), $18 - 8 = 10$ (the number of legs among an unknown number of cats), $10 - 4 = 6$ (one cat), $6 - 4 = 2$ (another cat), the last equality indicating not only that no more cats can be found, but that no combination of cats may have 10 legs.

This example demonstrates that, just as there exist multiple solutions of a single problem at different levels of complexity, one can observe the coexistence of rigorous arguments that differ by the levels of complexity. In addition to having experience with different ways of solving a problem, the teachers need to have experience with different proofs of the same proposition. In fact, this is an important characteristic of mathematics, as a field of disciplined inquiry. The development of mathematical knowledge often results from one's efforts to improve already existing proofs.

3. MANIPULATIVE-SUPPORTED PROOF: REPRESENTATION OF UNIT FRACTIONS AS THE SUM OF TWO LIKE FRACTIONS

The activities of this section stem from an episode shared with the author by a teacher who had observed first-grade students working on the task of finding all ways to cover a fraction circle one–half using other fraction circles[1]. A hidden depth of this activity, while perhaps not having been clear to the teacher, has great potential to provoke young children's intuition and curiosity. Indeed, in a course of manipulating fraction circles, a child could inquire:

- *How do we (you) know that all the ways to cover one–half have been found?* (Compare this question to the one asked in connection with the pet store problem: *How do we know that all combinations of animals have been found?*).
- *Can other unit fractions be covered with two unit fractions?*
- *Can any unit fraction be covered with two unit fractions?*

To support this line of inquiry in a teacher education classroom, electronic fraction circles can be created by using *The Geometer's Sketchpad*. Below, a few propositions about representations of unit fractions as a sum of two like fractions are presented. Consequently, proofs of these propositions will be technology-supported. In the words of one pre-service teacher,

> The electronic manipulatives helped me articulate mathematical proof through visual understanding. Sometimes it is difficult to consider which fractions are going to create a particular sum. But the manipulatives helped me to understand what was going on in the problem as well as understand why the answers were correct. I was thrilled at knowing there are alternative ways to teach children about fractions. I feel I have gained the necessary knowledge and resources to someday teach this to a classroom of my own.

Indeed, classroom observation of teachers working through carefully designed combinations of hands-on and technology-enhanced investigations indicated that their confidence steadily grew as the activities went along. Using technology, the teachers were able to make significant progress in connecting their informal explorations with formal symbolic mathematics. In this situation, traditionally poorly understood topics, like formal arithmetical operations with fractions, when highlighted from a different, sometimes advanced, perspective in which the teachers experience success, leads to a greater understanding of and confidence in those topics.

We begin with

Proposition 1: *There exist exactly two ways to represent 1/2 as a sum of two unit fractions.*

Proof. One way to partition fraction circle $1/2$ into two fraction circles is to cut it into two equal pieces, as shown in the left-hand side of Figure 10.3. This gives the representation $1/2 = 1/4 + 1/4$. In order to find a different representation, one has to use instead of $1/4$ a larger fraction circle and see if there exists a smaller fraction circle complementing the first one to $1/2$. The only fraction circle that is larger than $1/4$ and smaller than $1/2$ is the fraction $1/3$. An experiment with electronic fraction circles can show that, whereas $1/3 + 1/5$ is greater than $1/2$ (Figure 10.4), the fraction circle $1/6$ does work with $1/3$, as shown in the right-hand side of Figure 10.3. Furthermore, adding fractions numerically confirms that $1/2 = 1/3 + 1/6$. This completes the proof.

Remark 1: Note that, had we started looking for fraction circles that are smaller (instead of bigger) than $1/4$, our reasoning might have never come

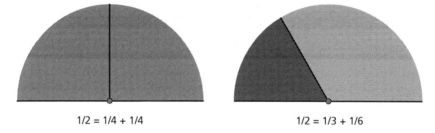

1/2 = 1/4 + 1/4   1/2 = 1/3 + 1/6

Figure 10.3 Covering one-half with two fraction circles.

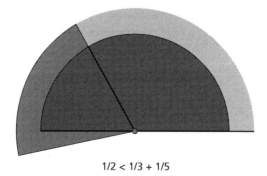

1/2 < 1/3 + 1/5

Figure 10.4 Rejecting fraction circle 1/5 experimentally.

to an end, as there exists an infinite number of unit fractions smaller than 1/4. Yet, the number of unit fractions larger than 1/4 and smaller than 1/2 is limited to 1/3 only. This situation is similar to the one discussed in the context of proof for the pet store problem, when focusing on the range for cats, rather than focusing on the range for birds, provided a more efficient line of reasoning.

Continuing in this vein, one can formulate and prove

Proposition 2: *There exist exactly two ways to represent 1/3 as a sum of two unit fractions.*

Proof. As in the case of 1/2, one way to partition fraction circle 1/3 into two fraction circles is to cut it into two equal pieces, as shown in Figure 10.5. This gives the representation $1/3 = 1/6 + 1/6$. In order to find a different representation, one has to use instead of 1/6 a larger fraction circle and see if there exists a fraction circle (smaller than 1/6) complementing the first one to 1/2. There are only two unit fractions smaller than 1/3 and bigger than 1/6. These are 1/5 and 1/4. Whereas, as shown in Figure 10.5, the fraction 1/4 can be complemented by the fraction 1/12 to sum up to 1/3 (numerically, $1/4 + 1/12 = 3/12 + 1/12 = 4/12 = 1/3$), no unit fraction exists to complement the fraction 1/5 in order to make 1/3. This fact can first be established experimentally as shown in Figure 10.6.

Indeed, although $1/5 > 1/6$ and $1/7 < 1/6$, the sum $1/5 + 1/7$ is greater than 1/3. Numerically, $1/5 + 1/7 = 12/35 > 12/36 = 1/3$. By the same token, trying 1/8 (which is also smaller than 1/6) shows that $1/3 > 1/5 + 1/8$. Numerically, $1/5 + 1/8 = 13/40 < 13/39 = 1/3$. This experiment with electronic fraction circles can be followed by an algebraic demonstration: The equation $1/5 + x = 1/3$ yields $x = 2/15$, thereby showing that x is not a unit fraction. Therefore, the two representations shown in Figure 10.5 are the only ways to partition 1/3 into a sum of two unit fractions. This completes the proof.

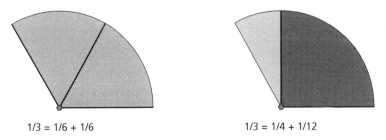

1/3 = 1/6 + 1/6   1/3 = 1/4 + 1/12

Figure 10.5 Covering one-third with two fraction circles.

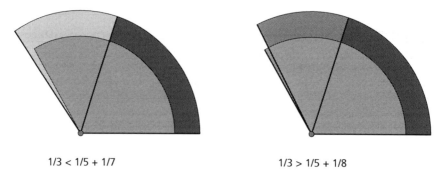

1/3 < 1/5 + 1/7   1/3 > 1/5 + 1/8

Figure 10.6   Trying to find more representations through trial and error.

• Based on a limited evidence of the above two propositions, one might think that *any* unit fraction can be partitioned in two like fractions in two ways only. This, however, is not the case, as the next proposition shows.

Proposition 3: *A unit fraction 1/4 can be represented as a sum of two unit fractions in exactly three ways.*

Proof. An obvious representation of 1/4 is through the sum of two equal unit fractions is 1/4 = 1/8 + 1/8. In this regard, it should be noted that, unlike the case of integers enabling only an even number to be represented as the sum of two equal numbers, any unit fraction can be represented as the sum of two equal fractions. This phenomenon, that is, the difference between the properties of integers and their reciprocals, can be explained algebraically by using the identities

$$n = \frac{n}{2} + \frac{n}{2} \text{ and } \frac{1}{n} = \frac{1}{2n} + \frac{1}{2n}.$$

Indeed, given integer n, its double, $2n$, is always an integer, whereas one-half of it, $n/2$, may or may not be an integer. In other words, the set of integers is closed under multiplication and is not closed under division. Experimenting with 1/5 (the largest fraction circle smaller than 1/4) one can discover that 1/4 = 1/5 + 1/20. Numerically, 1/5 + 1/20 = 4/20 + 1/20 = 5/20 = 1/4.

Now, only two possibilities to represent 1/4 as a sum of two unit fractions remain: using 1/6 and 1/7, as these two fractions are the only unit fractions that are larger than 1/8 and smaller than 1/5. One can check to see that 1/6 + 1/12 = 2/12 + 1/12 = 3/12 = 1/4. However, as the experiment can give the way to the use of algebra, the equation 1/7 + x = 1/4 yields $x = 1/4 - 1/7 = 3/28$, not a unit fraction. Figure 10.7 shows all three representations of 1/4 as a sum of two unit fractions.

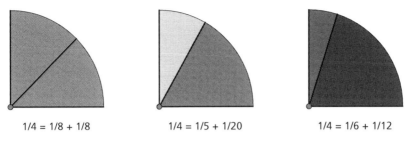

1/4 = 1/8 + 1/8   1/4 = 1/5 + 1/20   1/4 = 1/6 + 1/12

Figure 10.7   Three representations of $1/4$ as a sum of two unit fractions.

Analyzing the three representations,

$$\frac{1}{2}=\left\{\frac{1}{4}+\frac{1}{4},\frac{1}{3}+\frac{1}{6}\right\},\ \frac{1}{3}=\left\{\frac{1}{6}+\frac{1}{6},\frac{1}{4}+\frac{1}{12}\right\},\ \frac{1}{4}=\left\{\frac{1}{8}+\frac{1}{8},\frac{1}{5}+\frac{1}{20},\frac{1}{6}+\frac{1}{12}\right\},$$

one can come up with the following generalization:

Proposition 4: *A unit fraction $1/n$ has at least two representations as the sum of two unit fractions: through two equal fractions,*

$$\frac{1}{n}=\frac{1}{2n}+\frac{1}{2n},\tag{1}$$

and through the largest and the smallest possible fractions,

$$\frac{1}{n}=\frac{1}{n+1}+\frac{1}{n(n+1)}.\tag{2}$$

Proof. By adding the fractions using the rules of algebra, one gets

$$\frac{1}{2n}+\frac{1}{2n}=\frac{2}{2n}=\frac{1}{n}\ \text{and}\ \frac{1}{n+1}+\frac{1}{n(n+1)}=\frac{n+1}{n(n+1)}=\frac{1}{n}.$$

This completes the proof.

Another guess that one can make based on the limited evidence of the above three propositions is that as the denominator of a unit fraction increases, the number of ways it can be represented as a sum of two like fractions either does not change or increases. Once again, this is not the case. In order to show that this guess is mistaken, one can consider the fraction circle $1/5$ and show that, just as for the fractions $1/2$ and $1/3$, there exist only two ways to represent $1/5$ as a sum of two unit fractions. In this regard, the following important observation can be made. Whereas multiple examples may not be sufficient for proving a statement, a single example (called a counterexample) is sufficient for disproving a statement. Indeed, whereas having three boys named Tom in a class does not imply that every boy in the class bears this name, having a boy named Bill in the class does imply that not all boys in the class have name Tom.

Nonetheless, numerical examples are useful tools in the study of mathematics, for they can motivate proof. For instance, the fact that the fractions 1/3, 1/5, and 1/7 have exactly two representations as a sum of two unit fractions may prompt an inquiry into what the three denominators have in common. The first guess could be that these are odd numbers and, thereby, every unit fraction with an odd denominator has exactly two representations as a sum of two unit fractions. How could a teacher proceed from here if a student proposed such a conjecture?

Ideally, the teacher should know if this is true or not. Yet, pedagogical content knowledge should prompt the teacher to offer informal means of verifying students' emerging conjectures. For example, using a spreadsheet, one can find that the fraction 1/9 has three representations as a sum of two unit fractions (one of which is displayed in Figure 10.8). What is the difference between an odd number 9 and odd numbers 3, 5, and 7? At that point it, may become clear that, whereas 3, 5, and 7 (as well as 2—recall Proposition 1) are prime numbers, 9 is a composite number. One can also note that both 4 and 9 are square numbers with exactly three representations as a sum of two unit fractions. However, the next square number, 16, can serve as a counterexample (alternatively, a nonexample): Using the spreadsheet shown in Figure 10.8, one can discover that 1/16 can be represented as a sum of two unit fractions in five ways. The programming of the spreadsheet is discussed in Chapter 13.

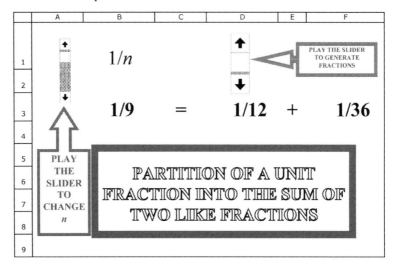

Figure 10.8 A non-trivial partition of 1/9 into the sum of two unit fractions.

Remark 2: Identity (2) is sometimes attributed to Fibonacci (Hoffman, 1998).

Remark 3: Unlike the case of integer n for which the larger the n, the larger the number of representations of n as a sum of two other integers, such a relationship is not true for its reciprocal, $\frac{1}{n}$.

4. CONTEXT-MEDIATED PROOF: EXPLORING UNIT FRACTIONS WITH A PRIME NUMBER DENOMINATOR

In this section, another type of mediation of a mathematical proof will be introduced—a proof mediated by context. Just as concrete objects can serve as situational referents for emerging mathematical symbolism, real-life context can mediate formal mathematical reasoning. Such mediation was provided in the above discussion of the role of counterexamples using boys' names. In order to have a context-mediated proof of a mathematical proposition, one has to situate the proposition into an appropriate context, so that any step of the proof will have a contextual referent. In this way, the learners of mathematics can use their real-life experience and common sense as they develop proficiency in formal mathematical reasoning.

To this end, consider

Proposition 5: *If n is a prime number, then the unit fraction $\frac{1}{n}$ can be represented as the sum of two unit fractions in only two ways, defined by Identities (1) and (2).*

In order to prove this proposition, consider the following context

Two Workers Problem: *Bill and Tom can complete a certain job in n days when working together. How many days does each of them need to complete this job when working alone?*

Through exploring this problem, a formal proof of Proposition 5 can be developed. To this end, let x and y represent, respectively, the number of days Bill and Tom need to complete the job when working alone. Several properties of the symbols x and y can be established. First, let us assume that we measure the completion of work in full days; under this assumption, the symbols x and y are positive integers. Second, the inequalities $x > n$ and $y > n$ hold; otherwise, Bill and Tom need fewer than n days to complete the job when working together. Indeed, if one of them can complete the job when working alone in n or fewer days (if $x \leq n$ or $y \leq n$), then with a co-worker, the job will be completed even faster. Third, let us assume that Tom is at least as capable as Bill; that is, the number of days it takes Bill to complete the job when working alone is always greater or equal to that of Tom. Symbolically, this assumption means $x \geq y$.

After establishing the properties of the symbols x and y, note that the unit fraction $1/x$ can measure Bill's daily capability. Indeed, $1/x$ repeated x times (days) yields one, a conditional unit of work. Likewise, the unit fraction $1/y$ represents the amount of work Tom can do per day. Then, the sum

$$\frac{1}{x} + \frac{1}{y}$$

represents the amount of work both individuals can do in one day when working together.

By the same token, if it takes them n days to complete the job when working together, then $1/n$ is their joint daily productivity. Indeed, the fraction $1/n$ repeated n times (days) yields the same conditional unit of work. This, in turn, implies the equation

$$\frac{1}{x} + \frac{1}{y} = \frac{1}{n}, \tag{3}$$

which can be interpreted as the representation of the unit fraction $1/n$ as the sum of two unit fractions, $1/x + 1/y$. In that way, a real-life context for Proposition 5 has been created.

According to Proposition 4, Identities (1) and (2) imply that the pairs $x = 2n$, $y = 2n$ and $x = n(n+1)$, $y = n+1$ are two solutions to Equation (3). The first solution means that the job can be completed jointly in n days, when Bill is as capable as Tom (each of them can complete a job in $2n$ days when working alone). The second solution means that Tom can complete the job when working alone in $n+1$ days; that is, although he cannot complete the job by himself in n days, he can do it in $n+1$ days, thereby expecting just a little help from a less capable collaborator. Now, we have to show that when n is a prime number and $2n < x < n(n+1)$, Equation (3) does not have solutions. This demonstration requires a certain level of algebraic skills.

To this end, Equation (3) can be rewritten in the form

$$\frac{xy}{x+y} = n,$$

from which it follows that $xy = nx + ny$ or $y(x-n) = nx$, whence the equation $y(x-n) = n(x-n) + n^2$. Because $x \neq n$, one can divide both sides of the last equation by $(x-n)$ and express y as a function of x and n in an equivalent form:

$$y = n + \frac{n^2}{x-n}. \tag{4}$$

Equation (4) allows one to see how the number of days for Bill (the variable x) affects the number of days for Tom (the variable y).

Now, we have to explore whether the expression

$$\frac{n^2}{x - n}$$

in the left-hand side of Equation (4) yields a whole number when n is a prime number and $2n < x < n(n + 1)$. Subtracting n from each side of the last two inequalities yields $n < x - n < n^2$. Therefore, one has to find how many divisors of n^2 reside between n and n^2. As was demonstrated through the development of the sieve of Eratosthenes in Chapter 6, when n is a prime number, its square, n^2, has only three divisors, 1, n, and n^2. In other words, there are no divisors of n^2 strictly between n and n^2. Therefore, there are only two solutions for the two workers problem. Proposition 5 has been proved.

5. MATHEMATICAL INDUCTION PROOF

A proof by mathematical induction differs from reasoning by induction in the following significant way: The former is a rigorous argument and the latter is not. An example of reasoning by induction that results in an incorrect generalization was presented in Chapter 6, in connection with exploring twin primes. Although the pairs (11, 13), (41, 43), (71, 73), and (101, 103) are four consecutive twin primes, with the difference 30 between the corresponding elements, the pair (131, 133) does not represent twin primes, as 133 is a composite number ($133 = 7 \times 19$). A simpler example of an incorrect generalization concerns the finding of the number of possible representations of a unit fraction $1/n$ as a sum of two unit fractions. Indeed, because for $1/2$ there are two representations: $1/2 = 1/4 + 1/4$ and $1/2 = 1/3 + 1/6$, and for $1/3$ there are also two representations: $1/3 = 1/6 + 1/6$ and $1/3 = 1/4 + 1/12$, one might generalize from the two instances that any unit fraction $1/n$ has two and only two representations as a sum of two unit fractions. But already the case $n = 4$ brings about a counterexample: In addition to the expected representations $1/4 = 1/8 + 1/8$ and $1/4 = 1/5 + 1/20$, there is a third one, $1/4 = 1/6 + 1/12$. These examples demonstrate two important things: (1) making a general statement based on several observed instances (reasoning inductively) may lead to an incorrect generalization; (2) in order to disprove a conjecture, one has to provide just one example (a counterexample) that defies the conjecture.

It should be noted that the transition from $n = 3$ to $n = 4$ in the above erroneous conjecture about a unit fraction $1/n$ was not justified. It was a guess for a special case (based on a limited experience with just two unit fractions, 1/2 and 1/3), rather than a formal argument in support of the general case. If one had justified the transition from n to $n+1$, that is, if one had rigorously demonstrated that, in general, the fact of having exactly two representations as a sum of two unit fractions for the fraction $1/n$ implies having exactly two representations for the fraction $1/(n+1)$, then by knowing that 1/2 has exactly two such representations as a sum of two unit fractions would imply the same for 1/3 and, therefore, for 1/4, and for 1/5, and for 1/6, and so on (i.e., for any fraction $1/n$). This kind of reasoning (i.e., a formal justification of the transition from n to $n+1$) constitutes the essence of the method of mathematical induction. Yet, the transition from n to $n+1$ in the case of unit fractions cannot be demonstrated.

Typically, mathematical induction proof starts with establishing the base clause and then proceeds with the completion of what Pólya (1954) referred to as "the demonstrative phase" (p. 110), or testing the transition from n to $n+1$. Such a phase can be supported by its representation in manipulative and/or computational environments. The following two propositions and their proofs show how this can be accomplished.

Proposition 6: *The formula*

$$1+2+3+\ldots+n = \frac{n(n+1)}{2} \tag{5}$$

holds true for all n = 1, 2, 3, ...

Proof. To begin, note that Formula (5) is true for $n = 1$. Indeed, both sides of the formula are equal to one, in this case. This establishes the base clause—a property followed by the demonstration of inductive transfer. A formal (algebraic) proof of inductive transfer can first be explained by using its manipulative representation. Figure 10.9 shows that when $n = 4$, twice the sum $1 + 2 + 3 + 4$ is represented by circles and squares

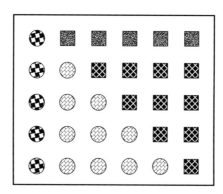

Figure 10.9 Visualizing inductive transfer in a manipulative environment.

arranged in a 4×5 rectangle. Transition from $n = 4$ to $n = 5$ (shown as the augmentation of the 4×5 rectangle by five circles and five squares in Figure 10.9) does not change the strategy of calculations. Indeed, one can see that the 5×6 rectangle consists of 15 (or $1 + 2 + 3 + 4 + 5$) circles complemented by as many squares. The validity of such a transition can be observed for other values of n.

This visual representation can be described in the language of algebra as follows. Making the so-called inductive assumption that twice the sum of the first n consecutive counting numbers can be found through the formula $2(1 + 2 + 3 + \ldots + n) = n(n + 1)$, which is equivalent to Formula (5), implies $2(1 + 2 + 3 + \ldots + n + (n + 1)) = (n + 1)(n + 2)$, because

$$2\big(1 + 2 + 3 + \ldots + n + (n + 1)\big) = \overbrace{2(1 + 2 + 3 + \ldots + n)} + \underline{2(n + 1)}$$

$$= \overbrace{n(n + 1)} + \underline{2(n + 1)} = (n + 1)(n + 2).$$

One can recognize in the underlined term the augmentation of the original rectangular arrangement by five identical circles and five identical squares (Figure 10.9). Now, using the already established base clause, the algebraic part of the proof (the justification of the transition from n to $n + 1$, such a transition resembling the domino effect—the fall of the first domino causes the fall of all others, all the way to infinity) can be put to work as follows: Being true for $n = 1$, Formula (5) is true for $n = 2$, and, thereby, for $n = 3$, and so on; that is, Formula (5) is true for all $n = 1, 2, 3,$

Proposition 7: *The sum $S(n)$ of all numbers in the $n \times n$ multiplication table is given by the formula*

$$S(n) = \left(\frac{n(n + 1)}{2} \right)^2 . \tag{6}$$

Proof. Formula (6) can also be proved by the method of mathematical induction. As was demonstrated in Chapter 9, a spreadsheet made it possible to computationally enhance the inductive development of Formula (6). Furthermore, in the process of proving Formula (6), it will be shown how the conditional formatting feature of a spreadsheet allows for the demonstrative phase to be visually enhanced.

The first step is to show that Formula (6) is true for $n = 1$. Indeed, when $n = 1$, the multiplication table consists of the unity only, whence $S(1) = 1$. The right-hand side of Formula (6) assumes the same value when $n = 1$. This elementary demonstration of the base clause establishes an important link between the concreteness of the multiplication table (Figure 10.10) and the abstractness of Formula (6).

The second step is to test the transition from n to $n+1$. In other words, assuming that Formula (6) holds true for n (making the inductive assumption), one has to show that, after replacing n by $n+1$, the structure of the formula does not change, that is,

$$S(n+1) = \left(\frac{(n+1)(n+2)}{2} \right)^2.$$

To visually support the second step—in other words, in order to show what augments the table when it acquires a new row and a new column—one can use the conditional formatting feature of a spreadsheet. This feature can highlight any augmentation of the table from its current state by a gnomon. As shown in Figure 10.10, conditional formatting highlights such a gnomon consisting of the numbers that belong to $S(11)$ but do not belong to $S(10)$. More specifically, $S(11) - S(10) = 2 \cdot 11 \cdot (1 + 2 + \ldots + 11) - 11^2$.

In general, the transition from n to $n+1$ yields the relationship $S(n+1) = S(n) + 2(n+1)(1+2+\ldots+(n+1)) - (n+1)^2$. Next, by utilizing Formula (5), one can show that $S(n+1) = S(n) + (n+1)^3$. Indeed,

$$2(n+1)(1+2+3+\ldots+(n+1)) - (n+1)^2 = 2\frac{(n+1)^2(n+2)}{2} - (n+1)^2 = (n+1)^3.$$

Finally, using the inductive assumption yields the following chain of equalities:

$$S(n+1) = S(n) + (n+1)^3 = \left(\frac{n(n+1)}{2} \right)^2 + (n+1)^3 = \frac{n^2(n+1)^2}{4} + \frac{4(n+1)^3}{4}$$

$$= \frac{(n+1)^2}{4}(n^2 + 4n + 4) = \frac{(n+1)^2}{4}(n+2)^2 = \left(\frac{(n+1)(n+2)}{2} \right)^2.$$

This concludes the proof of Formula (6) by the method of mathematical induction.

Remark 4: A difference in carrying out the transition from n to $n+1$ when proving Proposition 6 and Proposition 7 is worth noting. In the former case, this transition was based on the augmentation of the corresponding sum by just one term, $n+1$. In the latter case, the transition from the sum $S(n)$ to the sum $S(n+1)$ involved $2n+1$ terms, all located within a gnomon. As it turned out, the sum of numbers in the gnomon is equal to

	A	B	C	D	E	F	G	H	I	J	K	L
1												
2		SIZE		11		←	→					
3												
4		1	2	3	4	5	6	7	8	9	10	11
5	1	1	2	3	4	5	6	7	8	9	10	11
6	2	2	4	6	8	10	12	14	16	18	20	22
7	3	3	6	9	12	15	18	21	24	27	30	33
8	4	4	8	12	16	20	24	28	32	36	40	44
9	5	5	10	15	20	25	30	35	40	45	50	55
10	6	6	12	18	24	30	36	42	48	54	60	66
11	7	7	14	21	28	35	42	49	56	63	70	77
12	8	8	16	24	32	40	48	56	64	72	80	88
13	9	9	18	27	36	45	54	63	72	81	90	99
14	10	10	20	30	40	50	60	70	80	90	100	110
15	11	11	22	33	44	55	66	77	88	99	110	121
16												

Figure 10.10 Visualizing inductive transfer in a computational environment.

$(n + 1)^3$. However, the finding of this sum was part of the transition from n to $n + 1$. In that way, the above two mathematical induction proofs belong to different levels of complexity.

6. TRAPEZOIDAL REPRESENTATIONS

Brain Teaser (Van de Walle, 2001, p. 66): *"Find ways to add consecutive numbers in order to reach sums between 1 and 15."*

This section will show how the rich conceptual structure of the brain teaser allows for a practice in proof techniques that have not been explored so far in this chapter. To this end, we begin with developing an organized list to represent numbers in the range 1 through 15 through the sums of consecutive counting numbers.

There are four sums that start with one: $1 + 2 = 3$, $1 + 2 + 3 = 6$, $1 + 2 + 3 + 4 = 10$, and $1 + 2 + 3 + 4 + 5 = 15$.

There are three sums that start with two: $2 + 3 = 5$, $2 + 3 + 4 = 9$, and $2 + 3 + 4 + 5 = 14$.

There are two sums that start with three: $3 + 4 = 7$ and $3 + 4 + 5 = 12$.

There are two sums that start with four: $4 + 5 = 9$ and $4 + 5 + 6 = 15$.

Finally, there is only one sum that starts with either five, or six, or seven: $5 + 6 = 11$, $6 + 7 = 13$, $7 + 8 = 15$.

Whereas the above way of developing an organized list may be considered as a practice in proving that all required sums have been found, the brain teaser has much more to offer to teachers, in terms of the learning of mathematics. Indeed, already many interesting questions can be asked about the sums in the organized list. Among them:

- Is there another way of making an organized list?
- Which numbers in the range 1 through 15 were not represented as the sums of consecutive counting numbers?
- Which numbers in the range 1 through 15 were represented as the sums of consecutive counting numbers more than one time?
- What is special about the sums of two consecutive counting numbers?
- What is special about the sums of three consecutive counting numbers?
- How can one prove that the sum of three consecutive counting numbers is divisible by three?
- Can this property be extended to other combinations of numbers; that is, is the sum of four, five, six, and so on consecutive counting numbers divisible, respectively, by four, five, six, and so on? Why or why not?

The variety of questions that one can ask about the sums of consecutive counting numbers demonstrates that the inclusion of this task in a mathematics methods textbook for elementary teachers (Van de Walle, 2001) was apparently due to the current emphasis of education reform on open-ended problem solving. One of the main didactical values of open-ended mathematical tasks is their either explicit or implicit connection to big ideas, their rich conceptual structure, and the possibility of using the tasks over and over across the curriculum.

As an example of a rich conceptual structure emerging from a pure numerical exploration, Pólya (1965) introduced the notion of a trapezoidal representation of a positive integer N with n rows; that is, the representation of N as a sum of n consecutive counting numbers (rows):

$$N = k + (k + 1) + \ldots + (k + n - 1), \quad k = 1, 2, 3, \ldots. \tag{7}$$

Allowing for the sum of consecutive counting numbers to start from any positive integer k, rather than necessarily from one, can be viewed as a generalization of a triangular number. The triangular representation ($k = 1$) and the one-term sum ($k = N$) are included into the trapezoidal rep-

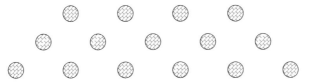

Figure 10.11 A trapezoidal representation of the number 15.

resentations of N with n rows. For example, fifteen has four trapezoidal representations: $15 = 15$, $15 = 7 + 8$, $15 = 4 + 5 + 6$ (see Figure 10.11), and $15 = 1 + 2 + 3 + 4 + 5$. Unlike triangular representations, trapezoidal representations may be not unique. By the same token, just as not all integers are triangular numbers, there are integers, like 16, that allow for the trivial trapezoidal representation only (i.e., a representation with one row [16 = 16]).

The following four propositions are aimed at the demonstration of how mathematical statements can be built on one another, so that one can break a complex proof into multiple, easy-to-understand steps. In particular, through these steps, a formula for the number of trapezoidal representations $T(N)$ of a prime number $N > 2$ will be found. For example, $T(3) = 2$, $T(5) = 2$, $T(7) = 2$, $T(11) = 2$, $T(13) = 2$, in which trivial representations with one row are included.

We begin with

Proposition 8: *The formula*

$$k + (k+1) + (k+2) + \ldots + (k+n-1) = \frac{n(2k+n-1)}{2} \tag{8}$$

holds true for n, k = 1, 2, 3, ...

Proof. Using the Gauss's method (Chapter 8), one can write

$$k + (k+1) + (k+2) + \ldots + (k+n-1) + (k+n-1) + (k+n-2) + (k+n-2) + \ldots + k$$

$$= (2k+n-1) + (2k+n-1) + (2k+n-1) + \ldots + (2k+n-1)$$

$$= n(2k+n-1).$$

Therefore,

$$k + (k+1) + (k+2) + \ldots + (k+n-1) = \frac{n(2k+n-1)}{2}.$$

This completes the proof.

Remark 5: A geometric interpretation of Formula (8) is presented in Figure 10.12 for $n = 4$ and $k = 3$.

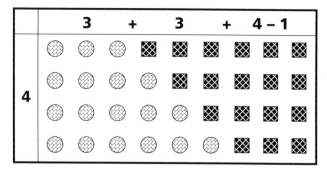

Figure 10.12   Developing Formula (8) for $n = 4$ and $k = 3$.

Remark 6: Formula (8) is a special case of Formula (11) from Chapter 8, where $x_1 = k$ and $d = 1$.

Let $N = k + (k + 1) + (k + 2) + \ldots + (k + n - 1)$. Then, according to Proposition 8,

$$2N = n(2k + n - 1). \tag{9}$$

Equation (9) is a two-variable equation; given N, each solution pair (k, n) determines the trapezoid with n rows, the top row having length k.

Proposition 9: *One of the factors in the right-hand side of Equation (9) is even and another is odd.*

Proof. If n is even, then $n - 1$ is odd and, therefore, $2k + n - 1$ is odd for all positive integers k. Likewise, if n is odd, then $n - 1$ is even and, therefore, $2k + n - 1$ is even for all positive integers k.

Now, one can formulate and then prove

Proposition 10: *Powers of two have only the trivial trapezoidal representation, that is, $T(2^m) = 1$, for a positive integer m.*

Proof. Substituting 2^m for N in Equation (9) yields $2^{m+1} = n(2k + n - 1)$. Note that the left-hand side of the last equation is an even number. Therefore, in order for the equation to have solutions, its right-hand side should be an even number, as well. Which combination of n and k makes the product $n(2k + n - 1)$ an even number? To answer this question, two cases need to be considered: n is even and n is odd.

If n is even, then $n - 1$ is odd and, therefore, $2k + n - 1$ is odd, as the sum of an even ($2k$) and an odd ($n - 1$) number. This implies that the product $n(2k + n - 1)$ is an even number only when $2k + n - 1 = 1$, whence $2k + n = 2$. The last equality, however, contradicts to the fact that $k \geq 1$ and $n \geq 1$. Indeed, $2k + n > 2$ for such values of k and n.

If n is odd, then $2k + n - 1$ is even. Therefore, the product $n(2k + n - 1)$ may only be even when $n = 1$. In this case, the equation $2^{m+1} = n(2k + n - 1)$ turns into $2^{m+1} = 2k$, whence $k = 2^m = N$, meaning that N can be represented through itself only (the trivial trapezoidal representation).

Finally, one can formulate and then prove

Proposition 11: *If N is a prime number, then it has exactly two trapezoidal representations, that is, $T(N) = 2$.*

Proof. According to Equation (9), N divides either n or $2k + n - 1$; otherwise, no combination of N, n, and k exists to satisfy the equation. Because no sum of n consecutive counting numbers may be equal to n $(n > 1)$—indeed, already $1 + 2 > 2$—this implies $n < N$. Therefore, N divides $n + 2k - 1$. In that case, n can assume two values only: $n = 1$ and $n = 2$; otherwise, N, a prime number, should have more than two divisors.

To clarify, two cases need to be considered: n is even and n is odd. If $n > 2$ is an even number, then $2k + n - 1$ is an odd number greater than one. Therefore, the equation

$$N = \frac{n}{2}(2k + n - 1)$$

implies the following contradiction: N, a prime number, has two different factors, each of which is greater than one. If $n > 2$ is an odd number, then $2k + n - 1$ is an even number greater than one. Once again, the equation

$$N = \frac{n}{2}(2k + n - 1)$$

yields the same contradiction: N, a prime number, has two factors, each of which is greater than one.

When $n = 1$, the equation

$$N = \frac{n}{2}(2k + n - 1)$$

turns into

$$N = \frac{1}{2}(2k + 1 - 1),$$

whence $k = N$, the trivial trapezoidal representation $N = N$. When $n = 2$, the equation

$$N = \frac{n}{2}(2k + n - 1)$$

implies

$$k = \frac{N-1}{2},$$

whence

$$N = \frac{N-1}{2} + \left(\frac{N-1}{2} + 1\right),$$

the only non-trivial trapezoidal representation of N. (For example, when $N = 11$, one has $11 = 5 + 6$). This completes the proof.

7. ACTIVITY SET

1. Prove by the method of mathematical induction the following identities concerning the sums of arithmetic sequences and give geometric interpretation to each identity in the case $n = 3$ using manipulatives:

$$1 + 3 + 5 + \ldots + 2n - 1 = n^2,$$

$$1 + 5 + 9 + \ldots + 4n - 3 = (2n - 1)n,$$

$$3 + 7 + 11 + \ldots + 4n - 1 = (2n + 1)n,$$

$$1 + 7 + 13 + \ldots + 6n - 5 = (3n - 2)n.$$

2. Prove by the method of mathematical induction the following identity:

$$x_1 + x_2 + x_3 + \ldots + x_n = \frac{2x_1 + d(n-1)}{2}n,$$

where $x_n = x_1 + d(n-1)$.

3. Prove by the method of mathematical induction the following identity and give geometric interpretation in the case $n = 3$ using manipulatives:

$$1 \cdot 2 + 2 \cdot 3 + 3 \cdot 4 + \ldots + n(n+1) = \frac{n(n+1)(n+2)}{3}.$$

4. Prove by the method of mathematical induction the following identity and give geometric interpretation in the case $n = 3$ using manipulatives: $1 \cdot 4 + 2 \cdot 7 + 3 \cdot 10 + \ldots + n(3n+1) = n(n+1)^2$.

5. Prove by the method of mathematical induction the following identity:

$$1^3 + 2^3 + 3^3 + \ldots + n^3 = \left(\frac{n(n+1)}{2}\right)^2.$$

6. Prove by the method of mathematical induction the following identities concerning Fibonacci numbers F_n:

$$F_1 + F_2 + F_3 + \ldots + F_n = F_{n+2} - 1$$

$$F_1 + F_3 + F_5 + \ldots + F_{2n-1} = F_{2n}$$

$$F_2 + F_4 + F_6 + \ldots + F_{2n} = F_{2n+1} - 1.$$

7. Prove that the number $N = 2^m\, p$, where p is a prime number and m is a positive integer, has exactly two trapezoidal representations.
8. Prove that the numbers $N = 2^m\, N_0$ and N_0, where m is a positive integer and N_0 is an odd number, have the same number of trapezoidal representations.
9. Prove that the number of trapezoidal representations of the number N is equal to the number of its odd divisors.

NOTE

1. Recall that a fraction circle, commonly used in the elementary classroom to illustrate the concept of fraction, is a manipulative representing a unit fraction and shaped as a sector of a whole circle.

CHAPTER 11

COMPUTATIONAL PROBLEM-SOLVING AND MODELING

The assumptions from which mathematics starts are simple; the rest is not.
—Eric Temple Bell
(Oxford Dictionary of Scientific Quotations, 2005, p. 52)

1. INTRODUCTION

A rich quality afforded the subject of mathematics is its potential to teach problem solving. The advent of technology into the mathematics teacher education classroom enabled new pedagogical opportunities by providing teachers with experience and skills needed for the successful teaching through problem solving (National Council of Teachers of Mathematics, 2000). A closely related mathematical activity is modeling. Teachers' training in modeling pedagogy is structured by their engagement in formulating and resolving problematic situations through the use of a variety of models that represent those situations. This suggests the fundamental relationship that exists among modeling, problem solving, and problem posing. Viewing problem solving and posing as two sides of the same coin emphasizes the importance of providing teachers with experiences in modeling through formulating, exploring, and resolving problematic situations that lead to new mathematical ideas and concepts. This chapter will show how using the

Topics in Mathematics for Elementary Teachers, pages 195–210
Copyright © 2010 by Information Age Publishing
195

computational power of a spreadsheet as a problem solving tool provides teachers with experience in modeling pedagogy, encouraging them to take intellectual risk through the formulation of problems that they can then offer to their own students.

2. MOTIVATION: MEASUREMENT MODEL FOR DIVISION

In Chapter 6, the measurement model for division was used to motivate the introduction of several divisibility tests. In this chapter, this model, conceptualizing division as repeated subtraction, will be utilized once again in order to motivate the development of computational problem solving and problem posing using a spreadsheet.

> **Problem 1:** *Andy has 86 marbles. He puts them in boxes containing 10 marbles each. How many boxes does Andy need?*

One way to solve this problem is to subtract 10 from 86 repeatedly as many times as possible within a set of positive numbers. The meaning of the digit 8 in the number 86 is the measure of 86, using 10 as the unit of measurement. In other words, dividing 10 into 86 determines how many sets of 10 objects can be created out of 86 objects. The digit 6, in turn, is the measure of remainder in the process of measurement. Therefore, the contextual meaning of the digit 6 is either an additional box that is required to augment the eight boxes given by the quotient, or no box at all. Such meaning of the remainder is likely to result from a classroom pedagogy that encourages problem solvers to inquire about the basic assumptions of the model and downplay a pure algorithmic (computational) approach.

In addition, there is enough evidence that questions one may raise about the meanings of mathematical algorithms involved in problem solving cannot be adequately answered without recourse to conceptual underpinning of those algorithms. Therefore, from a didactic perspective, it is hard to overestimate the significance of the conceptual approach to mathematical problem solving and the importance of the model as a problem-solving tool. So, the concept of remainder can become a tool in solving certain types of problems. In what follows, the notation $MOD(N, m)$ will be used to represent the remainder of N when divided by m. Recall that this notation was already used in Chapter 6 in connection with finding the greatest common divisor of two numbers through the Euclidean algorithm.

When one has conceptual understanding of a mathematical operation, then such an operation is likely to be perceived as a mathematical model of a problem situation, rather then just an algorithm that resolves the situation. In particular, a conceptual approach to division enables for the meaning of associated concepts (such as the quotient and the remainder) to emerge from mathematical activities that appropriately emulate the situation. Note that no arithmetical operation that involves the givens, 86 and 10, yields the answer to Problem 1. In order to get the answer, one has to have conceptual understanding of the operation that leads to the use of verbally defined functions conducive to use in computing applications. The answer—nine boxes—can be expressed formally in terms of the function *CEILING*(N, m), which returns the smallest number greater than N that is divisible by m. Therefore, the answer to Problem 1 can be expressed as *CEILING*$(86, 10)/10 = 9$. A similar function, *FLOOR*(N, m), returns the largest number smaller than N that is divisible by m. In that way, through the *FLOOR* function, the answer to the marbles problem can be expressed as *FLOOR*$(86, 10)/10 + 1 = 8 + 1 = 9$. Below, only the function *CEILING* will be used in developing spreadsheet-based computational algorithms.

3. SETTING A CONTEXT

In setting a context for problem solving, one has to keep in mind that context itself does not account for the mathematical content—the latter usually begins with a quantitative inquiry into the former, something that may be referred to as mathematization. The mathematical content of this chapter is limited mostly to elementary number theory (or, simply, arithmetic), an area of mathematics that provides many opportunities for computational problem solving. Following is an example of context that can be used as a milieu for solving and posing problems using a spreadsheet.

> *An architect was very creative while designing a new hotel. (A blueprint of its beginning is pictured in Figure 11.1.) The hotel was made up of a number of buildings adjacent to each other. Each building had one, two, three, or four floors, with one room on each floor.*

Below, different problematic situations that stem from this context will be developed, resolved, and then generalized through spreadsheet-enhanced modeling activities. In referring to the context, the following terminology will be used throughout the chapter. Any one-cell unit will be referred to as a *room*. A combination of one or several vertically arranged rooms will be

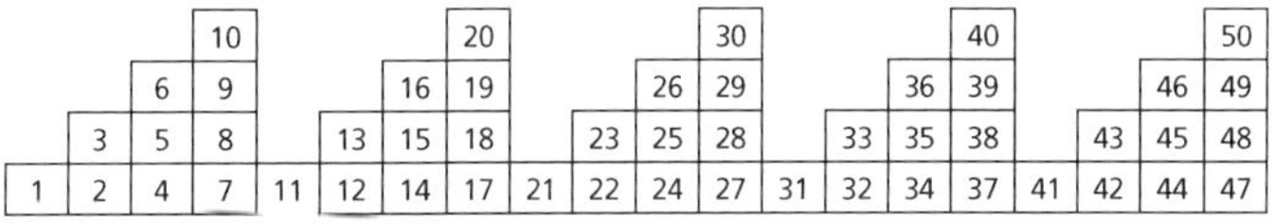

Figure 11.1 A blueprint of the 4-storied hotel.

referred to as a *building*. A combination of different buildings adjacent to each other will be referred to as a *block*. Finally, a *hotel* is a combination of several blocks. In such a way, there are 50 rooms, 20 buildings, and 5 blocks in the blueprint of the 4-storied hotel pictured in Figure 11.1.

4. FINDING THE NUMBER OF ROOMS GIVEN THE BUILDING NUMBER

Observing the blueprint of Figure 11.1, one can see that the number of rooms in each building varies from 1 to 4. Because such a variation occurs in a regular pattern, one may wonder if there is any relationship between a building number and the number of rooms in this building. With this in mind, the following simple problem can be formulated.

Problem 2: *How many rooms are in the 19th building of the 4-storied hotel?*

Solution: An answer to this question, three rooms, can be obtained from Figure 11.1 through simple counting, something that does not require using any mathematical model (operation). However, the limitation of one-by-one counting as a problem-solving strategy becomes obvious if a much bigger (say, a three-digit) number replaces 19. In order to move beyond counting, one can construct a table representation of a function that relates the building number to its height (the number of rooms). Such a table is shown in Figure 11.2.

From the table, one can see that all buildings with numbers 1, 5, and 9 have only one room. How can one describe the sequence $1, 5, 9, \ldots$? This is an arithmetic sequence with the difference 4. In particular, all numbers in this sequence have the same remainder when divided by 4, the remainder being equal to the first term of the sequence (see Chapter 8). A similar observation can be made about the sequences $2, 6, 10, \ldots$; $3, 7, 11, \ldots$; and $4, 8, 12, \ldots$. In that way, four arithmetic sequences with the difference 4 can be identified:

$$a_n = 1 + 4n, \quad b_n = 2 + 4n, \quad c_n = 3 + 4n, \quad d_n = 4 + 4n, \quad n = 0, 1, 2, 3, \ldots.$$

Therefore, each building can be associated with one of the four arithmetic sequences with the difference 4 (the height of the tallest building), the first

Building number	1	2	3	4	5	6	7	8	9	10
Number of rooms	1	2	3	4	1	2	3	4	1	2

Figure 11.2 Relating the building number to the number of rooms.

term of which determines the number of rooms in the building represented by this sequence. Using the *MOD* notation, one can conclude that the $MOD(B, 4)$ function yields the number of rooms in building B, except in the case of a zero remainder (the sequence d_n) when the number of rooms is 4. Now, one can find the number of rooms in a building—say, 519—not by counting, but rather, through calculating $MOD(519, 4) = 3$. In that way, there are 3 rooms in building 519.

The same learning environment can be developed for dealing with a different number of stories in a hotel.

Problem 3: *How many rooms are there in the 22nd building of the 5-storied hotel?*

Solution: Figure 11.3 shows the blueprint of the 5-storied hotel. Repeatedly subtracting 5 from 22, that is, dividing 22 by 5 using the measurement model for division yields the remainder 2. By using the conventional notation, one can write $MOD(22, 5) = 2$. In that way, one can solve the inverse problem: *Describe building 22 as a term of an arithmetic sequence.* It follows from the last equality that the first term of such a sequence is 2 and its difference is 5. Therefore, the arithmetic sequence sought has the form $f_n = 2 + 5n$ and $f_4 = 22$.

On a more general level, the following two problems can be posed.

Problem 4: *How many rooms are there in the kth building of the 4-storied hotel?*

Problem 5: *How many rooms are there in the kth building of the 5-storied hotel?*

The new level of generality suggests the need for the replacement of intuitive reasoning with formal reasoning, something that does require the development of a mathematical model. Once again, the measurement model for division can provide such a model. This process brings about the associated notion of remainder, which becomes a crucial tool in describing a model that allows for the variation of the building number and formulating the following strategy for resolving Problems 4 and 5.

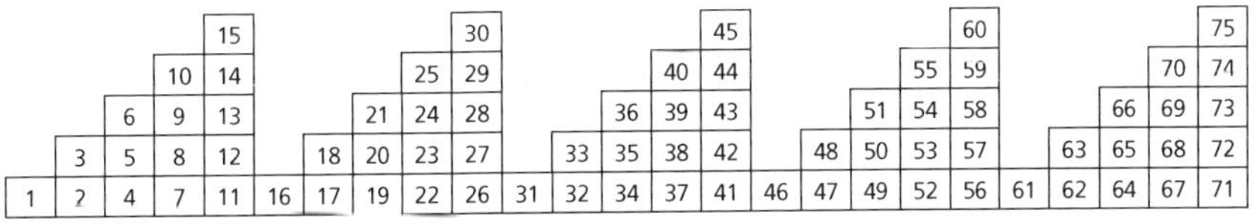

Figure 11.3   A blueprint of the five-storied hotel.

Solution to Problem 4: In order to find the number of rooms in the kth building of the 4-storied hotel, one has to divide 4 into k and, if remainder is 0, replace it with 4; otherwise, a non-zero remainder, $MOD(k, 4)$, represents the number of rooms in this building.

Solution to Problem 5: In order to find the number of rooms in the kth building of the 5-storied hotel, one has to divide 5 into k and, if the remainder is 0, replace it with 5; otherwise, a non-zero remainder, $MOD(k, 5)$, represents the number of rooms in this building.

It should be noted that the process of generalization from the specific number of stories to any such number requires a set of blueprints. By exploring various blueprints, one can see that the number of stories in a hotel coincides with the number of buildings in each block of the hotel. Furthermore, dividing the number of stories into the building number yields a remainder, which, in all cases but one, coincides with the number of rooms in this building. In that way, one can pose the following.

Problem 6: *How many rooms are in the kth building of the n-storied hotel?*

Solution: By setting $R(k, n)$ to represent the number of rooms in the kth building of the n-storied hotel, one has $R(k, n) = MOD(k, n)$, if $MOD(k, n) \neq 0$; $R(k, n) = n$, if $MOD(k, n) = 0$.

One can construct a spreadsheet environment for solving Problem 6 for different values of k and n. Figure 11.4 shows such a spreadsheet that includes two slider-controlled parameters—hotel type (the number of stories n) and building number k. In particular, because $MOD(319, 7) = 4$, there are four rooms in the 319th building of the 7-storied hotel.

5. FINDING BLOCK NUMBER GIVEN ROOM NUMBER

The next type of problems motivated by the architectural context can deal with relating room number to block number. Any such problem should specify the type of a hotel involved (i.e., the number of stories it has).

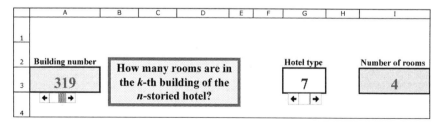

Figure 11.4 In the 7-storied hotel there are 4 rooms in the 319th building.

Problem 7: *To which block of the 4-storied hotel does room 49 belong?*

Solution: This problem is similar to Problem 1 and it can be reformulated as follows: *How many 4-storied hotel blocks does one need to arrange 49 rooms in groups of 10 (the sum of the first four counting numbers) rooms in each block?*

As in the beginning of this chapter, the reformulated problem can be solved with the help of the *CEILING* function using the information about the number of rooms in a block. In that way, as $CEILING(49, 10)/10 = 5$ (recall, $CEILING[49, 10]$ is the smallest number greater than 49 and divisible by 10), room 49 belongs to block 5 of the 4-storied hotel.

A similar problem can be posed in the context of the 5-storied hotel. In any block of such a hotel, the number of rooms is equal to $1 + 2 + 3 + 4 + 5 = 15$ (alternatively, the triangular number of rank five). In this case, one would arrange rooms in blocks, 15 rooms in each block. Now, one can solve the following.

Problem 8: *To which block of the 5-storied hotel does room 49 belong?*

Solution: Because 60 is the smallest number greater than 49 and divisible by 15 (alternatively, 60 is the smallest multiple of 15 greater than 49), one has $CEILING(49, 15) = 60$. Dividing 15 into 60 yields 4. Therefore, room 49 in the 5-storied hotel belongs to block 4.

Problem 9: *To which block of the 6-storied hotel does room 249 belong?*

Solution: There are $1 + 2 + 3 + 4 + 5 + 6 = 21$ rooms in a block of the 6-storied hotel. Next, $CEILING(249, 21)$ is the smallest multiple of 21 greater than 249; that is, $CEILING(249, 21) = 252$. Finally, dividing 21 into 252 yields 12, the block number to which room 249 belongs.

In general, one can formulate the following.

Problem 10: *To which block of the n-storied hotel does room r belong?*

Solution: Generalizing from special cases of Problems 7–9, three distinct steps have to be carried out. The first step is to find the triangular number of rank n by using the formula

$$t_n = \frac{n(n+1)}{2}$$

(see Formula [A1] in Appendix). The second step is to find the value of $CEILING(r, t_n)$, the smallest multiple of t_n greater than r. The third (and final) step is to divide t_n into $CEILING(r, t_n)$. Setting $B(r, n)$ to represent the block of the *n*-storied hotel to which room *r* belongs, one has the formula

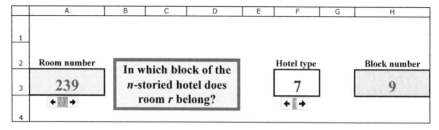

Figure 11.5 Computational environment for solving Problem 6.

$B(r, n) = CEILING(r, t_n)/t_n$, where $t_n = 1 + 2 + 3 + \ldots + n$ is the triangular number of rank n.

Figure 11.5 shows the spreadsheet designed to computationally model Problem 10. For example, in the 7-storied hotel, room 239 belongs to block 9. The spreadsheets computes $t_7 = 28$, $CEILING(239, 28) = 252$, and divides 28 into 252, yielding 9.

The advantage of having this computational environment for a teacher is that a multitude of problems can be formulated and solved instantly. The National Council of Teachers of Mathematics (1989) has referred to problem posing as "an activity that is at the heart of doing mathematics" (p. 138), and, acknowledging the advent of technology into the classroom, has noted that "computer programs can engage students in posing and solving problems" (p. 76). By gaining a research-like experience in curriculum development through the use of technology, teachers can use their technological expertise in problem posing as an agency for recognizing both the profound effectiveness of systematic reasoning and the complexity of mathematical ideas that can emerge from familiar situations. In particular, the pedagogical and mathematical power of a spreadsheet allows one to delve into the way the tool supports problem posing and inductively discover interesting results about mathematical structures involved—results that traditionally are not available to teachers because of the complexity of mathematics associated with the formal methods of exploring those structures (for more information see Abramovich & Cho [2008]).

6. EXPLORING FIBONACCI-K HOTELS

Other types of blueprints can be created for computational problem solving, in which the number of rooms in each building follows a certain sequence of numbers. For example, consider the first six Fibonacci numbers (1, 1, 2, 3, 5, 8) and the corresponding blueprint (Figure 11.6) that displays three blocks, each of which consists of six buildings, with Fibonacci numbers representing the number of rooms in each building of a block. Below, such

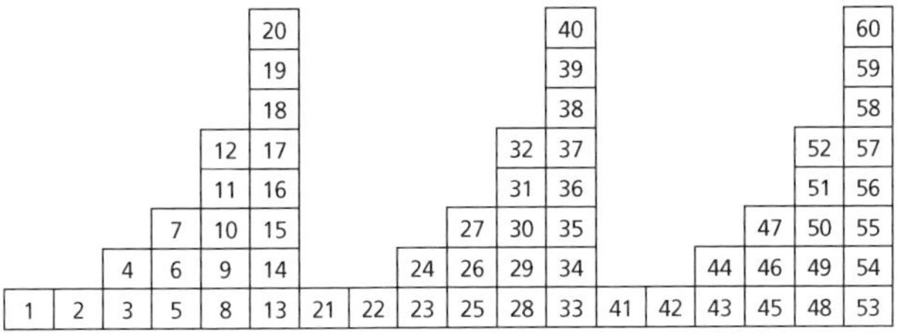

					20							40					60	
					19							39					59	
					18							38					58	
				12	17						32	37				52	57	
				11	16						31	36				51	56	
			7	10	15					27	30	35			47	50	55	
		4	6	9	14				24	26	29	34		44	46	49	54	
1	2	3	5	8	13	21	22	23	25	28	33	41	42	43	45	48	53

Figure 11.6 A blueprint of the Fibonacci-six hotel.

a hotel will be referred to as the Fibonacci-six hotel. In general, if a block consists of n buildings with the number of rooms in each building varying from F_1 to F_n, such a hotel will be referred to below as the Fibonacci-n hotel. Here, F_n is the nth Fibonacci number calculated through the formula

$$F_n = \frac{1}{\sqrt{5}}\left((\frac{1+\sqrt{5}}{2})^n - (\frac{1-\sqrt{5}}{2})^n\right),$$

introduced in Chapter 7 (see also Appendix, formula [A21]).

Problem 11: *How many rooms are there in the 17th building of the (8-storied) Fibonacci-six hotel?*

Solution: Exploring the chart of Figure 11.7, one can see that the number of rooms varies in the range $[1, 8]$ and the function $MOD(k,6)$ maps building k onto the segment $[0, 5]$. When $MOD(k,6) = 0$, the number of rooms in the kth building is the sixth Fibonacci number, when $MOD(k,6) = 1$, the number of rooms in the kth building is the first Fibonacci number; when $MOD(k,6) = 2$, the number of rooms in the kth building is the second Fibonacci number; when $MOD(k,6) = 3$, the number of rooms in the kth building is the third Fibonacci number; when $MOD(k,6) = 4$, the number of rooms in the kth building is the fourth Fibonacci number; finally, when $MOD(k,6) = 5$, the number of rooms in the kth building is the fifth Fibonacci number.

In order to solve the problem, one finds $MOD(17,6) = 5$ and then selects the 5th Fibonacci number $F_5 = 5$. Therefore, there are 5 rooms in the 17th building of the Fibonacci-six hotel.

Building number	1	2	3	4	5	6	7	8	9	10	11	12	13
Number of rooms	1	1	2	3	5	8	1	1	2	3	5	8	1

Figure 11.7 A chart for exploring the Fibonacci-six hotel.

Problem 12: *How many rooms are in the n-th building of the Fibonacci-k hotel?*

Solution: The flow chart of Figure 11.8 shows the process of solution. The spreadsheet that incorporates this model is shown in Figure 11.9. The programming of the spreadsheet is discussed in Chapter 13.

Problem 13: *To which block of the Fibonacci-six hotel does room 52 belong?*

Solution: By analogy with Problem 8, one has to find first the sum

$$\sum_{i=1}^{6} F_i$$

of six consecutive Fibonacci numbers. This sum can be found by using the formula

$$\sum_{i=1}^{n} F_i = F_{n+2} - 1$$

(Chapter 7, Formula [7]). The case $n = 6$ yields

$$\sum_{i=1}^{6} F_i = F_8 - 1 = 20.$$

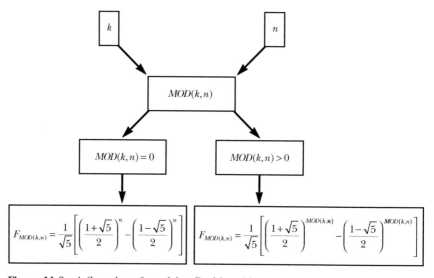

Figure 11.8   A flow chart for solving Problem 11.

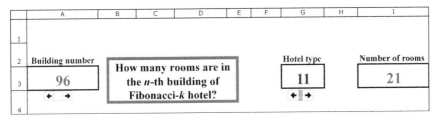

Figure 11.9   Spreadsheet modeling of Problem 11.

Next, one has to find the smallest number greater than 52 and divisible by 20. Using the conventional notation yields $CEILING(52, 20) = 60$. Finally, the block number to which room 52 belongs is $60 \div 20 = 3$. This answer, 3, can be confirmed by the blueprint of Figure 11.6.

In general, one can pose and then solve the following.

Problem 14: *To which block of the Fibonacci-k hotel does room r belong?*

Solution: The flow chart of Figure 11.10 shows the steps through which the problem can be solved. In addition, the spreadsheet of Figure 11.11 shows a numeric solution to this problem for $k = 6$ and $r = 63$. (The result can be confirmed by extending the diagram of Figure 11.6). The programming of such a spreadsheet is discussed in Chapter 13.

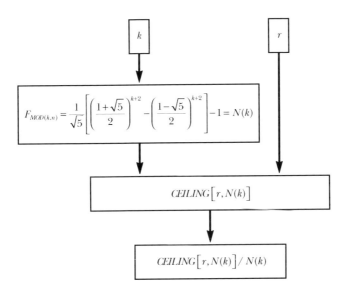

Figure 11.10   A flow chart for solving Problem 14.

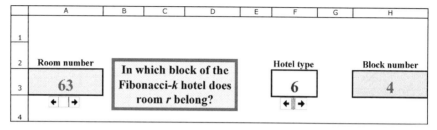

Figure 11.11   Spreadsheet modeling of Problem 14.

7. EXPLORING SQUARE-TYPE HOTELS

Consider the blueprint pictured in Figure 11.12, where each block consists of sub-blocks of identical buildings forming a square.

> **Problem 15:** *How many rooms are in the 25th building of the 4-storied square-type hotel?*

Solution: The first step is to find the total number of buildings in a block. In the specific case of Figure 11.12, this number can be found as $1 + 2 + 3 + 4 = 10$, the triangular number of rank four. The second step is to map the 25th building to the first block by evaluating $MOD(25, 10) = 5$. That is, the 5th and the 25th buildings have the same number of rooms. The blueprint shows that there are three rooms in the 5th building.

The question, however, remains how one can find the number of rooms given the building number that belongs to the 1st block. Unlike the situation described in Problem 2, the building number that belongs to the 1st block, in general, does not necessarily coincide with the number of rooms in this building. How can one formally (without using the blueprint) decide the number of rooms in the 5th building of the 1st block? To answer this question, one can construct a chart that relates the range of building numbers to the number of rooms in that range. Such a chart is shown in Figure 11.13.

One can recognize in the upper border of each range a triangular number, of which the rank appears in the cell immediately below. The problem now has been reduced to the following one: *Given an integer, find the rank*

				18	22	26	30						48	52	56	60						78	82	86	90
		8	11	14	17	21	25	29			38	41	44	47	51	55	59			68	71	74	77	81	85	89
	3	5	7	10	13	16	20	24	28		33	35	37	40	43	46	50	54	58		63	65	67	70	73	76	80	84	88
1	2	4	6	9	12	15	19	23	27	31	32	34	36	39	42	45	49	53	57	61	62	64	66	69	72	75	79	83	87

Figure 11.12   A square-type hotel.

Building range	1	2 – 3	4 – 6	7 – 10	11 – 15
Number of rooms	1	2	3	4	5

Figure 11.13   A chart in support of Problem 15.

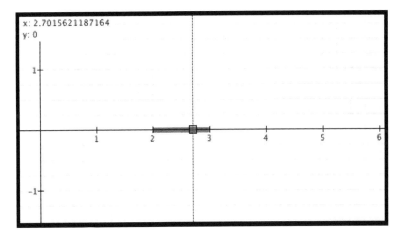

Figure 11.14   Computer graphing in support of Problem 15.

of the smallest triangular number that is greater or equal to this integer. In order to solve this problem, in the case of the 5th building, one has to find the positive root of the quadratic equation $n(n+1)/2 = 5$, and then evaluate the *CEILING* of this root (i.e., the smallest integer that is greater or equal to the root). This can be done graphically by graphing the last equation. As shown in Figure 11.14, the graph is a vertical line that crosses the *x*-axis in the interval [2, 3]. Therefore, the upper bound of this segment, 3, represents the number of rooms in the 5th building as well as in any building with a number that, when divided by 20, yields the remainder 5. This means that the 25th, 45th, 65th, 85th, and so on buildings all have three rooms. This sequence of building numbers is an arithmetic sequence, with the first term $b_1 = 5$ and the difference $d = 20$; its form is $b_n = b_1 = d(n-1) = 20n - 15$, $n = 1, 2, 3, \ldots$.

Problem 16: *How many rooms are in the k*th *building of the n-storied square type hotel?*

Solution: The first step is to find the total number of buildings in a block. This number is given by the sum

$$1 + 2 + 3 + \ldots + n = \frac{n(n+1)}{2} = t_n,$$

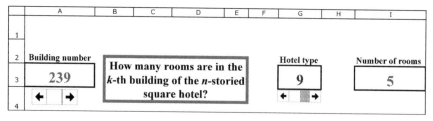

Figure 11.15 Spreadsheet modeling of Problem 16.

the triangular number of rank n. The second step us to map building k to the first block by evaluating $MOD(k, t_n)$ as both buildings, k and $MOD(k, t_n)$, have the same number of rooms. Finally, one has to find the positive root of the equation $MOD(k, t_n) = t_n$, and then find the smallest integer greater or equal to this root by using

$$CEILING(\frac{-1+\sqrt{1+8MOD(k,t_n)}}{2},1),$$

which returns the smallest integer greater or equal to the positive root of the quadratic equation $n^2 + n - 2MOD(k, t_n) = 0$. It is this integer that represents $R(k, n)$, the number of rooms in the kth building of the n-storied square hotel, assuming $MOD(k, t_n) > 0$. When $MOD(k, t_n) = 0$, one has $R(k, n) = n$. This process can be automated by using a spreadsheet, which, thereby, provides an alternative to the graphing approach shown in Figure 11.14. This spreadsheet is shown in Figure 11.15 and its programming is discussed in Chapter 13.

Problem 17: *To which block of the 4-storied square-type hotel does room 65 belong?*

Solution: The first step is to find the number of rooms in a block as the sum of four squares: $1^2 + 2^2 + 3^2 + 4^2 = 30$. The second step is to find the smallest number greater than 65 (room number) that is divisible by 30 (the number of rooms in a block) by evaluating $CEILING(65, 30) = 90$. The third step is to divide 90 by 30 to get 3 – the block number sought.

Moving towards the development of a spreadsheet for evaluating the block number given room number and hotel type, one can formulate the following.

Problem 18: *To which block of the n-storied square-type hotel does room r belong?*

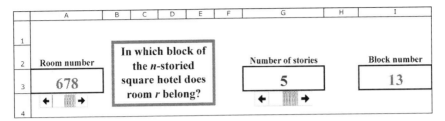

Figure 11.16 Spreadsheet modeling of Problem 18.

Solution: Let $B(r, n)$ represent the block number sought. The first step is to find the number of rooms in an n-storied block as the sum of n squares (Chapter 9, Formula [4]):

$$1^2 + 2^2 + 3^2 + \ldots + n^2 = \frac{n(n+1)(2n+1)}{6}.$$

The second step is to evaluate the function

$$CEILING\left(r, \frac{n(n+1)(2n+1)}{6}\right).$$

The third step results in the answer to the problem:

$$B(r,n) = CEILING\left(r, \frac{n(n+1)(2n+1)}{6}\right) / \left[\frac{n(n+1)(2n+1)}{6}\right].$$

Note that the sum of the first n consecutive squares is called the n-th square pyramidal number. A spreadsheet that integrates the last formula is shown in Figure 11.16. In particular, room 678 of the 5-storied hotel belongs to block 13. The programming of this spreadsheet is discussed in Chapter 13.

8. ACTIVITY SET

1. Using the blueprint shown in Figure 11.17, where each building in a block has two more stories than the previous one, construct formal models to investigate:
   – To which building does room 39 belong?
   – To which building does room 239 belong?
   – How many rooms are in the 13th building?
   – How many rooms are in the 15th building?
   – How many rooms are in the 115th building?

- To which block does room 49 belong?
- To which block does room 249 belong?

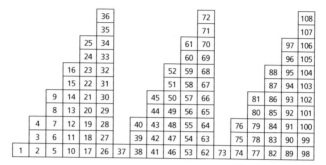

Figure 11.17 Exploration for Activity 1.

2. Using the blueprint shown in Figure 11.18, where each building in a block has three more stories than the previous one, construct formal models to answer the questions listed above (under Activity 1).

1	2	3	4	5	6	7	8	9	10	11	12	13	14	15
				35					70					105
				34					69					104
				33					68					103
			22	32				57	67				92	102
			21	31				56	66				91	101
			20	30				55	65				90	100
		12	19	29			47	54	64			82	89	99
		11	18	28			46	53	63			81	88	98
		10	17	27			45	52	62			80	87	97
	5	9	16	26		40	44	51	61		75	79	86	96
	4	8	15	25		39	43	50	60		74	78	85	95
	3	7	14	24		38	42	49	59		73	77	84	94
1	2	6	13	23	36	37	41	48	58	71	72	76	83	93

Figure 11.18 Exploration for Activity 2.

3. Using the blueprint shown in Figure 11.19, where the number of 4-storied buildings in each block varies across the Fibonacci number sequence, construct formal models to answer the questions listed above (under Activity 1).

1	2	3	4	5	6	7	8	9	10	11	12	13	14	15	16	17	18	19	20	21	22	23	24	25	26	27
10				20				30	34				44	48	52				62	66	70	74	78			
6	9			16	19			26	29	33			40	43	47	51			58	61	65	69	73	77		
3	5	8		13	15	18		23	25	28	32		37	39	42	46	50		55	57	60	64	68	72	76	
1	2	4	7	11	12	14	17	21	22	24	27	31	35	36	38	41	45	49	53	54	56	59	63	67	71	75

Figure 11.19 Exploration for Activity 3.

CHAPTER 12

NUMBERS AND OPERATIONS IN DIFFERENT BASES

Vygotsky rightly points out that as long as one operates only with the decimal system without being aware of the other bases, one has not mastered the system; rather one is bound by it. When one learns other bases, one can consciously choose one's system and thus a new level of conceptual control is achieved.

—E. E. Berg (1970, p. 379)

1. INTRODUCTION

The main goal of this chapter is to show how teaching arithmetical operations in the elementary classroom can be enhanced by the use of manipulative materials. To this end, in what follows, the operations will be studied in different base systems. This pedagogical approach is based on the notion that one's physical experience with a mathematical operation is primary, and the corresponding symbolic experience is secondary. It will be shown that a physical action, that underlies the symbolism of an operation, is invariant across various base systems. Here is an analogy: one can browse through the pages of a book and, to some extent, recognize the meaning of illustrations without knowing the language in which the book is written. The book, as a physical object, has invariant meaning across a linguistic manifold.

The Hindu-Arabic system of numbers, commonly used nowadays around the world to record operations in base-ten arithmetic, consists of ten sym-

Topics in Mathematics for Elementary Teachers, pages 211–229
Copyright © 2010 by Information Age Publishing

bols which are called digits. Implicitly representing a number as the sum of products of powers of ten and one of the (one-digit) numbers 0, 1, 2, 3, 4, 5, 6, 7, 8, 9, the very representation of the number is a string of digits (see Chapter 6). For example, a base-ten number 2376 is a concise representation of the sum of four products $2 \times 10^3 + 3 \times 10^2 + 7 \times 10^1 + 6 \times 10^0$ in which each coefficient in a power of ten (a digit) shows, respectively, the number of ones (10^0), tens (10^1), hundreds (10^2), and thousands (10^3) in the total amount of units described by the number.

In this chapter, arithmetical operations will be explored in several modified Hindu-Arabic number systems in order to better understand how the base-ten system works. More specifically, several non-decimal systems with bases B, $2 \leq B \leq 9$, will be introduced. Note that in the base B system there are only B digits: 0, 1, 2, ..., $B - 1$. In that way, the above-mentioned string of digits 2376, besides base ten, can be used to represent a number in bases nine ($2376_{base9} = 2 \times 9^3 + 3 \times 9^2 + 7 \times 9^1 + 6 \times 9^0$) and eight ($2376_{base8} = 2 \times 8^3 + 3 \times 8^2 + 7 \times 8^1 + 6 \times 8^0$). Already in base seven, the symbol 2376 cannot be used to describe a quantity as there is no digit 7 in base seven (just like there is no digit 10 in base ten). The citation at the beginning of this chapter explains a pedagogical purpose of introducing teachers to non-decimal base systems.

One of the recommendations of the Conference Board of the Mathematical Sciences (2001) for elementary teacher preparation states that mathematics education programs should provide the teachers with "a deep understanding of place value [in order for them to be able] to help their students use it as a foundation for the successful learning of integer arithmetic, and later ... symbolic calculations in algebra" (p. 5). Many concepts associated with base-ten system are often taken for granted by teachers as arithmetical operations have typically been committed to memory without a proper conceptual understanding. In that case, it is almost impossible for a teacher to appreciate difficulties that many young children experience with arithmetic.

For example, the equality $5 + 6 = 11$ might look counter intuitive if addition is understood on a physical level alone – the operation must result in the increase of a quantity. Without connecting symbolic meaning of the number 11 to its physical meaning, one might wonder as to why the sum $5 + 6$ is described by a number the digits of which are smaller than those in the corresponding summands. The same can be said about the equalities $8 \times 6 = 54$ and $264 \div 3 = 88$ which might appear counter intuitive also, as the product is recorded using smaller digits (in comparison with each of the factors), and the quotient is recorded using larger digits (in comparison with the dividend).

In order to develop a deep understanding of the decimal system needed for the teaching of base-ten arithmetic in the grade school, one has to experience difficulties by doing arithmetic in non-decimal bases. In such artificially created learning environments, automatism and memorization cannot be used as a support system and, thereby, have to be replaced by conceptual understanding. For example, in recording the sum 5 + 6 in base seven one has to perform addition conceptually as the memory typically does not include addition facts in a non-decimal system. In order to move away from pure memorization, a sequence of tasks on addition and subtraction in different bases will be offered below. These tasks will be supported by diagrams, which will provide physical experience with the notion of a base system. These tasks are designed to demonstrate the primordial nature of the physical experience over the symbolic one. The author's work with teachers suggests that learning to understand the meaning of an operation in a physical environment helps one to conceptualize a symbolic representation of an arithmetical operation in a particular base system. As the content of this chapter is somewhat unusual, we begin with sharing the voices of teachers regarding their experience of using manipulatives as support system in doing arithmetic in various base systems.

2. VOICES OF TEACHERS

Reflecting on different manipulative-based activities of partitioning numbers in two summands in different base systems, one teacher admitted:

> Honestly, if it weren't for the use of manipulatives I would probably not understand the base system, even today. The idea was actually very confusing, at first, even with the use of manipulatives. It wasn't until I got home and was able to play around with manipulatives for myself, that I was able to fully grasp the concept. Creating that visual representation in order to give students firm visual grasp on a concept before creating a number sentence or formula is the best way to help students learn and understand. There is no doubt in my mind that I would use manipulatives in my classroom in future work when using base-ten arithmetic.

Reporting original confusion with the basic facts developed in non-decimal bases (creating this confusion and then resolving it through the use of concrete objects was the author's pedagogical intent), another teacher agreed that manipulatives were helpful in overcoming difficulties with unfamiliar operations and concepts:

> I feel that using manipulatives is a great way to develop conceptual understanding of addition and multiplication in a base system. When working with base systems other than base ten, I find it to be confusing. All of the facts that I have memorized for base ten don't match with other base systems. I can't

rely on facts that I have memorized; I need to be able to apply the concept. By using manipulatives and drawing pictures, I was able to visualize what was actually happening in other base systems. I felt that it helped me to really understand the concept and have a good grasp on the material.

This was echoed in the reflections of yet another teacher who acknowledged the educational value of manipulatives in understanding the meaning of arithmetical operations in the absence of memorization:

> I have had very little experience with using manipulatives for developing a conceptual understanding of operations addition and multiplication in a base system until now. This course has taught me how to use manipulatives not only for addition but for multiplication as well. Multiplication, as I remember it, was focused more on the skill of memory than developing a conceptual understanding of its operations. The manipulatives are more effective to understand the representations in different bases. You can see the question you are posing and the answer in one representation.

Now, the reader may want to know more about manipulative-based learning environments that can be recommended for the teaching of arithmetic in general. In addition, an electronic spreadsheet will be used as a means for the verification of the correctness of hands-on operations and their symbolic description.

3. PARTITIONING NUMBERS IN DIFFERENT BASES

We begin with partitioning numbers in two summands to be carried out in different base systems. Two environments will mediate these operations: manipulative (supported by square tiles) and computational (supported by a spreadsheet). Whereas the use of manipulatives requires understanding of place value system in general, the development of computational environments requires understanding of how addition is defined in different base systems. The need to program a spreadsheet to perform a representation of a number as a sum of two numbers leads to new mathematical activities that are discussed in Chapter 13. In that way, a spreadsheet serves as an agency for mathematical activities, which are not directly associated with the original hands-on tasks. However, once the spreadsheet is constructed, it amplifies the combination of manipulative and arithmetic activities and supports the development of residual mental power that can be used in the absence of the tool. In the words of the early advocates of using computers as cognitive tools, before technology can amplify one's thinking, it provides an environment for reorganizing one's thinking by putting in place new, cognitively more challenging activities.

In Tasks 1–4 of this section, the same symbol, recorded as 12, will be used to represent two-digit numbers in different base systems. However, depending on a base system, the meaning of the first digit in the symbol 12 will vary from base to base. Because of that, say, in base nine, we suggest to read the symbol 12 as "one–two-base-nine," meaning that this symbol represents, for instance, a quantity of square tiles arranged in two groups: a group of nine tiles and a group of two tiles.

Task 1: *Represent base-ten number 12 (one ten and two ones) as a sum of two other base-ten numbers in all possible ways (without regard to order). How many different representations are there? Use manipulatives as thinking tools. Draw pictures of all your representations. Use the partitioning spreadsheet to confirm your findings.*

Solution: As we know, in base-ten system there are ten symbols (digits) used to record numbers as the strings of digits. Using these symbols, partitioning diagrams for the number 12 presented in Figure 12.1 can be recorded, respectively, as follows: $12 = 11 + 1$, $12 = 10 + 2$, $12 = 9 + 3$, $12 = 8 + 4$, $12 = 7 + 5$, $12 = 6 + 6$.

This recording can then be confirmed by a spreadsheet-based solution pictured in Figure 12.2 where the sum of numbers in two consecutive rows is equal to 12 repeated 6 times, as 6 is the number of partitions of 12 in a sum of two numbers without regard to order. The rule of arranging rods in two groups (separated by a vertical bar in the diagram) is as follows: a ten-block rod may be used to borrow a block (may be physically partitioned) only when no blocks remain immediately to its right.

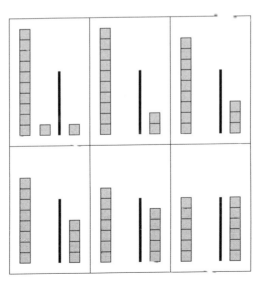

Figure 12.1 Diagrammatic solution to Task 1.

	A	B	C	D	E	F	G
1	**Base**		**Partition**				
2	10		12				
3	← ⬚ →						
4	12	11	10	9	8	7	6
5	0	1	2	3	4	5	6

Figure 12.2 Spreadsheet-based solution to Task 1.

Task 2: *Represent base-nine number 12 (one nine and two ones) as the sum of two other base-nine numbers in all possible ways (without regard to order). How many different representations are there? Use manipulatives as thinking tools. Draw pictures of all your representations. Use the partitioning spreadsheet to confirm your findings.*

Solution: Base-nine system differs from the decimal system in a number of ways. First, there are only nine symbols available to be used as digits. These symbols are 0, 1, 2, 3, 4, 5, 6, 7, and 8. Just like there are only ten digits in base ten, there are only nine digits in base nine. Using these nine symbols, partitioning diagrams for a base-nine number 12 presented in Figure 12.3 can be recorded, respectively, as follows: 12 = 12 + 0, 12 = 11 + 1, 12 = 10 + 2, 12 = 8 + 3, 12 = 7 + 4, 12 = 6 + 5.

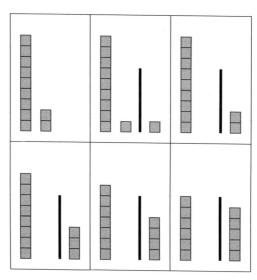

Figure 12.3 Diagrammatic solution to Task 2.

	A	B	C	D	E	F
1	**Base**		**Partition**			
2	9		12			
3	←	→				
4	12	11	10	8	7	6
5	0	1	2	3	4	5

Figure 12.4 Spreadsheet-based solution to Task 2.

This recording can then be confirmed by a spreadsheet-based solution pictured in Figure 12.4. Having a tool capable of partitioning numbers in two summands in a non-decimal base without recourse to manipulatives, prompts teachers' mathematical curiosity regarding the design of such a tool. A useful practice in doing addition in base nine is to add all numbers in the two consecutive rows of Figure 12.4, and compare the sum with 12 (one nine and two ones, or one–two-base-nine) repeated five times where five is the number of partitions of 12 in a sum of two numbers without regard to order. It should be noted that, just like in the decimal system, the rule of arranging rods in two groups (separated by a vertical bar in the diagram) is that a nine-block rod may be used to borrow a block (may be physically partitioned) only after no blocks remain immediately to its right.

Task 3: *Represent base-eight number 12 (one eight and two ones) as the sum of two other base-eight numbers in all possible ways (without regard to order). How many different representations are there? Use manipulatives as thinking tools. Draw pictures of all your representations. Use the partitioning spreadsheet to confirm your findings.*

Solution: Base-eight system differs from the decimal and base-nine systems in a number of ways. First, there are only eight symbols available to be used as digits. These symbols are 0, 1, 2, 3, 4, 5, 6, and 7. Just like there are only nine digits in base nine, there are only eight digits in base eight. Using these symbols, partitioning diagrams for the base-nine number 12 presented in Figure 12.5 can be recorded, respectively, as follows: 12 = 12 + 0, 12 = 11 + 1, 12 = 10 + 2, 12 = 7 + 3, 12 = 6 + 4, 12 = 5 + 5.

This recording can then be confirmed by a spreadsheet-based solution pictured in Figure 12.6. At that point, another question may be raised: How does the spreadsheet "know" (without "looking" at Figure 12.5) that in base eight, when numbers are listed in the descending order, 10 is followed by 7? One can also add (using the rules of base eight) all numbers in the two rows of Figure 12.6, and compare the sum with the number 12 repeated 5

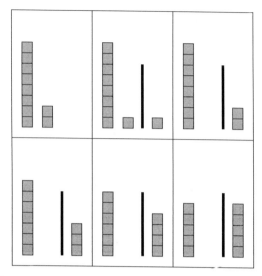

Figure 12.5 Diagrammatic solution to Task 3.

	A	B	C	D	E	F
1	**Base**		**Partition**			
2	8		12			
3	← ➡					
4	12	11	10	7	6	5
5	0	1	2	3	4	5

Figure 12.6 Spreadsheet-based solution to Task 3.

times – the number of partitions of 12 in a sum of two numbers without re-gard to order. It should be noted that, just like in other base systems, the rule of arranging rods in two groups (separated by a vertical bar in the diagram) is that an eight-block rod may be used to borrow a block (may be physically partitioned) only when no blocks remain immediately to its right.

> **Task 4:** *Represent base-seven number 12 (one seven and two ones) as the sum of two other base-seven numbers in all possible ways (without regard to order). How many different representations are there? Use manipulatives as thinking tools. Draw pictures of all your representations. Use the partitioning spread-sheet to confirm your findings.*

Solution: Base-seven system differs from the above three base systems in a number of ways. First, there are only seven symbols available to be used as digits. These symbols are 0, 1, 2, 3, 4, 5, and 6. Just like there are only eight digits in base eight, there are seven digits in base seven. Using these symbols, partitioning diagrams for the base-seven number 12 presented in Figure 12.7 can be recorded, respectively, as follows: $12 = 12 + 0$, $12 = 11 + 1$, $12 = 10 + 2$, $12 = 6 + 3$, $12 = 5 + 4$.

As before, this recording can be confirmed by a spreadsheet-based solution pictured in Figure 12.8. One can also add (using the rules of base seven) all numbers that belong in the two rows of the chart, and compare the sum with the number 12 repeated 5 times – the number of partitions of 12 in a sum of two numbers without regard to order. It should be noted that the rule of arranging rods in two groups (separated by a vertical bar in the diagram) is that a rod of seven blocks may be used to borrow a block only when no blocks remain to its right.

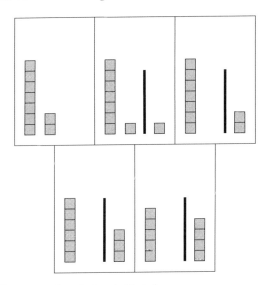

Figure 12.7 Diagrammatic solution to Task 4.

	A	B	C	D	E
1	**Base**		**Partition**		
2	7		12		
3	← →				
4	12	11	10	6	5
5	0	1	2	3	4

Figure 12.8 Spreadsheet-based solution to Task 4.

4. MULTIPLICATION IN DIFFERENT BASES

We begin with a task that can motivate the idea of multiplication regardless of a base system. The task is borrowed from a mathematics resource guide for the elementary schools in New York State (New York State Education Department, 1998, p. 36). The basic idea of the task is to geometrize the product of two numbers through the construction of a rectangle the dimensions of which are the two numbers (factors). Below, unless stated otherwise, a two-digit number will denote a base-ten number.

Rectangle Construction Problem

Give students 18 color tiles. Have them make as many rectangles as possible out of the tiles and record each rectangle on a piece of graph paper, noting the number of rows and columns of each rectangle, to find all the multiplication facts for the given number.

Figure 12.9 shows 18 tiles, which in Figure 12.10 are arranged in three different rectangles. The transition from the construction of rectangles to their symbolic description yields the following multiplication facts: $18 = 18 \times 1 = 1 \times 18$, $18 = 9 \times 2 = 2 \times 9$, $18 = 6 \times 3 = 3 \times 6$.

As was mentioned in Chapter 4, the commutative property of multiplication has a simple physical interpretation shown in Figure 12.10. Indeed,

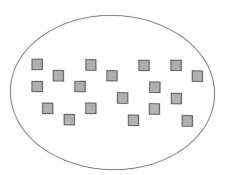

Figure 12.9 Tiles to be arranged in a rectangle.

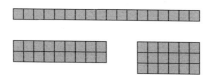

Figure 12.10 Three rectangles made out of 18 tiles.

geometrically, 18 groups of unit blocks are identical to one group of 18 blocks, 9 groups of 2 blocks are identical to 2 groups of 9 blocks, and, finally, 6 groups of 3 blocks are identical to 3 groups of 6 blocks.

Now, we will show how the blocks pictured in Figure 12.10 can be represented in non-decimal base systems. We begin with Figure 12.11 that shows the representations of the blocks in the following base systems: decimal system, base-eight system, and base-five system. Recording each of the three representations results in the symbols 18_{base10}, 22_{base8}, and 33_{base5}. But, as shown in Figure 12.10, the number of multiplication facts for each of the three numbers remains the same. The only difference is in the recording of the multiplication facts by using digits available in a particular base system. For example, $22_{base8} = 22_{base8} \times 1 = 1 \times 22_{base8}$, $22_{base8} = 11_{base8} \times 2 = 2 \times 11_{base8}$, and $22_{base8} = 6 \times 3 = 3 \times 6$. Note that the factors 6 and 3 represent unit blocks and have the same meaning in base eight as in any other base greater than six. Similarly, $33_{base5} = 33_{base5} \times 1 = 1 \times 33_{base5}$, $33_{base5} = 14_{base5} \times 2 = 2 \times 14_{base5}$, and $33_{base5} = 11_{base5} \times 3 = 3 \times 11_{base5}$.

Consider the case when 18 (reads one–eight) is a base-nine number, that is, $18_{base9} = 1 \times 9^1 + 8 \times 9^0$. How many rectangles can be made out of that number of blocks? The base-nine representation of this number and a single rectangle that 18_{base9} blocks can form are shown in Figure 12.12.

Can symbol 18 represent a base-eight number? To answer this question note that just like there is no digit 10 in base ten, there is no digit 8 in base eight. However, if 18 means one rod of eight blocks and eight unit blocks, than one has two rods of eight blocks and therefore this amount of blocks should be recorded as 20 (read two–zero) in base eight. How many rectangles can be created out of that number of blocks? All such rectangles are shown in Figure 12.13. So, the number 20_{base8} can be represented as the product of two factors in three ways (regardless of the order of factors): $20_{base8} = 20_{base8} \times 1$, $20_{base8} = 10_{base8} \times 2$, and $20_{base8} = 4 \times 4$. One can note that the first two multiplication facts resemble those from the decimal system and only the third multiplication fact does not look familiar.

Whereas there are three ways to factor a number represented by the amount of manipulatives shown in the top part of Figure 12.13, there are

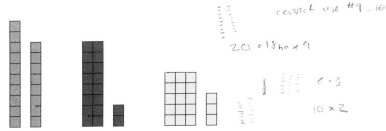

correct use #9 ..10

$20 = 18 \text{ box } 9$

$6 \cdot 3$

10×2

Figure 12.11 Representations of 18 (base-ten) tiles in different bases ($B = 10, 8, 5$).

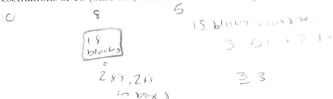

10 8 5

18 blocks

2 8's, 2 1's
in box 8

15 blocks

3 5's

$3\ 3$

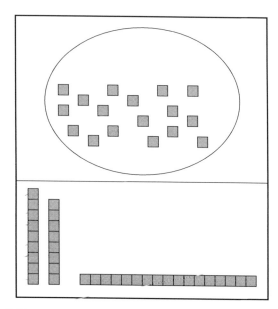

Figure 12.12   Different representations of the number 18_{base9}.

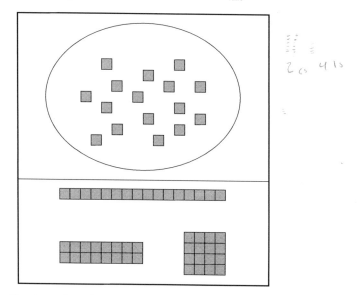

Figure 12.13   Hands-on factoring does not depend on a base system.

multiple ways, depending on a base system, to describe rectangles created in the bottom part of the diagram. Below these rectangles are described as multiplication facts in the decimal system as well in the base-nine, -eight, -seven, and -six systems.

In the decimal base, the three rectangles can be described as follows: $16 = 16 \times 1 = 1 \times 16$, $16 = 2 \times 8 = 8 \times 2$, $16 = 4 \times 4$.

In base nine, the three rectangles can be described as follows:

$$17_{base9} = 1 \times 17_{base9} = 17_{base9} \times 1, \ 17_{base9} = 2 \times 8 = 8 \times 2, \ 17_{base9} = 4 \times 4.$$

In base eight, the three rectangles can be described as follows:

$$20_{base8} = 1 \times 20_{base8} = 20_{base8} \times 1, \ 20_{base8} = 2 \times 10_{base8} = 10_{base8} \times 2, \ 20_{base8} = 4 \times 4.$$

In base seven, the three rectangles can be described as follows:

$$22_{base7} = 1 \times 22_{base7} = 22_{base7} \times 1, \ 22_{base7} = 2 \times 11_{base7} = 11_{base7} \times 2, \ 22_{base7} = 4 \times 4.$$

In base six, the three rectangles can be described as follows:

$$24_{base6} = 1 \times 24_{base6} = 24_{base6} \times 1, \ 24_{base6} = 2 \times 12_{base6} = 12_{base6} \times 2, \ 24_{base6} = 4 \times 4.$$

5. RECORDING MULTIPLICATION IN DIFFERENT BASES

In order to show how multiplication can be recorded in base nine, Figure 12.14 displays five blocks that are repeated seven times and then arranged into groups of nine blocks (labeling blocks by consecutive integers 1 through 9). In all, after three groups of nine blocks are created, eight blocks remain. Symbolically, the representation $3 \times 9 + 8$ has been created, thereby, indicating that the product 7×5 in base nine can be recorded as 38_{base9}. The meaning of multiplication and its physical representation do not depend on a base system. Therefore, the same diagram can be used to record the product 7×5 in other bases. For example, in base eight, one

1		1	2	3	4	5
2		6	7	8	9	1
3		2	3	4	5	6
4		7	8	9	1	2
5		3	4	5	6	7
6		8	9	1	2	3
7		4	5	6	7	8

Figure 12.14 Multiplying 5 by 7 in base nine.

has $(7 \times 5)_{base8} = 43_{base8}$. However, as there is no digit 7 in bases lower than base eight and there is no digit 5 in bases lower than base six, the product of two numbers described by the diagram of Figure 12.14 will be recorded in bases seven, six, and five, respectively, as follows: $(10_{base7} \times 5)_{base7} = 50_{base7}$, $(11_{base6} \times 5)_{base6} = 55_{base6}$, $12_{base5} \times 10_{base5} = 120_{base5}$.

6. DIVISION IN DIFFERENT BASES

The table pictured in Figure 12.15 shows the sequences of consecutive counting numbers generated in different bases. Using this table, one can see, for example, that $18_{base10} = 102_{base4}$. By using the measurement model for division, one can show that 102_{base4} is divisible by 21_{base4}. Indeed, Figure 12.16 shows the representation of 102_{base4}, in particular, one can see that 21_{base4} when subtracted twice from 102_{base4} yields zero. Using this approach, one can show that

$$110_{base4} \div 22_{base4} = 2$$

$$300_{base4} \div 120_{base4} = 2$$

$$20_{base9} \div 6 = 3$$

$$60_{base8} \div 14_{base8} = 4$$

$$110_{base7} \div 40_{base7} = 2$$

$$223_{base5} \div 41_{base5} = 3$$

$$140_{base6} \div 26_{base6} = 3$$

Figure 12.15 can also be used to identify prime numbers in non-decimal systems, that is, numbers with exactly two divisors. For example, the following is the list of prime numbers in base nine: 2, 3, 5, 7, 12, 14, 18, 21, ...

	A	B	C	D	E	F	G	H	I	J	K	L	M	N	O	P	Q	R	S	T	U	V	W
1																							
2		10		1	2	3	4	5	6	7	8	9	10	11	12	13	14	15	16	17	18	19	20
3		9		1	2	3	4	5	6	7	8	10	11	12	13	14	15	16	17	18	20	21	22
4		8		1	2	3	4	5	6	7	10	11	12	13	14	15	16	17	20	21	22	23	24
5		7		1	2	3	4	5	6	10	11	12	13	14	15	16	20	21	22	23	24	25	26
6		6		1	2	3	4	5	10	11	12	13	14	15	20	21	22	23	24	25	30	31	32
7		5		1	2	3	4	10	11	12	13	14	20	21	22	23	24	30	31	32	33	34	40
8		4		1	2	3	10	11	12	13	20	21	22	23	30	31	32	33	100	101	102	103	110

Figure 12.15 Consecutive counting numbers in bases four through ten.

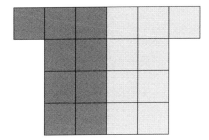

Figure 12.16 Division as repeated subtraction: the case $102_{base4} \div 21_{base4} = 2$.

7. ACTIVITY SET

1. Describe what you have discovered through the Tasks 1–4 (section 3). For which base system does the number 12 have the most (the least) number of representations?
2. In which base systems can 12 be partitioned in the sum of two equal numbers?
3. Formulate the test of divisibility by two for different base systems. Use manipulatives as thinking tools.
4. Find the products 12×2, 12×3, 12×4, and so on, in different base systems.
5. Add the first ten counting numbers in base five. Compare the result with the sum of the first ten counting numbers in base ten.
6. Represent base-ten number 15 (one ten and five ones) as the product of two other base-ten numbers. How many different representations are there? Use manipulatives as thinking tools. Draw pictures of all your representations. How many tiles would you give to students in order to show all the multiplication facts for this base-ten number?
7. Represent base-seven number 15 (one seven and five ones) as the product of two other base-seven numbers. How many different representations are there? Use manipulatives as thinking tools. Draw pictures of all your representations. How many tiles would you give to students in order to show all the multiplication facts for this base-seven number?
8. Base-eight number 14 (one eight and four ones) represent as the product of two other base-eight numbers. How many different representations are there? Use manipulatives as thinking tools. Draw

pictures of all your representations. How many tiles would you give to students in order to show all the multiplication facts for this base-eight number?

9. For a number represented by the amount of square tiles pictured in Figure 12.17, write all multiplication facts in the base systems four through ten by creating all possible rectangles out of the tiles, and interpreting each rectangle as a multiplication fact.

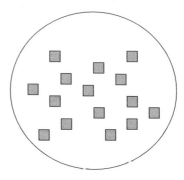

Figure 12.17   Arrange tiles in rectangles.

10. Show that the base-nine numbers 1, 4, 10, 17, 27, 40, 54, 71, where the first digit of the two-digit numbers represents the number of nines and the second digit represents the number of ones, are square numbers in base nine.

9									
▲		**1**	**2**	**3**	**4**	**5**	**6**	**7**	**8**
▼	**1**	1	2	3	4	5	6	7	8
	2	2	4	6	8	11	13	15	17
	3	3	6	10	13	16	20	23	26
	4	4	8	13	17	22	26	31	35
	5	5	11	16	22	27	33	38	44
	6	6	13	20	26	33	40	46	53
	7	7	15	23	31	38	46	54	62
	8	8	17	26	35	44	53	62	71

Figure 12.18   Multiplication table for one-digit numbers in base nine.

11. Show that the base-eight numbers 1, 4, 11, 20, 31, 44, 61, where the first digit of the two-digit numbers represents the number of eights and the second digit represents the number of ones, are square numbers in base eight.

8		1	2	3	4	5	6	7
▲ ▼	1	1	2	3	4	5	6	7
	2	2	4	6	10	12	14	16
	3	3	6	11	14	17	22	25
	4	4	10	14	20	24	30	34
	5	5	12	17	24	31	36	43
	6	6	14	22	30	36	44	52
	7	7	16	25	34	43	52	61

Figure 12.19 Multiplication table for one-digit numbers in base eight.

12. Do square numbers in bases nine and eight follow the pattern known in base ten: the difference between two consecutive square is an odd number? Why or why not? Carry out subtraction in the corresponding base, and explain your answer by using manipulatives.

13. Show that the Theon theorem (connecting two consecutive triangular numbers and a square number) remains true in any base system. *Hint*: In the multiplication table, whatever the base system, any element n^2 in the main diagonal and two elements $(n-1)n$ and $n(n+1)$, immediately to its left and to its right, respectively, satisfy the identity $n^2 - n(n-1) = (n+1)n - n^2$, whence $2n^2 = n(n-1) + (n-1)n$, from where it follows that

$$n^2 = \frac{n(n-1)}{2} + \frac{(n-1)n}{2}.$$

In other words, the Theon Theorem can be discovered in the multiplication table regardless of the base in which it was developed. In particular, this confirms that the meaning of multiplication does not depend on a system in which it is carried out.

14. Show that the first seven Fibonacci numbers in base four look as follows: 1, 1, 2, 3, 11, 20, 31, ...

15. Apply the Sieve of Eratosthenes to the sequence of consecutive integers in bases seven, eight, and nine. Describe what you have found in common with the Sieve of Eratosthenes developed in base ten.

16. Using the base-nine multiplication table shown in Figure 12.18, find the first five cubes in that base by adding numbers within the corresponding gnomons. Then verify your findings by multiplying the base of each cube three times by itself (see section 6 of Chapter 4). *Hint*: Adding all numbers in the 4th gnomon yields $(4 + 8 + 13 + 17 + 13 + 8 + 4)_{base9} = 71_{base9}$. On the other hand, $(4 \times 4 \times 4)_{base9} = (17_{base9} \times 4)_{base9} = 71_{base9}$.

17. Using the base-eight multiplication table (Figure 12.19), find the first five consecutive cubes in that base by adding numbers within the corresponding gnomons. Then verify your findings by multiplying the base of each cube three times by itself (see section 6 of Chapter 4).

18. Using the base-seven multiplication table (Figure 12.20), find the first five cubes in that base by adding numbers within the corresponding gnomons. Then verify your findings by multiplying the base of each cube three times by itself (see section 6 of Chapter 4).

7						
	1	**2**	**3**	**4**	**5**	**6**
1	1	2	3	4	5	6
2	2	4	6	11	13	15
3	3	6	12	15	21	24
4	4	11	15	22	26	33
5	5	13	21	26	34	42
6	6	15	24	33	42	51

Figure 12.20 Multiplication table for one-digit numbers in base seven.

19. Exploring the multiplication table with a variable base, one can discover that $(12 \times 12)_{base\,10}$, $(11 \times 11)_{base\,9}$, and $(10 \times 10)_{base\,8}$ have the same representation through a three-digit number 144 (reads one–four–four). Explain this phenomenon by using manipulatives.

20. Exploring the multiplication table with a variable base, one can discover that $(20 \times 20)_{base\,10}$, $(18 \times 18)_{base\,9}$, and $(16 \times 16)_{base\,8}$ have the same representation through a three-digit number 400 (reads four–zero–zero). Explain this phenomenon by using manipulatives.

21. Is it possible to find the coinciding squares in more than three bases? Why or why not?

22. A college bookstore has a textbook sale. As a part of the sale, the manager announced that any textbook a student can get for free if he or she can be smarter than the store's famous "Free Book" machine. The machine displays a book's price and offers a student to insert any number of dollars in the range $1 through $9 into the money slot. The machine then adds some amount of dollars in the same range ($1 through $9) and tells a student the resulting sum. If this sum is less than the price of a book, the student-machine interaction continues in the same vein. If a student reaches the book's price first, the machine refunds student's money and drops a free textbook into the basket. If the machine reaches the price first, a student pays the whole price for a textbook. Help a student to get a $73 book for free. Help a student to get an $80 book for free.

23. A college bookstore has a textbook sale. As a part of the sale, the manager announced that any textbook book a student can get for free if he or she can be smarter than the store's famous "Free Book" machine. The machine displays a book's price and offers a student to insert any number of dollars in the range $1 through $8 into a money slot. The machine then adds some amount of dollars in the same range ($1 through $8) and tells a student the resulting sum. If this sum is less than the price of a book, the student-machine interaction continues in the same vein. If a student reaches the book's price first, the machine refunds student's money and drops a free textbook into the basket. If the machine reaches the price first, a student pays the whole price for a textbook. Help a student to get a $56 book for free. Help a student to get a $54 book for free.

24. A college bookstore has a textbook sale. As a part of the sale, the manager announced that any textbook book a student can get for free if he or she can be smarter than the store's famous "Free Book" machine. The machine displays a book's price and offers a student to insert any number of dollars in the range $1 through $7 into the money slot. The machine then adds some amount of dollars in the same range ($1 through $7) and tells a student the resulting sum. If this sum is less than the price of a book, the student-machine interaction continues in the same vein. If a student reaches the book's price first, the machine refunds student's money and drops a free textbook into the basket. If the machine reaches the price first, a student pays the whole price for a textbook. Help a student to get a $60 book for free. Help a student to get a $63 book for free.

CHAPTER 13

PROGRAMMING DETAILS

Facility at creating spreadsheets is becoming required in many entry-level positions for high school graduates.

—Conference Board of the Mathematical Sciences (2000, p. 4)

1. INTRODUCTION

The purpose of this chapter is to provide details of the programming of a number of spreadsheet environments used to support an experimental approach to elementary mathematics concepts. The need for such a material to be included in the book stems from the following remark by a teacher: "I would like to learn how the tools we used [in the course "Topics in Mathematics for Elementary Teachers"] were created." Learning to develop spreadsheet-based computational environments for the elementary classroom could be a part of a separate course on the use of technology for teachers. All computational environments discussed in this chapter are based on Excel 2008 (Mac)/2007(Windows) spreadsheets, but they work equally effective with Excel 2004 (Mac)/2003(Windows) versions. Note that only basic techniques of spreadsheet programming will be considered in this chapter. Towards this end, it is assumed that the readers have basic familiarity with spreadsheets that includes the use of names (absolute references) and relative references in spreadsheet formulas. For a more advanced learning to develop spreadsheets like those used in chapters 9 and 11, a book by Neuwirth & Arganbright (2004) is recommended.

Topics in Mathematics for Elementary Teachers, pages 231–244
Copyright © 2010 by Information Age Publishing

It should be noted that syntactic versatility of spreadsheets enables the construction of both visually and computationally identical environments using syntactically different formulas. Below, the notation (**A1**)→ will be used to present a formula defined in cell **A1**. Many spreadsheet formulas incorporate the function $MOD(n, m)$ which returns a remainder of n when divided by m. Other formulas incorporate the function $INT(x)$ which returns the greatest integer smaller that x. Also, many spreadsheet formulas incorporate the conditional function **IF(_, _, _)** which includes three parts: a condition, an action that must be taken if the condition is true, and an action that must be taken otherwise. Whenever appropriate, spreadsheet formulas include names rather than absolute references. The use of names facilitates one's comprehension of spreadsheet programming as the names give meaning to the formulas involved. Some formulas are based on a special technique of using circular references, thereby, enabling for an interactive construction of non-constructively defined functions. In many cases, a spreadsheet becomes an agent of mathematical activities for its users, thereby, supporting the recommendation, "prospective teachers need to understand that the use of technology for complicated computation does not eliminate the need for mathematical thinking but rather often raises a different set of mathematical problems" (Conference Board of Mathematical Sciences, 2001, p. 48).

2. SPREADSHEETS USED IN CHAPTER 1

2.1. Spreadsheet Programming for Figures 1.14–1.15

Consider the equation

$$a_1 x + a_2 y + a_3 z = n, \tag{1}$$

which describes a partition of n into non-negative summands a_1, a_2, a_3. Equation (1) includes four parameters defined, respectively, in the slider-controlled cells **A2**, **E2**, **F2**, and **G2**, which, in turn, are given the names **n**, **a_1**, **a_2**, and **a_3**. (Note that the need to use the underscore symbol in the name **a_1** is because the shorter notation, **a1**, is recognized by a spreadsheet as the cell reference **A1**). The spreadsheets of Figures 1.14 and 1.15 are designed to generate the values of variables x, y, and z that provide solutions to Equation (1).

Consider Figure 1.15, where the ranges for the number of dimes (x) and the number of nickels (y) are, respectively, $[0, 2]$ and $[0, 5]$. This means that there may not be more than two dimes and five nickels in change for a quarter. How does the spreadsheet know when to stop generating values for the variables x and y that are beyond those ranges? This technology-motivated question becomes an agent for mathematical activities associated with the use of linear algebraic inequalities. First, by using the measurement model for division one can use dimes and nickels to measure quarter. Dividing 10 into 25 yields the quotient 2; dividing 5 into 25 yields the quotient 5. In other words, $2 = INT(25/10)$ and $5 = INT(25/5)$. In general, one can show that the variables x and y in Equation (1) satisfy the inequalities $x \leq INT(n/a_1)$ and $y \leq INT(n/a_2)$. This explains the use of the following spreadsheet formulas in establishing the ranges for the variables x and y (in Figure 1.15, the number of dimes and the number of nickels, respectively):

> (**D4**)→ =0; (**C5**)→ =0; (**E4**)→ =IF(D4<INT(n/a_1),1+D4," ");
> (**C6**)→ =IF(C5<INT(n/a_2),1+C5," ").

Formulas in cells **E4** and **C6** are replicated across row **4** and down column **C**, respectively.

The values of z (see the numbers in the range **D5:J11**) satisfying Equation (1) can be found as follows.

> (**D5**)→ =IF(OR(D$4=" ",$C5=" ")," ",
> IF(AND(n-D$4*a_1-$C5*a_2>=0,
> MOD(n-D$4*a_1-$C5*a_2,a_3)=0),(n-D$4*a_1-$C5*a_2)/a_3," ")).

The formula in cell **D5** is replicated across rows and down columns to cell **J11**.

Finally, the total number of solutions to Equation (1) generated by the spreadsheet can be counted as follows: (**A8**)→ = COUNT(D5:J11). For example, the number 12 in cell **A8** (Figure 1.15) shows the number of solutions to Equation (1) when $a_1 = 10$, $a_2 = 5$, $a_3 = 1$. In other words, there exist 12 ways to change a quarter using dimes, nickels, and pennies.

2.2. Spreadsheet Programming for Figure 1.16

Consider the equation

$$x + y + z = n, \tag{2}$$

which describes a partition of n into positive integer summands. The goal is to construct an environment that generates all solutions to Equation (2) assuming that the quadruple $(x, y, z, n) = (1, 2, 1, 5)$ is different from that of $(2, 1, 1, 5)$. Under this assumption, the number 5 can be partitioned in three summands in six ways: $5 = 1 + 2 + 2$, $5 = 2 + 1 + 2$, $5 = 2 + 2 + 1$, $5 = 1 + 1 + 3$, $5 = 1 + 3 + 1$, and $5 = 1 + 1 + 3$.

The difference between modeling Equation (1) and Equation (2) is that the former model partitions n into three specified summands without regard to their order, whereas the latter model partitions n into three summands in all possible ways with regard to order. The spreadsheet that models Equation (2) allows one to construct a table representation of a function that relates n to the sought number of solutions of Equation (2). Here are the details of the programming of such a spreadsheet (presented with reference to Figure 1.16).

Cell **B4** is given the name n.

(C4)→ **=1**; **(D4)**→ **=IF(C4<n,1+C4," ")**.
 The formula is replicated across row **4**.
(B5)→ **=1**; **(B6)**→ **=IF(B5<n,1+B5," ")**
 is replicated down column **B**.
(C5)→ **=IF(n-(C$4+$B5)>0,n-(C$4+$B5)," ")**
 is replicated across rows and down columns to cell **O17**.
(C1)→ **=3**; **(D1)**→ **=1+C1**
 is replicated across row **1**.
(C2)→ **=IF(n=2,0,IF(C$1=n,$A$1,C2))**
 is replicated across row **2**.

The use of a circular reference in the last formula (i.e., a reference to a cell in which it is defined) enables the spreadsheet to keep the value of already computed number of solutions of Equation (2) unchanged as its right-hand side (the content of cell **B4**) changes.

3. SPREADSHEETS USED IN CHAPTER 2

In Chapter 2, a spreadsheet was used to construct tree diagrams for three objects both in numeric and non-numeric formats. A numeric tree diagram can be easily transformed into a pattern/color-based diagram using the conditional formatting feature of a spreadsheet (Abramovich & Sugden, 2004).

3.1. Spreadsheet Programming for Figure 2.4

The following programming details are presented with reference to Figure 2.4.

(B6)→ **=1**; **(B15)**→ **=5**; **(B24)**→ **=10**.

(**I3**)→ =1; (**I6**)→ =5; (**I9**)→ =10.
  The range of cells **I3:I11** is replicated to cell **I29**.
(**N2**)→ =1; (**N3**)→ =5; (**N4**)→ =10.
  The range of cells **N2:N4** is replicated to cell **N28**.
(**P2**)→ =B6+I3+N2. (**R2**)→ = 1; (**R3**)→ =1+R2
  is replicated down column **R** (which is hidden from the view as it
  includes auxiliary numerical entries needed to arrange the sums
  (column **P**) of the denominations of coins in the increasing order
  (column **S**).
(**S2**)→ =SMALL(P$2:P$28,R2)
  is replicated to cell **S28**. As a result, all possible sums of three coins
  are arranged in the increasing order displaying ten different sums.

3.2. Spreadsheet Programming for Figure 2.5

The conditional formatting feature of a spreadsheet may be viewed as
a generalization of the common accounting practice of rendering negative amounts (payments, debts) in red, while other quantities are shown in
conventional black. The modern spreadsheet program allows for automatic
formatting of any cell, based on its current value. Often, it is not difficult
to specify the formatting or highlighting of a cell (or range of cells), which
satisfy some condition. However, when the range of cells, each of which has
a different numerical value, has to be uniformly formatted, it is not a specific value that defines formatting but rather, a general rule that describes
numbers in this range.

The spreadsheet shown in Figure 2.5 generates all possible combinations of three patterns in all possible orders. Assuming that each pattern is
assigned a numerical value, the sum of the values for a three-pattern combination does not depend on the order in which the patterns appear on the
screen; however, the visual perception of such a combination is a function
of the arrangement of patterns. To this end, the following simple programming can be used.

(**B6**)→ =1; (**B15**)→ =5; (**B24**)→ =10.
(**I3**)→ =1; (**I6**)→ =5; (**I9**)→ =10.
  The range of cells **I3:I11** is replicated to cell **I28**.
(**N2**)→ =1; (**N3**)→ =5; (**N4**)→ =10.
  The range of cells **N1:N3** is replicated to cell **N28**.

Highlight the range **B2:N28**. Open the dialogue box of Conditional Formatting (Format Menu).
Condition 1. Cell Value is equal to **1**. Choose format.

Condition 2. Cell Value is equal to **5**. Choose format.

Condition 3. Cell Value is equal to **10**. Choose format.

In order to hide numerical values (according to which a pattern was assigned to the cells), choose white color format for the numbers used.

4. SPREADSHEETS USED IN CHAPTER 4

In Chapter 4, a spreadsheet was used to generate the multiplication table as well as numbers with special properties in the table.

4.1. Spreadsheet Programming for Figure 4.6

The following programming details are presented with reference to Figure 4.6.

(B1)→ =1; **(C1)**→ =B1 + 1 is replicated across row **1**.

(A2)→ =1; **(A3)**→ = A2 + 1 is replicated down column **A**.

Highlight the range **B1:K1** and define the name *x*; highlight the range **A2:A11** and define the name **y**. **(B2)**→ =x*y, replicated to cell **K11**. As a result, the spreadsheet generates the 10 × 10 multiplication table.

4.2. Spreadsheet Programming for Figures 4.16 and 4.18

The following programming details are presented with reference to Figure 4.16.

Cell **A2** is given the name *n*. Cell **G1** is given the name *divisor*.

(B3)→ =1, **(C3)**→ =IF(B3<n,1+B3," ") is replicated across row **3**.

(A4)→ =1, **(A5)**→ =IF(A4<n,1+A4," ") is replicated down column **A**.

Highlight the range **B3:K3** and define the name **x**; highlight the range **A4:A13** and define the name *y*.

(B4)→ =IF(OR(x=" ", y=" "), " ", IF(MOD(x*y, divisor)=0, x*y, 0)).

Formula in cell **B4** is replicated across rows and down columns to cell **K13** yielding the products that are the multiples of the *divisor* (cell **G1**); in Figure 4.16, even products are displayed.

(I1)→ =n^2-COUNTIF(B4:N16,"0").

This formula enables the spreadsheet to count the number of the products displayed in the table by subtracting the number of empty cells (which numerical value is zero by default) from the total number of cells in the multiplication table. In Figure 4.16, the spreadsheet counted 75 even products.

4.3. Spreadsheet Programming for Figure 4.19

In comparison with Figure 4.16, a new chart is added to Figure 4.19. This chart dynamically calculates the percentage of even products as the function of the table's size. **(C23)→ =IF(n=1,0,IF(C22=n,I1/n^2,C23))** is replicated across row 23. Once again, the use of a circular reference in the formula defined in cell **C23** enables the spreadsheet to keep the value of already computed percentage number unchanged as the table changes its size.

One can format the cells in row 23 by choosing for number the percentage category with zero decimal places. One can see that in an even size table the percentage does not change (stays constant at 75%), whereas in an odd size table this percentage increases monotonically approaching 75%.

4.4. Spreadsheet Programming for Figure 4.23

In comparison with Figure 4.16, a new chart is added to Figure 4.23. This chart dynamically calculates non-multiples of three as the function of the table's size. **(C18)→ =IF(n=1,0,IF(C17=n,n^2-I1,C18))** is replicated across row 18. Once again, the use of a circular reference in the formula defined in cell **C18** enables the spreadsheet to keep the value of already computed number of non-multiples of three unchanged as the table changes its size. One can see that, regardless of the table's size, the number of non-multiples of three is always a square number.

5. SPREADSHEETS USED IN CHAPTER 6

5.1. Spreadsheet Programming for Figure 6.1

The following programming details are presented with reference to Figure 6.1.

The range **B1:AF1** is filled with counting numbers.

(B2)→ =IF(MOD(B$1,2)=0,"*"," ")

is replicated across row **2**. As a result, the days for Alan (every second day) will be marked with an asterisk

(B3)→ =IF(MOD(B$1,3)=0,"*"," ")

is replicated across row **3**. As a result, the days for Beth (every third day) will be marked with an asterisk

(B4)→ =IF(MOD(B$1,5)=0,"*"," ")

is replicated across row **4**. As a result, the days for Chuck (every fifth day) will be marked with an asterisk.

5.2. Spreadsheet Programming for Figure 6.2.

The following programming details are presented with reference to the upper part of Figure 6.2.

(B2)→ =2; **(C2)**→ =B2+1

is replicated across row **2**. As a result, the sequence of counting numbers (starting from two) is generated.

(B4)→ =IF(B2=2,B2,IF(MOD(B2,2)=0," ", B2))

is replicated across row **4**. As a result, all multiples of two are eliminated from the list of counting numbers.

(B6)→ =IF(B4=" "," ",IF(AND(MOD(B4,3)=0,B4>3)," ", B4))

is replicated across row **6**. As a result, all remaining multiples of three are eliminated from the list of non-multiples of two.

(B8)→ =IF(B6=" "," ",IF(AND(MOD(B6,5)=0,B6>5)," ", B6))

is replicated across row **8**. As a result, all remaining multiples of five are eliminated from the list of non-multiples of two and three.

(B10)→ =IF(B8=" "," ",IF(AND(MOD(B8,7)=0,B8>7)," ", B8))

is replicated across row **10**. As a result, all remaining multiples of seven are eliminated from the list of non-multiples of two, three, and five.

The bottom part of Figure 6.2 incorporates the same programming techniques applied to the range [32, 61] (row **15**).

5.3. Spreadsheet Programming for Figure 6.10

The following programming details are presented with reference to Figure 6.10. Cells **B2** and **B3** are slider-controlled and designated for two integers for which the GCD is sought. **(B4)**→ =IF (B3>0,MOD(B2,B3),0) is replicated down column B. In the Preferences menu one has to choose View and leave the box "Show zero values" blank. As a result, the spreadsheet generates the sequence of remainders until the last non-zero remainder is reached. **(A4)**→ **=IF (AND(B4>0, B5=0), "GCD="," ")** is replicated down column A. The right-hand side of Figure 6.10 (columns D and E) is based on the same programming; it shows how applying the Euclidean algorithm to two consecutive Fibonacci numbers generates remainders that are consecutive Fibonacci numbers ending with the number 1 as the last non-zero remainder.

5.4. Spreadsheet Programming for Figure 6.12

The following programming details are presented with reference to Figure 6.12.

(C1)→ **=COUNT(C3:C102)** is replicated across row **1**.
(C2)→ **= 1**; **(D2) = 1+C2** is replicated across row **2**.
(A2)→ **=100**; cell **A2** is given the name p.

Highlight the numbers in row **2** and define the name n. Highlight the numbers in column **B** and define the name k.

(C3)→ **=IF(AND(n>=k, INT(p*k/n)=p*k/n), p*k/n," ")**
  is replicated across rows and down columns. As a result, the spreadsheet generates the integer values of the expression $100k/n$ in the range $1 \leq k \leq 100$, $1 \leq n \leq 100$.

6. SPREADSHEETS USED IN CHAPTER 7

6.1. Spreadsheet Programming for Figure 7.14

The following programming details are presented with reference to Figure 7.14. Cells B4 and E4 are given, respectively, the names n and *term*. In cells C4 and D4, two Fibonacci numbers are generated using Binet's formula (Chapter 7, Formula [10]).

(C4)→ **=(1/SQRT(5))*(((1+SQRT(5))/2)^(n-2)-((1-SQRT(5))/2)^(n-2))**,
(D4)→ **=(1/SQRT(5))*(((1+SQRT(5))/2)^(n-1)-((1-SQRT(5))/2)^(n-1))**,
(F4)→ **=COUNT(B6:B105)**, **(A6)**→ **=0**, **(A7)**→ **=1+A6**
  is replicated down column **A**.
(B6)→ **=IF(AND(MOD(term-C\$4*A6,D\$4)=0, term-C\$4*A6>=0),**
  (term-C\$4*A6)/D\$4," ")
  is replicated down column **B**.
(C6)→ **=IF(\$B6=" "," ", A6+B6)**
  is replicated across rows and down columns.

7. SPREADSHEETS USED IN CHAPTER 8

7.1. Spreadsheet Programming for Figure 8.21

The following programming details are presented with reference to Figure 8.21. Cell **C5** is slider-controlled and it is given the name **d** (this name stands for the difference of an arithmetic sequence).

(**B3**)→ =1, (**B4**)→ =1, (**C4**)→ =B4 + **d**
is replicated across row **4**.
(**C3**)→ =B4 + C4
is replicated across row **3**.
(**H2**)→ =IF(C5=1,"Triangular", IF(C5=2,"Square",
 IF(C5=3,"Pentagonal", IF(C5=4,"Hexagonal",
 IF(C5=5,"Heptagonal", IF(C5=6,"Octagonal", IF(C5=7,"Nonagonal",
 IF(C5=8,"Decagonal","(d+2)-gonal")))))))).

This nested conditional function **IF** generates the name of a polygonal number as the function of the difference of the corresponding arithmetic sequence. In particular, in Figure 8.21 the value $d = 5$ (cell **C5**) generates the words Heptagonal numbers in cell **H2**.

8. SPREADSHEETS USED IN CHAPTER 9

8.1. Spreadsheet Programming for Figures 9.7 and 9.8

The following programming details are presented with reference to Figure 9.7.

Cells **D2**, **K2** are slider-controlled and given the names n and *MODULO*, respectively. Cell **P2** is given the name *sum*.

(**B4**)→ =1, (**C4**)→ =IF(B4<n,B4+1," ")
is replicated to cell **K4**,
(**A5**)→ =1, (**A6**)→ =IF(A5<n,1+A5," ")
is replicated to cell **A14**.

Highlight the range **B4:K4** and define the name *x*; highlight the range **A5:A14** and define the name *y*.

(**B5**)→ =IF(OR(x=" ", y=" ")," ", IF(MOD(x*y, MODULO)>0," ", x*y))
is replicated to cell **K14**,

(O5)→ = 1, (O6)→ =1+O5
   is replicated to cell **O14**,
(P5)→ =IF(n=0," ", IF(n=O5, sum, P5))
   is replicated to cell **P14**.

By changing the value of **n** from 1 to 10 through the slider attached to cell **D2**, the spreadsheet generates even products in the corresponding multiplication table, calculates the sum of the corresponding products in cell **P2**, and records each sum in the range **P5:P14**.

9. SPREADSHEETS USED IN CHAPTER 10

9.1. Spreadsheet Programming for Figure 10.8.

The following programming details are presented with reference to Figure 10.8.
Cell **A3** (with a hidden content) is slider-controlled and given name n. Cell **D2** (with a hidden content) is slider-controlled and given name x.
(B3)→ =1/n, (D3)→ =IF(x>n, IF(n+(n^2)/(x-n)>=x,
   IF(MOD(n^2, x-n)=0, 1/x," ")," ")," "),
(C3)→ =IF(COUNT(D3)=0," ","="),
(E3)→ =IF(COUNT(D3)=0," ","+"), (F3)→ =IF(COUNT(D3)>0,
   IF(n+(n^2)/(x-n)>=D2, 1/(n+(n^2)/(x-n))," ")," ").

9.2. Spreadsheet Programming for Figure 10.10

The following programming details are presented with reference to Figure 10.10.
Cell **D2** is slider-controlled and is given the name n.

(B4)→ =1, (C4)→ =IF(B4<n,B4+1," ")
   is replicated across row **4**. Highlight the range **B4:L4** and give the name x.
(A5)→ =1, (A6)→ =IF(A5<n,1+A5," ")
   is replicated down column **B**. Highlight the range **A5:A15** and give the name y.
(B5)→ =IF(OR(x=" ", y=" ")," ", x*y)
   is replicated across rows and down columns to cell **L15**.

Highlight the range **B5:L15**.
Open the dialogue box of Conditional Formatting (Format Menu).

Condition 1. Formula is = **AND(OR(x>n-1, y>n-1), COUNT(x)>0, COUNT(y)>0)**. Choose Format.

10. SPREADSHEETS USED IN CHAPTER 11

10.1. Spreadsheet Programming for Figure 11.4

The following programming details are presented with reference to Figure 11.4. Cells **A3** and **G3** are slider-controlled. **(I3)→ =IF(MOD(A3,G3)=0, G3, MOD(A3, G3))**.

10.2. Spreadsheet Programming for Figure 11.5

The following programming details are presented with reference to Figure 11.5.

Cells **A3** and **F3** are slider-controlled.

(H3)→ =CEILING (A3, 0.5*F3*(F3+1))/(0.5*F3*(F3+1)).

10.3. Spreadsheet Programming for Figure 11.9

The following programming details are presented with reference to Figure 13.20. Cells **A3** and **G3** are slider-controlled.

(I3)→ =IF(MOD(A3,G3)=0,(1/SQRT(5))*(((1+SQRT(5))/2)^G3 – ((1-SQRT(5))/2)^G3), (1/SQRT(5))*(((1+SQRT(5))/2)^MOD(A3,G3) – ((1-SQRT(5))/2)^MOD(A3,G3))).

Here, Binet's formula (Chapter 7, Formula [10]) is used.

10.4. Spreadsheet Programming for Figure 11.11

The following programming details are presented with reference to Figure 11.11. Cells **A3** and **F3** are slider-controlled.

(H3)→ =CEILING(A3,(1/SQRT(5))*(((1+SQRT(5))/2)^(F3+2) – ((1-SQRT(5))/2)^(F3+2))-1)/((1/SQRT(5))*(((1+SQRT(5))/2)^(F3+2) – ((1-SQRT(5))/2)^(F3+2))-1).

Here, Binet's formula is used.

10.5. Spreadsheet Programming for Figure 11.15

The following programming details are presented with reference to Figure 11.15. Cells **A3** and **G3** are slider-controlled.

(**I3**)→ =**IF(MOD(A3,G3*(G3+1)/2)=0, G3, CEILING(0.5***
 (-1+SQRT(1+8*MOD(A3,G3*(G3+1)/2))),1)).

10.6. Spreadsheet Programming for Figure 11.16

The following programming details are presented with reference to Figure 11.16.

Cells **A3** and **G3** are slider-controlled.

(**I3**)→ =**CEILING(A3,G3*(G3+1)*(2*G3+1)/6)/**
 (G3*(G3+1)*(2*G3+1)/6).

11. SPREADSHEETS USED IN CHAPTER 12

11.1. Spreadsheet Programming for Figures 12.2, 12.4, 12.6, and 12.8

The following programming details are presented with reference to Figure 12.2.

Cells **A2** and **C2** are given, respectively, the names *Base* and *Number*. Cell **A2** is slider-controlled.

(**A4**)→ =**Number**, (**D4**)→ =**IF(SUM(A4)=0," ",IF(A4=10,Base-1,A4-1))**
 is replicated across row **4**;

(**A5**)→ =**Number-A4**; (**B5**)→ =**IF(B4=" "," ",IF(A5+1=Base,10,A5+1))**
 is replicated across row **5**.

11.2. Spreadsheet Programming for Figure 12.15

The following programming details are presented with reference to Figure 12.15.

The range **B2:B8** is filled with counting numbers as shown. (**D1**)→ =**1** is replicated down column **D**.

(**E2**)→
 =**IF(INT(D2/10^0)-10*INT(D2/10^1)+1<$B2,IF(INT(D2/10^1)-**
 10*INT(D2/10^2)<$B2,100*(INT(D2/10^2)-10*INT(D2/10^3))+
 10*(INT(D2/10^1)-10*INT(D2/10^2))+INT(D2/10^0)-
 10*INT(D2/10^1)+1,100*(INT(D2/10^2)-10*INT(D2/10^3)+1)+

10*(INT(D2/10^1)-10*INT(D2/10^2)-\$B2)+INT(D2/10^0)-
10*INT(D2/10^1)+1),IF(INT(D2/10^1)-10*INT(D2/10^2)+
1<\$B2,100*(INT(D2/10^2)-10*INT(D2/10^3))+10*(INT(D2/10^1)-
10*INT(D2/10^2)+1)+INT(D2/10^0)-10*INT(D2/10^1)+1-
\$B2,100*(INT(D2/10^2)-10*INT(D2/10^3)+1)+10*(INT(D2/10^1)-
10*INT(D2/10^2)+1-\$B2)+INT(D2/10^0)-10*INT(D2/10^1)+1-
\$B2))

is replicated across rows and down columns to cell **W8**.

REFERENCES

Abramovich, S., & Cho E. K. (2008). On mathematical problem posing by elementary pre-teachers: the case of spreadsheets. *Spreadsheets in Education, 3*(1), 1–19. Retrieved September 21, 2009 from http://epublications.bond.edu.au/ejsie/vol3/iss1/1/.

Abramovich, S. (2005). Early algebra with graphics software as a type II application of technology. *Computers in the Schools, 22*(3/4), 21–33.

Abramovich, S., & Sugden, S. (2004). Spreadsheet conditional formatting: an untapped resource for mathematics education. *Spreadsheets in Education,* 1(2), 85–105. Retrieved August 21, 2009 from http://epublications.bond.edu.au/ejsie/vol1/iss2/3/.

Abramovich, S. (2010, to appear). Modeling as isomorphism: the case of teacher education. In R. Lesh, P. L. Galbraith, C. R. Haines, A. Hurford (Eds.), *Modeling Students' Mathematical Modeling Competencies: ICTMA 13.* New York: Springer.

Berg, E. E. (1970). *L. S. Vygotsky's theory of the social and historical origins of consciousness* (Doctoral Dissertation, University of Michigan). Ann Arbor, MI: University Microfilms, Inc.

Bruner, J. S. (1964). Some theorems on instruction illustrated with reference to mathematics In E.R. Hilgard (Ed.), *Theories of Learning and Instructions* (pp. 306–335). Chicago: The National Society for the Study of Education.

Bruner, J. S. (1973). *Beyond the Information Given: Studies in the Psychology of Knowing.* New York: Norton.

Conference Board of the Mathematical Sciences. (2001). *The Mathematical Education of Teachers.* Washington, DC: The Mathematical Association of America.

Cuisenaire, G., & Gattegno, C. (1963). *Numbers in Colour: A New Method of Teaching the Process of Arithmetic to All Levels of the Primary School.* London: Heinemann.

Dewey, J. (1910). *How we think.* New York: D. C. Heath & Co.

Dewey, J. (1929). *The Quest for Certainty.* New York: Minton, Balch & Co.

Topics in Mathematics for Elementary Teachers, pages 245–247
Copyright © 2010 by Information Age Publishing

Hardy, G. H. (1929). *Bulletin of the American Mathematical Society, 35,* 778–818.

Hoffman, P. (1998). *The Man Who Loved Only Numbers: The Story of Paul Erdos and the Search for Mathematical Truth.* New York: Hyperion.

Hofstadter, D. (1999). *Godel, Esher, Bach: An Eternal Golden Braid.* New York: Basic Books.

Loweke, G. P. (1982). *The Lore of Prime Numbers.* New York: Vantage Press.

National Council of Teachers of Mathematics. (1989). *Curriculum and Evaluation Standards for School Mathematics.* Reston, VA: Author.

National Council of Teachers of Mathematics. (1991). *Professional Standards for Teaching Mathematics.* Reston, VA: Author.

National Council of Teachers of Mathematics. (2000). *Principles and Standards for School Mathematics.* Reston, VA: Author.

New York State Education Department. (1996). *Learning Standards for Mathematics, Science, and Technology.* Albany, NY: Author.

New York State Education Department. (1998). *Mathematics Resource Guide with Core Curriculum.* Albany, NY: Author.

Neuwirth, E., & Arganbright, D. (2004). *Mathematical Modeling with Microsoft® Excel.* Belmont, CA: Thomson Learning.

Oxford Dictionary of Scientific Quotations. (2005). Edited by W. F. Bynum and R. Porter. New York: Oxford University Press.

Pólya, G. (1945). *How to Solve It?* Princeton, NJ: Princeton University Press.

Pólya, G. (1954). *Induction and Analogy in Mathematics.* Princeton, NJ: Princeton University Press.

Pólya, G. (1963). On learning, teaching, and learning teaching. *The American Mathematical Monthly, 70*(6), 605–619.

Pólya, G. (1965). *Mathematical Discovery: On Understanding, Learning, and Teaching Problem Solving* (volume 2). New York: John Wiley & Sons.

Pólya, G. (1981). *Mathematical discovery: On understanding, learning, and teaching problem solving* (combined edition). New York: Wiley.

Posamentier, A. S., Smith, B. S., & J. Stepelman. (2006). *Teaching Secondary Mathematics.* (7th ed.). Upper Saddle River, NJ: Pearson Education.

Senk, S. L., Keller, B., & Ferrini-Mundy, J. (2004). Teacher preparation: K–12 mathematics. In S. L. Ganter & W. Barker (Eds.), *The Curriculum Foundations Project: Voices of the Partner Disciplines* (pp. 145–155). Washington, DC: The Mathematical Association of America.

Shulman, L. S. (1997). Disciplines of inquiry in education: An overview. In R. M. Jaeger (Ed.), *Complementary Methods for Researchers in Education* (pp. 3–19). Washington, DC: American Educational Research Association.

United States Department of Education. (2000). *Before it's too late. A Report to the nation from the National Commission on Mathematics and Science Teaching for the 21st century.* Washington, DC: Author.

Van de Walle, J. A. 2001. *Elementary and Middle School Mathematics* (4th ed.). New York: Addison Wesley.

Van Hiele, P. M. (1986). *Structure and Insight: A Theory of Mathematics Education.* Orlando, FL: Academic Press.

Vygotsky, L. S. (1987). Thinking and speech. In R. W. Rieber & A. S. Carton (Eds.), *The collected works of L. S. Vygotsky* (vol. 1, pp. 39–285). New York: Plenum Press.

Vygotsky, L. S. (1978). *Mind in Society*. Cambridge, MA: Harvard University Press.

Vygotsky, L. S. (1962). *Thought and Language*. Cambridge, MA: The MIT Press.

Wells, D. (1986). *The Penguin Dictionary of Curious and Interesting Numbers*. London: Penguin Press.

APPENDIX

SOME USEFUL FORMULAS

Sums of the first n terms of arithmetic sequences:

$$1+2+3+\ldots+n = \frac{n(n+1)}{2} \tag{A1}$$

$$1+3+5+\ldots+2n-1 = n^2 \tag{A2}$$

$$1+4+7+\ldots+3n-2 = \frac{n(3n-1)}{2} \tag{A3}$$

$$1+5+9+\ldots+4n-3 = n(2n-1) \tag{A4}$$

Let x_n and d be, respectively, the n-th term and difference of an arithmetic sequence, then:

$$x_n = x_1 + d(n-1) \tag{A5}$$

$$x_1+(x_1+d)+(x_1+2d)+\ldots+\left(x_1+(n-1)d\right) = \frac{2x_1+d(n-1)}{2}n \tag{A6}$$

$$x_1+(x_1+d)+(x_1+2d)+\ldots+\left(x_1+(n-1)d\right) = \frac{x_1+x_n}{2}n \tag{A7}$$

Topics in Mathematics for Elementary Teachers, pages 249–252
Copyright © 2010 by Information Age Publishing
249

The sums of consecutive squares and cubes:

$$1^2 + 2^2 + 3^2 + \ldots + n^2 = \frac{n(n+1)(2n+1)}{6} \tag{A8}$$

$$1^3 + 2^3 + 3^3 + \ldots + n^3 = \frac{n^2(n+1)^2}{4} \tag{A9}$$

Fibonacci identity for unit fractions:

$$\frac{1}{n} = \frac{1}{n+1} + \frac{1}{n(n+1)} \tag{A10}$$

The relationship between the least common multiple and the greatest common divisor of two integers:

$$LCM(a,b) \cdot GCD(a,b) = a \cdot b \tag{A11}$$

Theon theorem:

$$\frac{n(n+1)}{2} + \frac{(n-1)n}{2} = n^2 \tag{A12}$$

Five basic algebraic identities:

$$n^2 - m^2 = (n-m)(n+m) \tag{A13}$$

$$(n+m)^2 = n^2 + 2nm + m^2 \tag{A14}$$

$$(n-m)^2 = n^2 - 2nm + m^2 \tag{A15}$$

$$(n+m)^3 = n^3 + 3n^2m + 3nm^2 + m^3 \tag{A16}$$

$$(n-m)^3 = n^3 - 3n^2m + 3nm^2 - m^3 \tag{A17}$$

Let C_n^m and $\overline{C}_n^m$ represent the number of m combinations out of n objects taken without and with repetitions, respectively. Then:

$$C_n^m = \frac{n!}{m!(n-m)!} \tag{A18}$$

$$\overline{C}_n^m = \frac{(n+r-1)!}{n!(r-1)!} \tag{A19}$$

where

$$n! = 1 \cdot 2 \cdot 3 \cdot \ldots \cdot n \tag{A20}$$

Closed formula for Fibonacci numbers:

$$F_n = \frac{1}{\sqrt{5}}\left[\left(\frac{1+\sqrt{5}}{2}\right)^n - \left(\frac{1-\sqrt{5}}{2}\right)^n\right], \quad n = 1,2,3,\ldots \tag{A21}$$

Identities among Fibonacci numbers:

$$F_1 + F_3 + F_5 + \ldots + F_{2n-1} = F_{2n} \tag{A22}$$

$$F_2 + F_4 + F_6 + \ldots + F_{2n} = F_{2n+1} - 1 \tag{A23}$$

The sum of angles in an n-sided polygon:

$$S(n) = 180°(n-2) \tag{A24}$$

The Law of Cosines:

$$c^2 = a^2 + b^2 - 2ab\cos C \tag{A25}$$

where a, b, and c are three sides of a triangle and C is the angle opposite to side c.

Double angle formula:

$$\sin 2\alpha = 2\sin\alpha \cdot \cos\alpha \tag{A26}$$

De Moivre's formula:

$$(\cos\alpha + \sin\alpha)^n = \cos n\alpha + \sin n\alpha \tag{A27}$$

Let $P(m, n)$ be the polygonal number of side m and rank n, $t_n = P(3, n)$. Then:

$$P(m,n) = P(m,n-1) + (m-2)(n-1) + 1, \quad P(m,1) = 1 \tag{A28}$$

$$P(m,n) = 0.5(m-2)(n+1)n - (m-3)n \tag{A29}$$

$$P(m,n) = \frac{n(n-1)}{2}(m-2) + n \tag{A30}$$

$$P(m,n) = P(m-1,n) + t_{n-1} \tag{A31}$$

$$P(m,n) = t_{n-1}(m-2) + n \tag{A32}$$

The Rule of Product (explains the multiplicative structure of a tree diagram): If an object A can be selected in m ways and if, following the selection of A, an object B can be selected in n ways, then the ordered pair (A, B) can be selected in mn ways.

Made in the USA
Middletown, DE
20 January 2022

59068921R00146